Binoo K. John has been a journalist for over three decades. Among the publications he has worked with are *Sunday*, *India Today*, *The Indian Express*, *Mail Today* and *DNA*. He worked both as an editor and reporter, covering a range of subjects, including Indian politics, Kerala, cricket and football.

Top Game is his fourth non-fiction book. The others are *The Curry Coast: Travels in Malabar 500 Years After Vasco da Gama; Under a Cloud: Life in Cherrapunji, the Wettest Place on Earth* and *Entry from Backside Only: Hazaar Fundas of Indian-English*. His lone work of fiction is *Last Song of Savio De Souza*.

John lives in Delhi with his wife Rebecca and son Zubin. He tweets at @binoojohn

TOP GAME

Winning, Losing and a New Understanding of Sport

Binoo K. John

SPEAKING TIGER

SPEAKING TIGER BOOKS LLP
125A, Ground Floor, Shahpur Jat, near Asiad Village,
New Delhi 110049

Published by Speaking Tiger Books in paperback 2021

ISBN: 978-93-5447-055-4
eISBN: 978-93-5447-060-8

10 9 8 7 6 5 4 3 2 1

Typeset in Sabon LT Std by SÜRYA, New Delhi
Printed at Shree Maitrey Prntech Pvt. Ltd., Noida

To
KC, KC and PC,
for taking me there

CONTENTS

CONTENTS

Author's Note and Acknowledgements

This book is an attempt to decipher the many unknowns in sport—but primarily the many theories that help in winning and the possible reasons why a number of extraordinary sportspersons never reach the top. Such an endeavour is, of course, complex and many of the conclusions I have drawn are liable to be questioned. The consequent debate, I hope, will help in advancing the cause of sport and the science on which it is based. The scope, range and ambition of this book is wide—but so are the pitfalls.

I selected four individual sports to discuss the basic notions of success and failure in sport: tennis, sprints, the marathon and boxing. Tennis, because it is the most evolved among popular individual sport. Sprints and marathons are primal—or the most basic of athletic activities—which we all can indulge in. Boxing is perhaps the most written about sport and while it has primal qualities too, there is an absolute finality of winning and losing.

Football or cricket are collectives of individual action so such games have not been analysed separately, though many aspects of these games have been looked at.

This book is extensively footnoted, considering that data, statistics and analyses form its bedrock. No individual interviews were done for this book since it needed to be based on published data or reports. Even top sportsmen do not know why they win so consistently. 'I don't know' is what they often say with a shrug during post-match interviews when asked, for example, to explain how they pulled through in a gruelling five-setter. This book hopes to tell them why they win and also to console the losers and show them a new way. One hundred years of sports history find mention here and there in this book. Authorial interventions are many, and at least two chapters are my own assessments of sporting theories.

All conclusions that I draw are supported with evidence from sport history, so newspaper reports are the main data suppliers and are strewn through the book. In addition, about fifty books about various sports form part of my bibliography. All reports and quotes have been attributed. If there are any omissions, they are inadvertent and will be corrected in future editions.

Sport is not country-specific and so this book is global in interest and in sourcing. Sportspersons from around the world pop up in these pages, each of them adding to its mystery and glory. It is only in sport that a right hook which landed on someone's face in 1938 is still a matter of interest and debate. For such matters at least, the book will be loved, I think.

This book was a solitary venture and possible only due to the support extended by my wife Becky during the five years and three total rewrites that it took for this manuscript to be sculpted into shape. During these years I also indulged in journalism, writing an average of twenty stories a year for various publications. I visited the Australian Open for three years to get an idea of how champions work, play, talk and win.

I must thank Ranjona Banerji and other editors for looking at the manuscript. My experience in writing four other books helped as I ran this marathon, often stopping for breath and slowing down in fear, as others passed me by. A Bengaluru-based foundation rejected the proposal. Some publishers even refused to look at the manuscript, others scoffed at it. Most Indian publishers prefer writers with Western degrees, an elitist pedigree or an American or English agent's gushing words. That's just how things are: one young Indian debut writer in 2020 had got three awards and a doctoral fellowship offer even *before* her novel was published. I am at the opposite, unlit end of this creative spectrum. But Speaking Tiger stood by me over the years since the contract was signed.

So this book emerged out of darkness and cynicism that often clouded my vision. But like soccer teams that emerge from the dark tunnel in coloured jerseys and put up a sterling display, this book too, I hope, will work like a compelling game.

New Delhi BINOO K. JOHN
March 2021

INTRODUCTION

Desire, Defeat and the Unending Search for Glory

My notions of winning and losing in sport were initially gathered during the ten years I spent trying to become a sportsman. First, I tried cricket at the only cricket nets in my hometown—Thiruvananthapuram, the capital of Kerala. As a child, I played cricket and thought I had potential. A senior player who played for the Kerala team commented that I bowled like the great leg spinner, B.S. Chandrasekhar. Encouraged by his comment, I decided that Test cricket was my life and future. The only cricket nets were in the Central Stadium and attended by senior players, at least three or four of whom played in the Ranji Trophy championships.

My dreams came to an end one fine day, when a gentle wind was blowing, and the smell of frying vadas from a roadside vendor's cart wafted in the air. That was the day the coach told me I had no future in cricket and threw me out of the nets. In shock, my head reeled and my body trembled in despair. This was my young mind's first collision with failure. Maybe it was the moment when this book was born.

I remember clearly, fifty years later, how on that day I sat on the steps of the Central Stadium, unable to understand what had happened to me. Above and beyond my fall, came the thought that I would be ridiculed in school. While sitting on those steps, steeped in despair and with thoughts of a dark future swirling around in my young mind, I heard the sound of basketball players to my right. On my left was the cinder track where for two or three years I had watched a young man practicing for the 100-metre race all on his own. He never made it. The basketball court on my right was only a few feet away from the nets. Many days later, I found myself on the basketball courts ready to renew my sporting career in a new sport. I had walked into the welcoming hands of PC Sir, guide and inspirer extraordinaire.

PC was among the few who laid the foundation of Kerala's rise in basketball. He trained about twenty-five to fifty kids, coaxing them and conducting matches—he played with us and taught us tricks with the ball. He could spin the ball on his finger for as long as he wanted and did stunts with his Jawa bike. He carried out his role as a guide efficiently and enthusiastically, successfully producing players who helped Kerala become a basketball power at the university and national level. He encouraged all types of players—the losers, the winners, the mediocre (like me)—and taught us all the higher values of life.

Maybe realizing that I would not become a major player, he encouraged me to write the test for referees. After I became a referee, he took me along to umpire matches in schools and colleges. During the District League matches when clubs appeared without a manager, he asked one of us to act as coach or manager, which we did happily. Once he asked me to be the manager of the girls' school team and I was thrilled to bits because the most beautiful girl in the town played for the team. I realized she knew my name and I was even more delighted. My sporting career had reached its zenith! I was to be the manager of many such local teams and although we never got paid, I loved the refereeing and coaching career which went side by side with my playing career. PC taught us to become scorers too. He was everything to many of us. He suggested marathon bicycle rides to the tip of the Indian peninsula, then called Cape Comorin, now Kanyakumari. Though I couldn't go, I lent my new bicycle to a friend who went for the ride to the tip of the country. When he returned the cycle, it smelt of the sea and specks of sparkling sand clung to the tyres.

PC helped schools to organize tournaments. He took us on his Jawa bike to these tournaments, riding the bike like a champion through the narrow streets, fully in command as he drove his bike adeptly. We loved his Jawa. He also liked to spend time at the coffee house near the stadium. At other times, I used to see him in the watch shop that his father owned near the stadium—he would bend over the minuscule dials, the magnifying lens held close to his eyes. And I would think of how he revelled in both the minuscule and the mighty—how he traversed the entire length!

It was in the Central Stadium where ten years of my life were spent that we learnt about winning and how to take defeats in our stride and plod along. We joked and laughed at our fate while spending time in that stadium, that cauldron of failed hopes. For me, though cricket was gone, basketball reigned. About thirty years later I returned to another sport, this time to tennis.

When I played my first match in the International Tennis Federation (ITF) veterans' circuit (fifty-five plus) in Raipur, Madhya Pradesh, my past whizzed through my mind. I lost 6-0, 6-2, to an equally old Sardar with a round arm service action and a wobbly knee. He consoled me saying that he had been playing for forty years, which was why he won his matches. I had been losing for forty, so I wasn't dismayed at being on handshaking terms with defeat for half a century. A defeat in Raipur wasn't going to hurt.

Back to the past. Unfortunately, at some point PC's career too got stuck. His aspirations had not taken him to the place he intended to reach. That yawning gap between ambition and the realization that he could not reach the pinnacle stretched like it did before many of us. He never became the coach of the Indian national team which he should have, nor for any length of time of the state team. However, he did get a chance to referee international matches and, I think, a junior Indian team too. He retired as a government-paid coach, a defeated man. I lost touch but every now and then I would hear disappointing stories about the man we respected very much, our friend and guide.

Around the year 2010, a man was found lying unconscious near a seedy bar in the city. He was taken to hospital where he was declared brought dead. No one recognized him until a police constable lifted the dirty blood-splotched sheet of a government hospital and saw the face of the once famous basketball coach. No obituaries were written for him because he died in the outhouse without connections.

Sport can kill you with its all-embracing love.

This book is one which comes out of despair as well as a deep love for sport after fifty years of observing various sports from a close range as a player, referee, autograph-seeker, organizer, frenzied spectator, reporter and editor. I have felt the power of sporting triumph and the stink of defeat.

To experience success and stardom along with despair at such close quarters haunted me. I once scaled the wire mesh of the university stadium (a kilometre from the Central Stadium) to see the cricketer Mansoor Ali Khan Pataudi up close. Many years later I told Pataudi (who by a quirk of fate had become my editor), while sitting in the verandah of his bungalow in Delhi, the story of my first glimpse of him, making him smirk.

It was in the same stadium I found myself in the middle of a football riot after a local team was dressed up as the famous Bengal soccer team of the 1970s for a fraudulent exhibition match. When the Kerala Ranji Trophy team was all out for a mere 33 runs, I stood stunned in the stands of the same stadium, feeling more humiliated than the players. I always backed teams that failed in sports, as the Davids seldom slayed the Goliaths.

It took a long time, half a century or more, to understand the lure of sport, the logic, the triumphalism, the failures. It took ages to reconcile all these as if all that I had learnt had to be fit into a balance sheet and then tallied. In this balance sheet, the losses always mounted. The blood-red stamps of loss and failure are spread all over the sheet—my failures are scarlet. However, if only this book is read, all that sweat will sparkle like it does on a victor's face, when his body is luminous with exertion and pride.

With all its flaws, this book had to be written.

CHAPTER ONE

Parenting, Nationalism and the Creation of Champions

There are many ways to win in sport and many theories to back them. Yet there is no definitive understanding of what exactly makes a champion. Or for that matter, why a much-heralded potential champion eventually never became a topper in his sport. Theories abound, and each coach and many scientists have their own theories of success and failure. Some advocate continuous strenuous practice. Others sit back and prefer to watch genes play their role in moulding a champion. Some others say winning is all in the mind and tutor their wards like Fagin trained pickpockets in Charles Dickens's *Oliver Twist*. Coaches the world over have produced champions using varying strategies.

There is no single strategy that is convincing enough. That could be because we still do not have any clue why a player who was spotted quite early in life, practiced well, was focused and devoted to the sport, burnt out like a flickering candle in the wind. To uncoil this mystery, we perhaps need to first understand the making of a champion. The theories that have been studied in detail in the last three decades are genetic factors, sheer ambition inculcated from childhood, sweatshop theories, 'accumulative advantages', place of birth and growing up, theories of practice and endurance, the science of muscle fibre and lung power and so forth.

The primary factor in the creation of champions is the role of parents, and then come strenuous practice, an environment that drives a young player to stretch his or her limits, and to a limited extent, the head start of a good physique that genes offer. All other theories have to follow these factors. The early planning and parental push have been the most elemental in creating champions. In such cases, parents mostly use their children to recreate and accomplish through them the shattered dreams of their own youth. The child becomes the parent redux.

After I looked at the bio-sketches of the Association of Tennis Professionals' (ATP's) Top 100 ranked players of 2018, I realized that sixty of them were introduced to and/or taught the game by their parents or members of the family. All of them were taken to tennis clubs when they were young children by their parents or uncles. For example, Tracy Austin's mother spent all her time in a neighbourhood tennis club and so did her three daughters. Tracy, a former World Number One professional tennis player, became a champion at fourteen but burnt out by the age of twenty-one after winning three Grand Slam titles in a career that also included the women's singles titles at the 1979 and 1981 US Open championships.

The onset of genius or the early promise of talent or qualities of being a champion have also been closely studied. Dr K. Anders Ericsson in his classic study of genius (referred to in detail elsewhere in this book) says: 'From many interviews with international-level performers in several domains, Bloom (1985) [B.S. Bloom, educational psychologist] found that these individuals start out as children by engaging in playful activities in the domain. After some period of playful and enjoyable experience they reveal "talent" or promise. At this point parents typically suggest the start of instruction by a teacher and limited amounts of deliberate practice. The parents support their children in acquiring regular habits of practice and teach their children about the instrumental value of deliberate practice by noticing improvements in performance.'

The parental accomplishment is vicarious but that is the way champions grow. There are scientists who believe that if you want to create a world champion or a prodigy, you can. Just follow a rigorous schedule from childhood. Professor Laszlo Polgar, Hungarian educational psychologist, is among them. To prove his belief that geniuses are made, not born, he groomed his daughters Judith and Susan to become Grandmasters in chess, while Sofia, the third one, settled down to be an International Master. He was obsessed with the art of creating geniuses and collected biographies of about 400 great 'geniuses'. 'When I looked at the life stories of geniuses, I found the same thing. They all started at a very young age and studied intensively,' he is quoted as saying. He also searched everywhere to find a wife who could help him with his experiment. Finally, he married Klare, who was from a Hungarian-speaking region in Ukraine. The Polgar experiment began in 1970 'with a simple premise that any child has the inane capacity to become a genius in any chosen field as long as education starts before their third birthday and they begin to specialize at six.' Judith was a perfect fit for her father's 'genius is made' theory.

At the age of six, the now retired Grandmaster Judith, could defeat her father. Judith is often described as the greatest women chess player ever, having beaten Garry Kasparov as well. The fact that two of her siblings did not match up to her calibre could be used as an indication for the other prevalent theory that geniuses are indeed born.

'A Father's Love of Sport Inspires a Daughter's Career' (*New York Times*) is the epic tale of Zbigniew Macur narrated by his daughter Juliet Macur, a celebrated sports journalist and columnist. The parental role in the moulding of a child is brilliantly drawn out by Juliet Macur.[1] She pays unbounded tribute to her father who was a constant presence on the sidelines as she worked hard to build a sporting career.

She writes, 'He (Zbigniew Macur) was the rebounder when I shot basketballs, the pitcher when I took batting practice, the coach who measured my long jumps and taught me to throw a baseball like a rocket. On our epic road trip around the country when I was 10—which we took in our old, red Volkswagen bus with an engine he had to rebuild along the route—he was the timekeeper for my mile runs in 22 states. He was my ski instructor who never fell on the slopes and my Trivial Pursuit partner who never lost.'

'He didn't miss a single one of my high school basketball games, a perk of his starting work before dawn and ending early. Every time I looked in the stands he was there, quiet and smiling. When I rowed for Columbia, he and my mother were at every regatta too ... He never cared if I won. What mattered was that I tried my best and—what a concept—that I had fun. So I grew to love sports because of his love of sports.'

Zbigniew spent some years of his childhood slaving in the Dachau concentration camp. The Allied army rescued

---

[1] Juliet Macur, 'A Father's Love of Sports Inspires a Daughter's Career', *New York Times*, 16 November 2015.

him when he thought he was about to die and he went on to become a soccer star.

Juliet may have become a journalist after she failed in sport, but many champions in most sport in all countries are created by the ambition of parents. The stories of how Richard Williams drove his daughters Serena and Venus to tennis fame just like Juliet Murray drove her sons Andy and Jamie to become professional tennis players are well known.

Ambition and desire don't arrive early in children. These are higher faculties of the brain and gather force later in life. So during that early phase, this elemental part of a child's make-up is supplied or buttressed by the parent and by coaches, in some cases. Their ambition is the prop for the child. Often their desire to take revenge on fate and destiny for letting them fail becomes the child's burden. Top stars find it difficult to bring up kids to their level due to various reasons explained later. During the hard training period, children often do not understand what it is all for. They do it *for* their parents and *because* of them. At some stage in their growth, this parental ambition is bluetoothed onto the children themselves. From then on the child drives himself or herself.

Not all parents are equipped to coach their children, yet they force their kids to submit to their ambition.[2] Enzo Calzaghe, an itinerant musician turned boxing trainer, used 'tough love' to transform his son Joe into a boxing champion. Joe has been the longest reigning World Boxing Organization (WBO) super-middleweight champion in the history of boxing. Many experts ridiculed Calzaghe's coaching because he did not use training pads to bind his son's hand correctly. They also believed that

---

[2] *The Times*, 19 October 2018.

he had little knowledge of tactics, that he was too much of an amateur.

However, he had one attribute that trumped all his deficiencies—he could, Calzaghe Jr recalled, '... kick up my arse and keep pushing me. If it wasn't for him I would never have laced up the gloves in the first place ... We stuck together through the ups and downs, even when people were saying I should get rid of him because he had never boxed. But he knew exactly what to say at the right time.'

There are many stories of failed parents transfixing their 'stalled ambition', as Nobel prize-winning novelist V.S. Naipaul calls it, onto their children. I pick up the story here of young American Olympian gold medal-winning slalom skier, Mikaela Shiffrin,[3] (two gold medals in the Sochi Winter Olympic Games, 2014, and one gold and one silver in the Olympic Games in South Korea, 2018) written so passionately by journalist Nick Paumgarten.

In the life of the sixteen-year-old Mikaela, so very much part of the American story, everything baffles us, everything makes us wonder, and some of it makes us cower in dread at this unrelenting search for fame and glory. Mikaela's mother Eileen was a skier too but gave up the sport and became a nurse. After she married Dr Jeff Sheffrin (who passed away in 2020), the forgotten ambition was rekindled. In marriages the reverse is often the case and the woman has to forget her ambition, but then it wasn't that Eileen herself went back to skiing. She vowed to make their daughter a skiing champion, inflicting her ambition on the child. Mikaela's story is 'as stark an example of nurture over nature, of work over talent, as anyone in the world of sport,' writes Paumgarten. Eileen

---

[3] *New Yorker*, 27 November 2017.

and Jeff were fiercely determined and 'committed early on to an incremental process and clung stubbornly to instilling a work ethic' in little Mikaela. 'Kids with raw talent rarely make it,' Jeff Shiffrin, Mikaela's father, told the *New Yorker*. 'What was it Churchill said? Kites fly higher against a headwind.'

Eileen watched videos, read up all she could, and charted out her daughter's life as only a mother could. Every second in her daughter's life, all the calories she consumed were accounted for. As a toddler, Mikaela was dragged around the living room and the driveway on skis. The Shiffrins wanted to wring as much training as possible out of every minute of the day and every vertical foot on the course. They favoured K. Anders Ericsson's deliberate practice over competition and were also followers of the 10,000-hour theory that practice for as many hours was essential and Daniel Coyle's book *The Talent Code: Greatness isn't born. It's grown* was their scripture.

The 10,000-hour theory is not really applicable to skiing because each event is only for a few minutes, yet Mikaela spent all her time working on her skills and physical fitness. After one such hectic schedule, all overseen or chalked out by her trainers and her mother, she said, 'I've never puked, I've come close. I'd pass out before I puke (out of overexertion). We have a grading scale. I rate nine fairly often,' she told the *New Yorker*.

She travelled with her mother and did not feel any remorse for having to stick to the tortuous route to the Olympic medal. 'The motivation comes from within,' Mikaela said. With no regret, not even a slight loosening of her killing schedule, like an automaton, Mikaela moved from one drill to another, a dangerous ski down a treacherous Austrian Alps slope, one second cut from her timing, another lunge at the Olympic medal.

In the 2018 South Korea Olympics, Mikaela Shiffrin won a gold medal and a silver but lost in her favourite slalom event, finishing fourth due to scheduling changes which resulted in many of her events getting packed together. She had puked before the event. 'First of all, to come away from this Olympics with two medals is insane, especially after the schedule changes on the front end and then having the combined pushed forward,' Mikaela said after the event.

This may be as much of a tiger mom story as it is about inculcating ambition and the desire to win. This is quite often a dangerous path for fear of burnout, among other factors. But the story of sporting success is still very often that of tiger parents driving their children to make up for their own stalled, derailed, unachieved ambitions.

*

The notion of being born a genius attracts or fascinates all of us. Most of us believe that genetic quality is the reason for sporting and academic excellence. The fact is that only a minuscule percentage of people of any country, any society, show high achievement and so a lack of spectacular genes is a good excuse for our lack of achievement, our failure to reach the top. Creative geniuses are even less in number. A large majority of us are caught or trapped in a swirling vortex of mediocrity from which a leap of faith and endeavour requires superhuman effort. In India, the most common form of escaping this mediocrity is joining sweatshop schools which train you to get into medical and engineering schools. These schools base their approach on Professor Polgar's theory that geniuses can be manufactured. The more time you spend trying to solve mathematical puzzles, the greater the chance is that you will pass a maths exam. This notion has an eerie parallel to the sport practice theory—the more you practice, the better is your chance of winning.

More recently, Malcolm Gladwell in *Outliers: The Story of Success* has outlined his theory that anything can be achieved if you put in 10,000 hours of practice. He was borrowing Ericsson's theory. All this falls in the same line of thinking. Gladwell says that achievers are invariably the beneficiaries of 'hidden advantage and extraordinary opportunities and cultural legacies that allow them to learn and work hard and make sense of the world in ways others cannot. It makes a difference where and when we grew up.'

Gladwell goes to ridiculous extents to study success. He tries to show that the date of birth could matter to a large extent in creating champions after studying an ice hockey team's composition and profile. He also mentions demographic patterns as a factor.

In *The Best: How Elite Athletes Are Made*,[4] the authors make the fantastic claim that younger siblings have a sporting advantage in big families and reaches conclusions like: in major league baseball, younger brothers outperform their older brothers; among brothers who have played Test cricket, the younger brothers have had a more successful career than their elder siblings and so on. Sports is awash with such theories but there is no truth to any such theorizing as I set out to prove in this book.

*

State intervention closely aligned with a jingoistic form of nationalism has also been considered a major force in creating champions. Many powerful powerful and often

[4] A. Mark Williams and Tim Wigmore, *The Best: How Elite Athletes Are Made*, Nicholas Brealey, 2020.

authoritarian world leaders, prime ministers, dictators, monarchs and the rest of them, had ideas about their nation's physical culture and sought to create a nation of physically well-built men. A nation full of muscle-bound men who wouldn't squirm at the thought of taking up a spade to dig, possessing powerful limbs to march and of course, the daring to take up the gun to shoot, are part of every demagogue's plan. In this national endeavour if not physical, then even sedentary and skilled sports like chess would do. Indian Prime Minister Narendra Modi's effort to get the entire country to do yoga falls directly into this old and global pattern.

Dictatorial regimes appointed powerful men to make 'men out of boys'. Certain castes or communities of societies were written off as feeble and incapable of producing geniuses or champions or generals.[5] As late as 1980, a US millionaire entrepreneur, Robert Graham, who developed shatter-proof glasses, started a sperm bank in California that would preserve sperm from men of the highest intellectual calibre, 'to be accessed only to inseminate healthy intelligent women.' In the US in the 1920s and '30s feeble or 'unintelligent' women were sought to be sterilized so that their physically and mentally 'weak' offspring would not pollute the genetic pool.

Anglo-German physical culture expert Eugene Sandow, during a visit to Bombay in the early part of the 1900s wrote in the journal *The Parsi*:[6] 'I have been a fairly keen observer of the Parsis during my stay in the city and the result of my observation is that the proportion of well-built strong men and women is very small indeed. The majority are small in stature and weak in limbs.'

---

[5] Siddhartha Mukherjee, *The Gene: An Intimate History*, Scribner, 2016.

[6] Prashant Kidambi, *Cricket Country: The Untold History of the First All India Team*, Penguin India, 2019.

In 1920, Alexander Ilyin Zhenevsky, commissar of Soviet chess, wrote that chess 'in some ways even more than sport, develops in a man boldness, presence of mind, composure, a strong will and most important, a sense of strategy.'[7]

The Soviet Union has a long history of mass-producing champions in sport like other communist dictatorships, such as former East Germany, some Eastern European states and now China. The Soviet Union initially mass-produced chess prodigies under the Zhenevsky blueprint. The Russian domination of chess still continues although not as masterfully. In 1991, the year Soviet Union broke up, the top nine chess players in the world were from the USSR.

It wasn't always left to sport commissars to make a game a national sport and wrap a country with muscles. Individuals (I don't mean coaches), mostly intellectuals, officials, godmen and eccentrics took it upon themselves to spread a physical culture. In India we have the well-known case of the great Bengali intellectuals, Satyajit Ray and Rabindranath Tagore and their families, trying to popularize judo in Bengal starting from the early part of the twentieth century. In 1866 a Bengali intellectual, Rajnarayan Basu, called for the revival of 'national gymnastic exercises'.

Shinzo Takagaki, considered the father of judo, was invited to Shantiniketan by Rabindranath Tagore. He trained girls and boys together there, something unheard of in the 1930s. One of Takagaki's students was Amita Sen, mother of noted economist Amartya Sen, according to John Stevens in *The Way of Judo: A Portrait of Jigoro Kano and His Students*.

[7] D.T. Max, 'The Prince's Gambit', *New Yorker*, March 2011.

This effort was part of the vigorous physical education movement that drew on 'British inspiration and support', according to Prashant Kidambi:[8] 'During the late 19th century educated middle class Indians had begun to chafe at the self-image of effeteness that had become an integral part of their identity. They sought to counter the negative stereotype about their physical degeneration and lack of manliness and courage which had first been propagated by the British colonizers but came to be internalised by Indians. They elevated indigenous wrestling, gymnastics and yoga over British sports such as cricket and racquets.'

So, physical culture became closely aligned with nationalist projects. In the late nineteenth century, for instance, the nationalist Bal Gangadhar Tilak exhorted people in Maharashtra to 'attend to one's body' and build physical strength and encouraged the setting up of local gymnasiums. In an article in the *Indian Express* on physical culture, Murali K. Menon writes: 'The early 1900s were incendiary times in Bengal, when nationalism acquired a muscular profile. The British, who were masters at cultural emasculation, had for long stereotyped the Bengali male as "effete". Thomas Macaulay wrote that, "Whatever the Bengali does he does languidly. His favourite pursuits are sedentary. He shrinks from bodily exertion and though voluble in dispute, he seldom engages in personal conflict and scarcely ever enlists as a soldier."'

According to Menon, Bengalis jumped into physical activity exhorted by the likes of Swami Vivekananda and Aurobindo Ghose. Soon a bodybuilding culture spread in Bengal. In 1904, when the Prussian Eugen Sandow, the man who started bodybuilding as a sport, visited Calcutta, he was afforded a reception fit for a rock star at Howrah

[8] Kidambi, *Cricket Country*.

Station. Among the famous bodybuilders from Bengal were Bishnu Charan Ghosh (brother of Paramahansa Yogananda), who became a yoga guru; Manotosh Roy, who became the first Asian to win a Mr Universe title in 1951; and the 'Pocket Hercules' Manohar Aich, who won a Mr Universe title in 1952, when he was past 40.

Judo and bodybuilding were easy choices if it came to imagining a nation full of hunks with rippling muscles. Boxing was a predictable choice too as a symbol or metaphor for ultra-nationalistic projects. More so as it involved the destruction or beating to pulp of the opposing nationalist, a war inside a square.

Boxing was predictably the right sport for Adolf Hitler. The Fuehrer had been a boon to German boxing. He had extolled it in his autobiographical political manifesto, *Mein Kampf*, and insisted that it be taught in German schools. What made for good fighters—courage, resolve, speed, cold-blooded calculation—made for good soldiers too, he said. In the Reich sports culture, the *Daily Worker* had wisecracked, boxing was second only to Jew-baiting in popularity. The Nazis initially had little use for professional athletes. They served the wrong gods—themselves. Heavyweight boxer Max Schmeling, moreover, was dark and brooding and had an almost Asian cast, a far cry from the lithe and cheery Aryan blonds of Leni Riefenstahl's films.

But Schmeling's ability to confound his critics, to rebound from defeat, to prevail by sheer force of character and will, embodied the Nazi vision of a renascent Reich. When he knocked out US heavyweight champ Joe Louis in 1937, the Nazis embraced Schmeling. *Schmeling's Victory: A German Victory* was the title of the film of that fight, which was shown throughout Germany by Hitler's personnel decree to enormous audiences of rapturous fans. Aptly, one American writer called Schmeling. 'The first nationally sponsored heavyweight'.[9]

The Joe Louis–Schmeling rematch in 1938, which Louis won in two minutes, was viewed by 70,000 people and heard by 100 million on the radio and was spoken of in some quarters as the biggest sporting event for a century. The very arrival of Schmeling in New York for the great fight in 1938 was a political, or rather, a racial event. Racial hatred and suspicion simmered everywhere. In one version, a US customs official told Schmeling as he landed in the US, 'Here's your stamp, my good young man. Go now and knock that nigger out, good and clean, understood?'

Schmeling, who loved being a Nazi idol (he carried an autographed picture of Adolf Hitler with him), wrote an exaggerated account of his arrival, suggesting that he was the victim of racial hatred. He wrote that people called him an 'Aryan show-horse' and representative of the 'master race'. But other reports said that his welcome was quite peaceful. Joe Louis, foretelling a Muhammad Ali type of bravado, said, 'Either me or him will drop early. There ain't gonna be no decision. All the judges can stay home that night.'

When it was announced that some of the proceeds would be given to help migrants, Joseph Goebbels complained about it in his diary: 'Jews are once again trying to sabotage the Schmeling fight by giving the surplus to German immigrants. They want to prevent him from fighting at all. But the Fuehrer determines that Schmeling is to fight.'

Not just with Schmeling, Hitler was to use sport as no leader ever had. The 1936 Berlin Olympics was the first

[9] David Margolick, *Beyond Glory: Joe Louis Vs Max Schmeling and a World on the Brink*, Bloomsbury, 2006.

event that would showcase Hitler's superior race theory though Jesse Owens spoiled the party. India won the hockey gold and that was more a Dravidian medal than anything! It was to be hockey wizard Dhyan Chand's last Olympics and he describes rather gushingly the visit of the Nazi chieftains Hermann Göring and Joseph Goebbels to the Olympic mess:[10] 'One day while we were in the dining hall, who should walk in but the burly Hermann Göring clad in his military attire. We were after him in a trice to get his autograph. Later some of us obtained Dr Goebbels' autograph.' But creditably, it was only the Indian and American contingents that did not do the Nazi salute in the opening ceremony.

According to Daniel James Brown in the stirring book *The Boys in the Boat: Nine Americans and Their Epic Quest for Gold at the 1936 Berlin Olympics,* Hitler was anti-sport and was opposed to the idea of hosting the 1936 Olympics. 'The year before he had damned the games as the invention of "Jews and Freemasons."' The very heart of the Olympic ideal—that athletes of all nations and all races should commingle and compete on equal terms—was antithetical to his National Socialist party core belief that the Aryan people were manifestly superior to all others.

The man who was responsible for Hitler's change of mind was Joseph Goebbels himself. He convinced Hitler about the possibility of presenting Germany as a civilized and modern state. While standing at the site of the Olympic Stadium, Hitler ordered, on the request of the architect, that the adjoining racing track should be destroyed to allow the expansion of the stadium. He ordered a sports complex for a unified 'Reichssportfeld'. 'It will be the task of the nation,' he announced.

---

[10] Boria Majumdar and Nalin Mehta, *Olympics: The India Story*, HarperCollins, 2012.

Sporting messages are part of history. Although 'God Save the King' was sung as India's national anthem in Berlin, by the time of the London Olympics in 1948 (no Olympics were held in between), India was a newly emerging nation full of nationalistic pride. 'While the Indian hockey team won gold at the London Olympic hockey stadium in 1948, defeating the English 4-0 in the final, much more than the Olympic victory was scripted. It was a newly independent nation's declaration against the forces of colonialism, retribution for humiliation meted out by the English for almost 200 years and finally a statement to the world about the significance of "sport" in an era of decolonisation. Hockey, the victory demonstrated, held the promise of being the new opiate of the masses,' Boria Majumdar and Nalin Mehta[11] write over sixty years later, with their fists pumping the air, as it were.

The authors go on to describe the role of hockey in the moulding of Indian nationalism. Hockey according to them, '... was at once a source of exhilaration, pride and national bonding. The sport for many in the country offered a substitute to religion as a source of emotive attachment and spiritual passion and for many since it was among the earlier of memorable post-independence experience, it infiltrated memory, shaped enthusiasm and served fantasies.'

This hockey euphoria was not to last, as we know. European countries captured the game, changed its rules, its texture and its pitch, made the game into a power-packed one. They took skill completely out of the game. It took India many years to learn the game anew as artificial turf changed the game entirely. So even as a national

[11] Majumdar, Mehta, *Olympics: The India Story*.

sport, as a national 'bond', hockey declined, and cricket took its place. Being identified as a national sport that drip-feeds doses of nationalism into the country's arteries, then, is no guarantee against a game's decline. Gradually, the country, ditched hockey and switched to cricket for bonding purposes.

After India's 1983 World Cup victory, cricket became closely identified with the rise of the nation-state. The gradual opening up of the economy was also inspired by the tag of 'World Cup winners', which India got long after the hockey wins became just memories, and by the new millennium the country had wiped out those hockey feats from its collective consciousness.

It is not nationalism that helps a sport or champions to develop, but rather the other way around. A nation captures a sport for its own uses: to hold it up as a lesson for its youth. In a country like India with a diverse culture and population, sport can work as a bond or a common cause.

Ronojoy Sen,[12] who has chronicled India's sporting history and links with nation-building in *Nation at Play*, says that though sport was patronized by the royal families for a long time during colonial rule, the British too worked hard at it. The link between this physical culture and nationalism can first be seen in Bengal. As discussed, this is seen as a sort of revenge against the general impression that Bengalis were an effete non-martial race, a notion propagated by some British journalists and British parliamentarian Lord Macaulay himself who derided the Bengali physique. Journalist G.W. Stevens is quoted by Sen: 'By his legs you shall know a Bengali. The Bengali's leg is either skin and bones ... or else it is very fat and

[12] Ronojoy Sen, *Nation At Play: A History of Sports in India*, Columbia University Press, 2015.

globular, also turning at the knees with round thighs like a woman's. The Bengali's leg is the leg of a slave.'

In fact, the impression then was that Bengalis were not interested in physical activity and thus did not contribute to the national cause, imperialism and so on. In reaction to this, as we have seen, sport and physical culture were encouraged by Bengal's nationalist and intellectual leaders, and this movement then merged with the Swadeshi movement and became an anti-colonial effort.

As discussed earlier, among the famous Bengali intellectuals who added muscle to this physical culture movement was Swami Vivekananda. Writes Sen, 'Swami Vivekananda, the great Hindu reformist leader hailed from the Simla area, and was said to have been tutored by Khetubabu, one of Calcutta's famous wrestlers. Vivekananda who was an inspiration for the militant wing of Bengal's national movement was proficient in several sports: lathi play, fencing, boxing, gymnastics, swimming and horse riding. He also once won the first prize in gymnastics in the Hindu Mela. But Vivekananda is perhaps best remembered for announcing: "You will be nearer to heaven through football than through the study of the Gita," adding that one "will understand the Gita better with your biceps, your muscles, a little stronger." Oddly, we have no record of Vivekananda playing football, but he was an avid cricketer, apparently even playing one match for the Town Club.'

In 1872, Nabagopal Mitra, a teacher of art, had set up a National School '... for the cultivation of arts, music and for physical training.'[13] This was in keeping with the overall sense of enlightenment in nineteenth-

[13] Tapati Guha-Thakurta, *Monuments, Objects, Histories: Institutions of Art in Colonial and Post-Colonial India*, Columbia University Press, 2004.

century Bengal. 'Scientific' methods of representation, or the arts, and 'physical training' were considered as important for Bengali youth as training in chemistry or botany, according to the author Tapati Guha-Thakurta. All this was related to the desire and project to physically invigorate the youth of the country, just as in later years other countries did or Hitler did with specific and virulent intent.

A sort of national awakening was sought to be attained in all sport and it did happen in some sports in India—football and hockey in the early part of the twentieth century and later, cricket. The general feeling however has remained that Indians, like other South Asians, are a non-athletic race, or lack any significant genetic pool advantages. But such notions will be rebutted in later chapters.

While nationalism was fertile ground for the rise of various sports in many countries, it also raised contentious questions about whether a sport is being imposed on a nation by colonial powers and if a country should follow such a sport. This question has been dealt with by Ramachandra Guha in his popular book, *A Corner of a Foreign Field*:[14] 'A follower of Professor Edward Said might dismiss cricket as a relic of colonialism. To quote one literary critic, "the continuing popularity of cricket in India demonstrates the hegemony of colonial ideals of masculinity on the unconscientised post-colonial consciousness."'

Guha points out that India embraced cricket just as the US created its own form of cricket—baseball—instead of following a colonial game: 'In 1966, when India played the West Indies in Calcutta, *The Times* of London

[14] Ramachandra Guha, *A Corner of a Foreign Field: The Indian History of a British Sport*, p. 335, Pan Macmillan, 2003.

marvelled at the playing of this English game between two coloured countries. For "the wily anti-colonialists of the Sukarno type" it remarked, the India–West Indies Test would be seen as a most subtly corrupting trick of neo-colonialism.' The lead, according to Guha, had come from the top with India's first prime minister, Jawaharlal Nehru, and second President, Sarvapalli Radhakrishnan, being avid fans of cricket.

National effort and encouragement by the state has produced champions, both individuals and teams. A country can indeed play a major role, but at the highest level, other sorts of expertise, environments and support, including corporate support, are required.

Many Olympic athletes from all over the world train in specialized centres of excellence in countries other than their own in order to reach exceptional levels of achievement from merely being in superior training academies or competing against or only sharing a space with the best international professional sports stars. Such academies are bubbles of superior achievement and just being there is enough for sportspersons to improve their performance. So a nation or any community for that matter, apart from appropriating a sport for larger purposes, also needs to provide the environment for the growth of that particular sport.

Perhaps a good example of statist or corporate intervention lies in the story of Japanese tennis star Kei Nishikori. His rise in tennis was the result of a private initiative founded by Masaki Morita, the younger brother of Sony founder Akio Morita, according to a report in *Time* magazine.[15] Nishikori was the Japan junior champion in 2001. 'Morita offered a scholarship to Nishikori to leave his hometown in the western Shimane

[15] *Time*, 19 January 2015.

prefecture—best known for tea ceremonies and ancient shrines—for the IMG academy [originally known as the International Management Group] in Florida which had produced Andre Agassi and Maria Sharapova, among many other tennis stars. Though it meant travelling more than 12,000 km to live in an unfamiliar culture, Nishikori had no doubts.' 'I knew immediately I wanted to go to Florida. I would do anything for tennis,' Nishkori said.

The private initiative in Japan was because of nationalistic pride and a sense of underachievement in tennis. The private effort really paid off since Nishikori reached the Top Five. Japan felt the need for a global star and had the wherewithal to create one since it was an economic superpower. In the 1990s, apart from Kimiko Date-Krumm and Ai Sugiyama, the only big player Japan had in tennis was Shuzo Matsuoka, at the forty-sixth rank.

Therefore, a state and sport are linked in many ways. Apart from the sheer accident of being born in a particular place, an athlete absorbs many aspects of the country, its culture and its facilities on the way to becoming a champion. It is here that his failures too are rooted.

India has made no national effort to win medals nor create champions. Whatever has been achieved is due to accident or fate. There has never been an Indian mind that worked singularly on the development of Indian sport. This is because sports federations have been usurped by people not really interested in the job, nor even committed to sport. Now the government has funding schemes for athletes for the Olympics, but it's a long way off from a national ambition which the Chinese show now and the USSR and East Germany showed earlier.

CHAPTER TWO

Are You Born Great or Do You Achieve Greatness?

About 100 years ago it was British scientist Francis Galton, cousin of Charles Darwin, who first put forward the theory of genetic collusion in the creation of geniuses. He found that eminent individuals in the British Isles were more likely to have relatives who were also eminent. 'By natural ability, I mean those qualities of intellect and disposition, which urge and qualify a man to perform acts that lead to reputation. I do not mean capacity without zeal, nor zeal without capacity, nor even a combination of both of them, without an adequate power of doing a great deal of very laborious work ...

'If a man is gifted with vast intellectual ability, eagerness to work, and power of working, I cannot comprehend how such a man should be repressed.' Galton's theory gave rise to eugenics, which ultimately resulted in the theory of the purity of certain races and the 'sterilization of failures'. Based on such theories, Hitler decided to exterminate races which he considered impure. Before Hitler, this theory of incompetent races was put to practice in the US itself and in the famous *Buck vs Bell* case which went all the way up to the Supreme Court, it was ruled that permitting the sterilization of the unfit did not violate rights. A woman called Carrie Buck was sterilized to prevent the propagation of 'inferior' human beings when she was diagnosed as 'feeble-minded'. It is frightening to think that as late as 1927 or even the early '30s, women classified as 'feeble-minded' or 'idiots' were sent to the US Virginia State Colony for confinement from where they never came out. Siddhartha Mukherjee says:[16] 'It was the Hotel California of mental illness; patients who checked in rarely ever left.' The idea was to prevent the 'contamination' of the population with 'morons and idiots'.

Many basic theories about the creation of champions or geniuses have always clashed. Science has not been able to get a fix on genius. The effort started over a century ago by Francis Galton continues even now. In the case of sporting geniuses, the task is even more daunting and inconclusive because sport is played out in the open in front of a million eyes and so laboratory experiments on sportsmen don't make any sense.

Various thinkers have tried to analyse what a genius really is. Some have rubbished the notion of genius and precocity, while others have celebrated it. 'Genius in popular conception is inextricably tied up with precocity—doing something really creative, we're inclined to think requires the freshness and exuberance and energy of youth,' wrote novelist Ben Fountain. This thinking is applied generously in sport, thus quelling the aspirations and life-long effort of many sportsmen in many games. Orson Welles made the film *Citizen Kane* at the age of twenty-five. Sporting achievement is naturally linked to

[16] Siddhartha Mukherjee, *The Gene: An Intimate History*, Scribner, 2016.

youth, so if a player hasn't reached a high ranking at the age of twenty-five, or given an indication that an explosive performance is imminent, he or she is normally written off.

There are areas where someone displays a flicker of creativity and genius and then burns out. Harvard psychologist Howard Gardner, who has worked on creativity has said that 'lyric poetry is a domain where talent is discovered early, burns brightly and then peters out at an early age.' But others have discounted this theory. David Galenson, economist at the University of Chicago, looked through forty-seven major poetry anthologies since 1980 and concluded that there is no evidence to prove the notion that lyric poetry is a young person's game. Some poets do their best work at the beginning of their career, while others take their time honing their talent. An example is that 42 per cent of Robert Frost's anthologised poems were written when he was around the age of fifty.

Here there is no direct link with sport but there are various sports where late flowering or peaking (after the age of thirty) is common. A genius in sport or poetry is, however, not just because of great genes. The performing genes in anyone grow side by side with the non-performing or retarding genes. 'Genetic wellness and genetic illness were not discrete neighbouring countries. Rather wellness and illness were contiguous kingdoms bounded by their often transparent borders,' says Siddhartha Mukherjee, doctor and author of the ground-breaking *The Gene: An Intimate History*. This profound observation itself puts paid to the journalistic habit of classifying winners and top rankers in sports as people of genetic brilliance.

Experiments in search of the sports gene, however, have to continue. For instance, on 27 July 2016, came this news agency report from Berlin: 'Researchers from the Max Planck Institute of Molecular Physiology in Berlin, Germany have further developed cryo-electron microscopy, a technique that can be used to explain the cause of muscle diseases and identify features that make the musculature of top athletes so efficient.'

Scientists seem to be veering around to the view that ultimately, you have to be born an athlete. Although there is evidence to the contrary, many scientists still hold on to the view that genes matter more than anything else. 'All top athletes probably have genes that enable them to achieve top performances,' said Stefan Raunser, from the Max Planck Institute.

The surmise here is that science will finally announce why Usain Bolt was able to run as fast as he did. This is because technology now enables scientists to observe and analyse muscle proteins as well as other molecules at work in a muscle. 'With cryo-electron microscopy, we can observe the natural changes in the interplay of muscle proteins. It would also enable us to discover whether this interplay differs in Bolt's muscles from that in other people's muscles,' Raunser told the news agency.

Special protein constellations could result in the optimal development of muscle strength. In addition, given that skeletal muscle contains both fast muscle fibres capable of rapid bursts of power and slow ones that are suitable for endurance activity, Bolt's musculature may be composed of a particularly effective combination of fibres, according to the report.

This is how it works, according to Max Planck scientists: The main actor is the protein actin which accounts for 20 per cent of the weight of the musculature and also the motor protein myosin, which converts chemical energy into actual movement. The actin uses myosin molecules like a track. When several million myosin molecules move along this track simultaneously, the muscle contracts.

David Epstein[17] tells us the fascinating story of photographer Dan McLaughlin who, inspired by the 10,000-hour-practice theory of achieving excellence, gave up his career as a photographer and set out to become a golfer who would make it to the Professional Golfers' Association of America (PGA) tour. His aim was to practice 10,000 hours (going by a slightly flawed interpretation of the Anders Ericsson deliberate practice theory) after starting from scratch and using the expertise to gain entry to the professional circuit in 2016 after a ten-year odyssey of 'deliberate practice'. His plan was to log every single hour along the path to 10,000 and to show 'there's no difference between experts and me or other people not just in golf but in every other field.' The 10,000 hours was to be specifically cognitively engaged practice, not just hitting the ball or putting. The McLaughlin experiment failed. At the end of logging over 6,000 hours of 'deliberate' practice in five years after giving everything up, he ended up nowhere. *Atlantic*[18] magazine tracked him down to find out where the experiment had taken him.

When McLaughlin set out, three books which pop up elsewhere in this study had been the guiding force—Malcolm Gladwell's *Outliers,* Geoff Colvin's *Talent Is Overrated* and Daniel Coyle's *The Talent Code*. Of course, Anders Ericsson was at the centre of the deliberate practice theory which would be the ultimate guide. It was

---

[17] David Epstein, The Sporting Gene: *Inside the Science of Extraordinary Athletic Performance*, Portfolio, 2014.

[18] Stephen Philips, 'The Average Guy Who Spent 6003 Hours Trying to Be a Professional Golfer', *Atlantic* magazine, 11 August 2017.

as if McLaughlin was the man who would prove that talent is nothing and hard work is everything—soon he and Ericsson were in partnership. They would change the way achievement in sport was perceived and would, in fact, show the way to sporting glory.

Ericsson was impressed by the idea and said that in particular, he was taken with McLaughin's commitment to 'deliberate' practice, something he said *Outliers* glossed over by implying mastery is simply a matter of accumulating hours. 'My feeling was, "Wow, this is really exciting."'

McLaughlin was as convinced as Ericsson that at the end of it all he would be the master professional golfer and would tweak his nose at Tiger Woods. 'Enlisting a coach, McLaughlin collected data on his performance and sent it to Ericsson, who plotted his improvement. McLaughlin built his game from the hole out. For months, all he did was putt. Gradually, he moved farther from the flag, adding clubs. Eighteen months in, he played his first full round. At peak practice, he was putting in four hours on the practice green and driving range and playing 18 holes daily. He was stingy in tallying hours toward the 10,000 mark, only counting concentrated practice,' Stephen Philips wrote in the *Atlantic*.

The progress wasn't good and McLaughlin wasn't sure if he was on the right track. Other scientists and intellectuals joined in, among them Robert Bjork, professor of cognitive psychology at the University of California, whose research was on 'deliberate difficulty'. Mark Guadagnoli, professor of neuroscience at the University of Nevada said, 'You want to increase arousal so (the brain encodes) information at a deeper level. It's like using a laser to engrave something versus a ballpoint pen.' McLaughlin incorporated these principles and in 2014, Bjork had a look at his game and commented, 'I could watch him and think it was remarkable for someone who hadn't played before. Or, I could look at him and say the whole idea of making the pro tour was unrealistic.'

That is what it turned out to be. McLaughlin gave up after 6,000 hours. Ericsson, however, was optimistic. 'The first person gets stuck but over time people figure out how to get to the top,' he reasoned.

The reason why McLaughlin probably failed in his herculean effort is that he started deliberate practice at the age of thirty. As I say here and discuss again later, any activity in which a high level of expertise has to be gained must start at childhood. If a child does not start any sport (or activity) at least at the age of ten or twelve, there is no way he/she can reach any level of expertise. This is because sport is closely linked to memory and other cognitive faculties of the brain which diminish drastically by the time one reaches thirty.

In fact, Ericsson himself suggests this, though he does not seem to have told McLaughlin this at any time during his epic but failed effort. The abstract of Ericsson's ground-breaking 1993 study mentions, 'In most domains of expertise, individuals begin in their childhood a regimen of effortful practice (deliberate practice) designed to optimize improvement. If not 10,000 hours specifically, almost all of today's champion players, or those in the top 10 or 25 of any sport, would have put in at least 5000 hours. The early part of those hours are done as a slog, due to fear of parents or coaches. Tennis champ Andre Agassi is frank about his loathing of those long hours in his incredible autobiography *Open*. His Iranian father forced him to hit at least 1000 balls a day. His rise as a champion is no doubt due to that. But he promised himself that he would never put his children through such a grind. Despite all such evidence, the actual number of 10,000 can be questioned as well as the rigour involved in these hours ... Such hours which are not just time spent out on the field but actual "deliberate practice".' This Ericsson theory also goes against the theory of the genetic factor being the most important in the creation of genius in sport or any other activity.

Vashti Cunningham is a US high jump champion, who was considered a sure shot for the Olympic gold in Rio de Janeiro.[19] She didn't finish even in the top ten, with just a 1.88-metre jump (1.94 metres was needed to qualify) with the winning height being 1.97 metres.[20] But here the description of her genetic pool is important and with this height clearance at the age of nineteen, she is sure to leap higher.

Journalist Adam Kilgore wrote in the *Washington Post*: 'The daughter of a freakishly athletic football player and a South African ballerina, Vashti was a genetic jackpot. She's lithe and strong, rangy but graceful. Her legs are so long that when she sits on the floor her knees come even with her forehead. She inherited Randall's [her father, quarterback and punter, Randall Cunningham's] competitive verve, she likes to watch his old game films because "he had like, a personality when he played" she said. "We kind of have the same thing."'

Many leading athletes and sportsmen too believe that genes play a part in making them great. The detonations of excellence that top players are capable of are attributed often to what they inherited. Olympic medal-winning Jamaican sprinter Yohan Blake is one of them.[21] He

---

[19] Adam Kilgore, 'Vashti Cunningham, Randall's daughter, is about to jump out of his shadow', *Washington Post*, 10 March 2016.

[20] Ibid.

[21] *HT* Correspondent, Interview, 'Sprinter Yohan Blake wants to play in IPL for KKR or RCB after retirement', *Hindustan Times*, 4 December 2019.

expressed his faith in the theory of the sports gene in an interview given in New Delhi.

To the question, 'Do you feel sprinters are born or can they be trained to become one?' Blake's reply was, 'I think it's genetics, when you are born fast. I don't think you can really make a sprinter. You can help him get better but you can't give him speed. You have to be born with that, you have to be born with fast muscles.'

To understand the role of genes in sporting achievements, we need to look at David Epstein's *The Sporting Gene*, Ed Caesar's *Two Hours: The Quest to Run the Impossible Marathon*, and ongoing studies by Greek sports psychologist Yiannis Pitsiladis of the University of Brighton, UK, as well as Ericcson and the others.

Emphasizing the natural talent aspect or genetic pool of athletes, Epstein points to the case of a German tennis talent camp managed by psychologist Wolfgang Schneider. In 1978, 106 of the most promising eight- to twelve-year-old tennis players were selected from that camp. Of these, ninety-eight made it to the professional level, ten rose to the top 100 and a few reached the Top Ten. In the five-year study, tennis players Steffi Graf and Boris Becker were termed natural athletes. 'We called Steffi Graf the perfect tennis talent. She outperformed the others in tennis-specific skills and basic motor skills and we also predicted from her lung capacity that she could have ended up as the European champion in the 1500 metres,' Schneider is quoted as saying. What this suggests is that despite practice, there needs to be natural talent. Otherwise all participants in many such sports camps should climb to the same level. This never happens even if such regular camps are held over long periods. The genetically blessed have a better chance of making it. The question is: Can anyone be genetically blessed?

Based on the studies that researchers have conducted in many developed countries and even South Africa, Epstein concluded that 'a nation succeeds in a sport not only by having many athletes who practice prodigiously at sport-specific skills, but also by getting the best all-round athletes into the right sports in the first place. The truth is even at the most basic level, it's always a hardware and software story, just as the reverse is true. Sport skill acquisition does not happen without both specific genes and a specific environment and often the genes and the environment must coincide at a specific time.'

The argument of how essential it is to have athletic parents in order to excel is heard more regarding athletics than skill games. While it may be true in a large number of cases, most champion athletes or top rankers in other games did not have parents who were champion athletes. While the basic body frame is genetically gifted, the rest of it, which include the pace, the speed, the endurance, the strategy, among other factors, have to be acquired by hard work.

The 10,000-hour or the ten-year theory for creating geniuses was first put out in a 1993 study of musicians in the Music Academy of West Berlin now widely accepted as the best study on the creation of high-achievers. It was done by three psychologists, led by Anders Ericsson.[22] The premise here was that musicians were much easier to study in a control group. The musicians, most of them experts considering they had got admission into this renowned Academy, were graded as 'best', 'good' and 'music teachers'. They were asked to make diary notes about the hours they spent practicing. The first indication that practice is a major factor in the creation of geniuses

---

[22] K. Anders Ericsson, Ralf Th. Krampes, Clemens Tesch Roman,'The Role of Deliberate Practice in the Acquisition of Expert Performance', *Psychological Review*, 1993.

came when it was found that the top two groups spent on an average 24.3 hours compared to 9.3 hours for the lower or third group.

Ericsson and his co-authors conclude: 'In most domains of expertise, individuals begin in their childhood a regimen of effortful activities (deliberate practice) designed to optimize improvement. Individual differences, even among elite performers, are closely related to assessed amounts of deliberate practice. Many characteristics once believed to reflect innate talent are actually the result of intense practice extended for a minimum of 10 years. Analysis of expert performance provides unique evidence on the potential and limits of extreme environmental adaptation and learning.'

Ericsson's theory thus says that there is no genetic gift by which you go on to win an Olympic medal. It has to be earned: 'The simplicity of these accounts is attractive, but more is needed. A truly scientific account of exceptional performance must completely describe both the development leading to exceptional performance and the genetic and acquired characteristics that mediate it. This account must specify the critical differences between exceptional and ordinary performers. It must also show that any postulated genetic differences can be hereditary and are plausible from an evolutionary perspective.'

Ericsson identified three phases in the creation of a genius. The first phase begins with an individual's introduction to activities in the domain and ends with the start of instruction and deliberate practice. The second phase consists of an extended period of preparation and ends with the individual's commitment to pursuing activities on a full-time basis. The third phase consists of a full-time commitment to improving performance and ends when the individual can make a living as a professional performer in the domain.

During all three phases, the individual requires support from parents, teachers and education institutions. The framework needs to be extended with a fourth phase to accommodate eminent performance. During the fourth phase, individuals go beyond the knowledge of their teachers to make a unique innovative contribution to their domain.

Ultimately, the individual has to put in ten years of practice to reach the level of extraordinary achievement. Ericsson feels that those who do not make it at the third stage have had inappropriate training during the early and middle phases of training, such as in music, which formed the basis of his study.

In his 2016 book *Peak*,[23] following by his ground-breaking *The Road to Excellence*, Ericsson argues vehemently against the idea of natural talent and says that whoever is pictured thus has had preliminary practice before he came to the attention of the public. He questions the depiction of Mozart as a musical genius who was born great. He was made to practice hard during his young days by his father. Some of the musical notes ascribed to Mozart are actually by his father.

Ericsson also says that most Nobel Prize winners do not even have Mensa IQ or very high intelligence quotient, thereby emphasizing that great discoverers achieved what they did by hard work and deliberate practice with a clear goal in mind. To bolster his argument, Ericsson looks at a 2006 study of young chess players, not Grandmasters, by three British researchers.[24] These children between the ages of nine and thirteen had been playing the game for about four years on average.

---

[23] K. Anders Ericsson and Robert Pool, *Peak: Secrets from the New Science of Expertise*, Bodley Head, 2016.

[24] Merim Bilalic and Peter McLeod of Oxford University, Fernand Gobet of Brunel University.

Ericsson's study[25] is a passionate attempt at proving that you need to work hard for any achievement in work, in sport and life in general. In the initial part the study says that IQ is not necessarily linked to various achievements. One of the early conclusions of the study is that acquired knowledge and skills are important to attain expert performance, irrespective of IQ and memory power.

The study of sport just as of any other subject, shows that over the last century, every sport has improved considerably. Who are the people who have driven this tremendous advancement in sport? Ericsson and many others suggest that those are the people who practice relentlessly. The study also gives us the instance of Tchaikovsky, nineteenth-century Russian composer, who asked two of his greatest violinists to play his violin concerto. Both refused, deeming the score unplayable. Today, however, the concerto is considered part of any standard repertory.

*

In the twentieth century, humankind worked relentlessly to push the horizons of knowledge and other achievements. Study after study shows that in every sphere, we humans have put in more work than we ever did in the preceding centuries.

Herbert A. Simon and William G. Chase, in 'Skill in Chess' in the *American Scientist*, July–August, 1973, first described the ten-year rule for achieving excellence after studying International Masters and found that almost all of them had put in at least ten years of playing chess.

What then is deliberate practice? If we look at sports stars who are major achievers, we know that it is not

[25] Ericsson, *Peak*.

just the relentless nature of their efforts but how they worked at various aspects of their game, not just spending time on the courts or stadiums. 'Deliberate practice is an effortful activity that can be sustained only for a limited time each day during extended periods without leading to exhaustion. To maximise gains from long term-practice individuals must avoid exhaustion and must limit practice to an amount for which they can recover on a daily or weekly basis,' says Ericsson.

In real sport, there are various examples to prove Ericsson's theory that there is nothing called natural talent. The athletes who are regularly described as 'raw talent' by sports reporters are actually not people who just started running or hitting the ball with ferocity the day they could lay their hands on a bat or racquet. Nor did they swim the fastest from the day they were dropped into the deep end of the pool.

American five-medal winner and star swimmer (four golds, one silver in the Rio Olympics) Katie Ledecky is reported to have finally got the time to attend a concert by 'Boss' Bruce Springsteen after years of wanting to only when someone surprised her with tickets. She had been a 'Boss' fan ever since she was a child but never got the time: 'I have been listening to Bruce Springsteen music riding in my family's car throughout my youth going to early morning practices and to swim meets. I have over 400 Bruce Springsteen songs on my iPod, including recordings of his live performance ... I never had the opportunity to attend a Springsteen show because of my training and meet schedule but I finally had a break in my training after the Olympics that coincided with Bruce's show at the Nationals Park.'

Ledecky's achievement of winning five freestyle Olympic medals, with two world records, is incredible and there is no doubt that it is strenuous and never-ending practice that made her perfect. For about eight years till she was nineteen at Rio, she put in eight hours of practice a day minimum since she started at 4 or 5 a.m.—that would come to 19,200 hours of practice over eight years even if we count for just 300 days a year.

A tennis star in the Top Twenty in 2017, Nick Kyrgios is among those who are frequently described as having raw talent, even by the ever-caustic John McEnroe. There is a widespread belief among tennis reporters that he is not interested in the game but reached where he is because he is a natural or raw talent. In other words, his genes do the work for him and if he merely followed his instinct, he could win matches. This belief has gained ground after he tanked matches and also because of his one-liners about hating practice, loving Pokemon, adoring NBA basketball. The generally accepted belief is that Kyrgios is God's gift to tennis though he is a brat, due mostly to his lazy, languorous gait. He is not seen as a young man in mission mode. The truth lies somewhere else.

The fact is that Kyrgios has practiced as hard as anyone else after his brother Christos introduced him to tennis, even though he also spent time playing basketball. In an interview,[26] his mother said that during his teenaged days there were many overnight car journeys to country town parks where the family would stay in caravans while Nick played in tournaments, which shows how early his parents had introduced him to tournament play—by the age of twelve he had already won a national title in Australia. That confidence gained from early tournament play is clearly visible now in his on-court performance.

Kyrgios himself feels that he is a natural and tennis came easily to him, so in this case he is a classic mix of

[26] Interview of Kyrgios and his mother by Mick Dickson, *Daily Mail*, 17 June 2017.

hard work on top of a genetic foundation. 'I sometimes wonder what would have happened had I stuck with basketball. But the "path" I've chosen is not the word. I originally played tennis because my brother Christos was playing and my parents wanted me to and I found it came pretty easily to me,' he said in the interview.

The 'coming easily' is his inheritance, in the sense that he had the physical build for the game. His mother Norlaila, who is Malaysian, was a national college badminton champion and his father had played in a season of professional soccer in Melbourne. Kyrgios is thus what genetic theory supporters would say 'the right mix'. But then the question remains of what happened to Christos who started first before his brother edged past him? As of now there cannot be answers as to how only one among siblings inherits the right genes from sporting parentage. The same is the case with Jamie and Andy Murray. Even among twins we see that one person breaks away mostly during adolescence and reaches heights while the other sibling is left behind.

But Kyrgios also has a self-destructive trait which can be seen in people following many professions. Is a destructive, which lives right beside his physically supreme genes, at work here? I watched Kyrgios in one of his most disastrous displays—at the 2017 Australian Open fourth round against Italian player Andreas Seppi, which he tanked at 6-2. I had no doubt that his mind was in a self-destructive mode. He never ran for his shots and deliberately hit wide, generally showing that he did not care a damn about winning a match. Here was one player who didn't mind losing. In fact, he asked for failure to come and hug him. He has the dominant psyche of those who cut their noses to spite someone else or everybody. However, in truth, Kyrgios plays or practices as much as his peers. He has never shirked Davis Cup responsibilities and has a caring nature, often encouraging youngsters to take to the game.

*

It is almost universally believed that Cassius Clay (he later changed his name to Muhammad Ali when he joined the Nation of Islam) was a natural—a robust, well-built human being, with all the physical attributes needed to take him to the top of boxing. This is the perception regarding all heavyweight boxers: 'Born champions', 'Born boxer', 'A natural boxer who can blast his way through any wall' and so on. Here too the truth lies elsewhere.

Ali was no 'genetic' natural, his father was a painter of signs, a bit of a vagabond, a bit of a 'womanizer' and a prodigious imbiber of alcohol. Clay Senior was once stabbed by a woman whose door he knocked on at night. With that bleeding injury he went to a friend and asked for a bottle of whisky, saying, 'A bit to be poured on the wound and the rest to be swallowed.'

Clay Junior inherited only a few of these characteristics and instead of painting signs, he shouted out loud. He wasn't a natural sportsman by his own admission, and so did not take to basketball. This is what he said and is quoted by David Remnick, again proving that practice is most influential in the creation of champions though genes too play an important part. 'I was not that bright and quick in school, couldn't be a football or a basketball player 'cause you have to go to college and get all kinds of injuries and pass examinations. A boxer can just go into a gym, jump around, turn professional, win a fight, get a break and he is in the ring.'

Clay Junior didn't just jump into the ring. A Louisville

cop to whom Clay went to complain about his bicycle being stolen, talked him into joining a gym which the cop himself ran on the side with money he made from emptying parking meters. When he asked him, 'Well, do you know how to fight?', Clay replied, 'No ... but I'd fight anyway.'

That's how it started.

Cassius Clay had more intention than gravitas. After the first practice bout with another boy at the gym, which he won by a split decision, he shouted: 'I am the greatest of all time!'

But boy, did he practice hard. He was maniacal about going to the gym for he soon saw destiny there. Clay's discipline from the age of twelve on convinced Martin (Joe Martin, the cop) that he had a future as a boxer. Cassius woke between 4 and 5 a.m., ran several miles and then worked out at the gym in the afternoon, staying long past the hour when his peers had gone home for dinner. 'All he wanted to do was run and train and spar,' said Jimmy Ellis, a contemporary at the Columbia Gym who won the WBA heavyweight championship when it was stripped from Ali in 1967 for his refusal to go to Vietnam. 'As long as there was someone to box, he'd take them on.'

This then, is a recurring story of all world champions. They all stayed back at the gym or court or stadium and sweated it out long after the others had gone for dinner. This is where the story of the world champion lies.

Remnick says that at the age of fifteen, Clay had a sure sense of his destiny—this is another mental aspect that one sees in every champion. Destiny and the very notion of greatness is embedded in a champion's mind from his young days. How it gets embedded is mostly by chance, like in the case of Clay who met the cop just because his bike was stolen, a moment that changed his life and the sport of boxing for ever.

In *Ali*: *A Life* by Jonathan Eig,[27] there is a detailed summary of the practice that Clay put in. In the first bout against Charles L. 'Sonny' Liston, when Clay was the total underdog, he practiced like hell. 'While Clay was running the streets every morning and punishing his body in brutal sessions and with brawny, sparring partners at the Fifth Street Gym, Liston was coasting and the Nilon brothers, concessionaires of the Philadelphia stadium, were letting him coast. In the air conditioned Surfside Civa auditorium in North Miami Beach, Liston worked out with a skipping rope…and running a mile or two outside when the mood struck him, which wasn't often. Liston sparred but none of his sparring partners were as big or as fast as Clay. At night Liston ate hot dogs, drank beer, played cards and screwed around with prostitutes. He was training like a man who believed he could knock out his opponents with a hard stare …

'Clay on the other hand was not only in top shape he was a diligent student of his sport who watched countless hours of fights on film, especially [those featuring world middleweight champion] Jake LaMotta versus Sugar Ray Robinson, [six times the world boxing champion], big bruising punches going against a faster smoother man. When someone asked how he felt about being listed as a ten to one underdog, Clay explained calmly why the people who slotted him as such were wrong.

He said, "I go to bed fighting, eat fighting, and even dream fighting."'

This should be the cardinal rule for every professional athlete wanting to reach and remain at the top. Most Indian athletes do no such thing. They are happy to be where they reach and do just enough to remain where

---

[27] Jonathan Eig, *Ali: A Life*, Houghton Mifflin Harcourt, 2017.

they are. For example, a member of the Indian women's medal-winning long relay team, whom I had met in Patiala, left the team and went back to her village during the Covid lockdown in 2020, saying she felt happy in her village. As a result these athletes plateau out and then decline. In this lack of full-fledged determination lies the story of many failures. Most Indian sportspersons are unable to develop the drive required to go further. Their ambitions are mostly local, to be recognized and adulated in their village or city. Their aspirations do not seem to last. Often this is because of the depressing and regressive nature of the environment most of them come from.

Success and failure are not assured even for the greats. Sporting life means to be in a constant state of preparation, if not by physical training, then by mental strength. Even greats like Roger Federer sometimes have the intuition that they are not going to win a particular match. Often they realize the mind is not in the right place. Federer lost in the US Open 2017 to the Argentine Juan Martín del Potro. After the loss Federer said, 'It has been a tough tournament. I struggled if I ran into a good guy. I knew I was going to lose. And going in I knew I was not in a safe place. I'm out of this tournament because I wasn't good enough, in my mind, my body and my game.'

Many players have expressed similar feelings about not being in the right frame of mind. The proper frame of mind surely helps you cut out the unforced errors, the lazy returns. To me, unforced errors in any game are the errors you make because your mind is not in the right place at that point of time.

*

Mike Tyson's coach, Kevin Rooney, who took over from boxing manager and trainer Cus D'Amato, says of his ward, 'Eat, sleep and train. Mike loves to train.' Which is why Mike Tyson is considered one of the best heavyweight boxers ever. In fact, there cannot be a world champion in any sport who does not love to train. The gifted athlete for whom winning comes naturally is a myth. Winning and training are strongly connected.

David Epstein, who plugs the gene theory, however, has his doubts about the Ericsson theory: 'All the data in support of the 10,000-hour rule (of Anders Ericsson) have been what scientists call "cross-sectional" and "retrospective". That is, researchers look at subjects who have already attained a skill level. A study that is restricted to only pre-screened performers is hopelessly biased against discovering evidence of innate talent.'

Daniel Willingham, an expert on implicit-explicit learning, says: 'The unexpected finding from cognitive science is that practice does not make perfect. Practice until you are perfect and you will be perfect only briefly. What's necessary is sustained practice. By sustained practice I mean regular ongoing review or use of target material (for example, regularly using new calculating skills to solve increasingly more complex math problems ...). This kind of practice past the point of mastery is necessary to meet any of these three important goals of instruction, acquiring facts and knowledge, learning skills or becoming an expert.'

Apart from genes and relentless practice, what else is required for the big performance? An ideal environment for the sport is highly essential. For example, Greek researcher Yannis Pitsiladis of the University of Brighton, UK, aims to groom an athlete to break the two-hour barrier in competitive marathons, preferring Kenyan runners since, overall, the Kenyan environment is suited for endurance running. Since 1998, the marathon record has dropped by three minutes and eight seconds, which in itself is an awesome achievement. The very idea is to take human physical achievement to its pinnacle. Even cutting two minutes from the marathon timing is an unimaginable feat. 'What excites me is understanding the limits of human performance. What can man do?' says Pitsiladis.

Pitsiladis is of the view that practice alone does not make perfect. Many elite marathoners run 120 miles a week. Perhaps even 75 miles a week may work just as well, he feels. He should know because few in the world have spent so much time and energy on one single athletic event trying to stretch the limits of human achievement.

Long-distance running itself goes counter to the Ericsson theory since people from the Rift Valley in Kenya and some others from Eastern African countries have performed admirably well and now monopolize long- and middle-distance events. Why should this happen if the 10,000-hour rule is the only criteria? Is it the argument that other long-distance aspirants are not practising the way they should? Pitsiladis believes the runner to break two hours would be someone from a rural East African village at an ideal altitude who was accustomed to daily activity. This fits the profile of Eliud Kipchoge perfectly.

He also believes that the mark can be broken only in a place near the Dead Sea where the air pressure is optimum. 'A quarter-mile below sea level at the Dead Sea, where the barometric pressure is high, there is about 5 per cent more oxygen to breathe. The naturally enriched air had been shown to increase exercise capacity in those with chronic lung disease. Would it do the same, Pitsiladis wondered, for the world's fastest distance runners?'[28]

---

[28] Jere Longman, 'Man vs. Marathon', *New York Times*, 11 May 2016.

Parallel to Pitsiladis' effort is the Nike's Building2 project, which resulted in Kipchoge breaking the two-hour barrier. Nike's effort was to make the top runners run in controlled conditions, cutting out all possible time-wasting that could be taking place in a competitive marathon run, even the act of taking water from the aid desks on the way or cutting out the bends and turns in the race course.

In the Nike-sponsored first unsuccessful attempt on a race track in Italy, all external conditions were to the liking of Kipchoge. Before the race, Kipchoge told Alex Hutchinson,[29] 'Most of the people were saying they will die before they see a man running under two hours. But I think I will prove them wrong.' He did, and how well!

So on the foundation of a good genetic pool or let's say, the right type of physique that he/she inherits, an athlete must work hours in ideal conditions and a conducive environment. More importantly, he/she must be backed by the annoyingly overwhelming and constant desire to excel, to win, that only the great possess.

*

There is no doubt that physical attributes (height, weight, eyesight and so on) are inherited. It is not known if one is born with strong lungs or a sturdy heart. But some hereditary factors may come into play, in endurance sport for example. There can be no doubt that in high-skill sport, genetic factors have no role to play. Skill has to be developed by hard work even if one or both the athlete's parents are Olympic winners.

Other scientific areas may shed some light on this issue. Evolutionary biology is an exciting field these

[29] Alex Hutchinson, *Endurance: Mind, Body, and the Curiously Elastic Limits of Human Performance*, HarperCollins, 2018.

days. Animals have developed or evolved sexual and other physical attributes to serve certain survival purposes, writes Ferris Jabr.[30] His article points out that Charles Darwin in *The Descent of Man*, 'explained sexual selection which he thought could explain two of animal kingdom's most conspicuous and puzzling features—weaponry and adornment. Sometimes males competing fiercely for females would enter a sort of evolutionary arms race, developing ever-greater weapons—tusks, horns, antlers—as best-endowed males of each successful generation reproduced at the expense of their weaker peers ... among species whose female chose the most attractive males based on their subjective taste, males would develop outlandish sexual ornaments.'

If animal species can evolve physical features that help them in the noble task of propagating their own species, will the same apply to sporting ability in humans? Will humans of the future have fully athletic muscles, or muscles and tendons tuned towards greater performances in sport? It is tempting to say that it is not very likely since sport is not a matter of the survival of a species. Also, ability in sport is not genetically transferred, though the physical nature of the human body is.

In his analysis of beauty in birds and animals, Ferris Jabr points out that sexual ornaments have become prominent in many species as a result of evolution. So is it an evolutionary possibility that human beings may eventually develop very long fingers (to grip and control racquets perfectly), disproportionately long legs (jumps and sprints in athletics) and so on? 'Think of the bright elastic throats of anole lizards, the Faberge abdomens of

[30] Ferris Jabr, 'How Beauty Is Making Scientists Rethink Evolution', *New York Times*, 14 January 2019.

peacock spiders and the curling, iridescent, ludicrously long feathers of birds-of-paradise. To reconcile such splendours with a utilitarian view of evolution, biologists have favoured the idea that beauty in the animal kingdom is not mere decoration—it's a code. According to this theory, ornaments evolved as indicators of a potential mate's advantageous qualities, its overall health, intelligence and survival skills, plus the fact that it will pass down the genes underlying these traits to its children. A bowerbird with especially bright plumage might have a robust immune system, for example, while one that finds rare and distinctive trinkets might be a superb forager. Beauty, therefore, would not confound natural selection—it would be very much part of it.'

Just looking at the time we have clipped from marathon races over the last 100 years is evidence enough that endurance, skill and muscles for higher sporting activity will develop, helped by scientific training over long periods. Genetically, too, there might be taller and stronger men in the next 200 years.

*

In the case of excellence in life in general too—landing good jobs, running a successful business, earning well—there is some evidence that the atmosphere at home and mental conditioning helps. An element of practice is also involved because academic excellence calls for time to be devoted to devouring lessons. *Time* magazine in a special issue[31] tracked nine families whose children are in top jobs and generally seen as achievers—the idea was to find out the secret of success, which is an ongoing passion of many scholars. In one such family, Gino Rodriguez, the father,

[31] Charlotte Alter, 'Ordinary Families, Extraordinary Kids', *Time*, 5 September 2016.

knelt down at the bed of each of his daughters while they slept and whispered the mantra: 'I can, I will.' He did this for twenty years. This subconscious suggestion for a long period, Gino felt, would transform into real achievement in life. 'You talk to the subconscious. You don't talk to the conscious. That's the one that listens.'

One by one, the girls achieved success in life. Ivelesse Rodriguez graduated from Harvard Business School, Rebecca Rodriguez is a medical director at the Westside Family Health Centre and Gina Rodriguez won a Golden Globe for Best Actress. Here, in a funny reversal of the Ericsson theory, the practicing was done by someone else—the father who did all the whispering for twenty years.

This suggests that external factors became crucial in the development of excellence. So like the Kenyan runners who grew up in a certain environment which helped stamina, these *Time* magazine families had a positive environment and factors that motivated kids or boosted their self-confidence. 'Of the nine families, eight had a parent who was an immigrant or an educator and five had a parent who was both. Many parents were involved in political activism of some kind. Most recall a conflict-heavy family life, but that conflict was rarely between parents. Many had a strong awareness of mortality as children. And most said they grew up with much more freedom than their friends did.'

The *Time* story consists of classic middle-class success stories and in an advanced society like the US, which can provide the right environment for success in various aspects of life, there would be myriads of them.

Success stories of even those who have had disjointed family lives or even lived their childhood on the streets (boxing champions like Mike Tyson, for example) go into sustaining the American dream—these poor and disadvantaged youngsters eventually escaping their hard lives and finding opportunities in the first-world environment where top-class sports and training facilities are common. Developed societies everywhere are also bubbles of excellence. It is there that ideas sprout and change our lives. This is also the reason why developed countries produce the greatest sportsmen and also the reason why developed countries form the top five or ten medal-winning countries in the Olympics.

The rest stagger along.

CHAPTER THREE

Why Wealthy Nations Dominate the Podium and the Link Between Olympic Medals and Economic Might

The Olympic Games are the showpiece of physical prowess and the single event that prompts and inspires a global physical culture. The quadrennial event is the one marker of the human intention and ability to stretch the boundaries of time, space, speed, strength and skill. It drives nations to higher levels of physical achievement and thousands of athletes to desperation, a few of them to immortality.

For all nations, the staging of the Olympics itself is a sign of supremacy in the comity of nations. The large majority of the world's 150 odd countries cannot even dream of hosting the Olympics in the near future. The approximate cost of $30 billion is far too much an unnecessary burden for many countries. They may at best participate in the hosting bid to announce that they too are on this planet and they too have inhabitants who nurture ambitions. The Olympics is a display of wealth and advancement as much as it is a show of sporting skills and physical prowess.

While poor nations or even developing nations cannot dream of hosting the Olympics, they cannot even aspire to win a medal. Even for huge economies like India, the Olympics is a quadrennial event to indulge in self-flagellation: a country with one billion people but no medal, is the oft-heard lament. For emerging economies or backward economies, the situation is the same. For such countries, the Olympics is an event which constantly downgrades them. It is a humiliating experience which takes place every four years. Some host nations which did not heed the dark clouds of a sliding economy have paid heavily; for example, Greece went bankrupt about six years after hosting the 2004 Olympics.

Built into all this is the notion of national self-confidence, pride and a certain jingoism. The Olympics is also a 'nationalism' project. Remember that all medal-winners at the Olympics rush to cover themselves with the national flag after their victory is confirmed, unlike say, at a Grand Slam final.

As India's pride and self-respect grew with its rising status as an economic power and it became the biggest market in the world for many high-end products, the country started putting more money into sport and its infrastructure grew phenomenally. Six medals in London and four in Rio is a big leap for India in the Olympics, but we finished overall at the shameful rank of sixty-seven in Rio, 2016. For a big economy it was below even a pedestrian performance. But India had just turned the corner about a decade before and it takes time for any country to turn itself into a sporting power. India now has private and focused programmes like the private Quest for Gold and the government's funding programme, the Target Olympic Podium Scheme (TOPS), but the terribly mismanaged sports federations have made the sport situation impossible. However, India satisfies its nationalistic urges by being a major power in cricket, a game that only ten countries play.

I studied the medal tallies from the 1960 Rome Olympics onwards to substantiate my conclusion that wealth and Olympics superiority is closely linked. There are a few exceptions, of course.

But first, a look at the Rio Olympics, 2016. No backward country, no African or Asian nation and no underperforming economy figured prominently in the top fifteen of the Rio medal list. Have a look at the five top medal-winners (gold, silver and bronze) as of 17 August 2016.

US	28, 28, 28
UK	19, 19, 12
China	17, 15, 19
Russia	12, 12, 14
Germany	11, 8, 7
Italy	8, 9, 8

The top five medal tally at the end of the Rio Olympics was:

US	38, 35, 32
UK	24, 22,14
China	22,18, 25
Germany	14, 8, 13
Russia	13, 16, 19

The final top five tally showed that all were economically advanced nations, which means that the medal tally roughly corresponds to ranking in terms of wealth or gross domestic product (GDP).

US (No. 1 in GDP in 2016)	46, 37, 38 = 121
UK (GDP rank–5)	27, 23, 17 = 67
China (GDP rank–2)	26, 18, 26 = 70
Russia (GDP rank–12)	19,17, 20 = 56
Germany (GDP rank–4)	17, 10, 15 = 42

The other wealthy nations were close behind:

6. Japan (GDP rank–3) 12, 8, 21 = 41
7. France (GDP rank–6) 10, 18, 14 = 42
8. S Korea (GDP rank–11) 9, 3, 9 = 21
9. Italy (GDP rank–8) 8, 12, 8 = 28
10. Australia (GDP rank–13) 8, 11, 10 = 29

Here then, is the line-up of the world's powerful sporting nations. This has been the line-up for most of the Olympics since 1960. These nations also form the so-called First World: advanced countries, with huge per capita incomes, though in some cases, small in size. All these ten countries have also hosted the Olympics, some of them twice over. The per capita criteria is significant—how much money there is per citizen, which together with GDP is a more accurate indicator of economic health and affluence. So a country like India, which was 7th in the 2016 GDP ranking, is not really affluent; its rank by per capita in 2017 was 122. Apart from other problems India faces, ranging from bureaucratic sports bodies, corruption and lack of consistent discipline in many sportspersons, this basic fact—that there isn't enough money to allocate towards creating champions, is one major reason why the country performs so badly at the Olympics. We may be one of the world's largest economies, but we are a poor nation.

There are of course exceptions, which only prove the rule. At the Rio Olympics, Canada, though a wealthy nation, finished twentieth with only four golds. Among the small and poor nations, only Jamaica and Kenya (six golds each) were in the top twenty. These two countries dominate the track events due mostly to individual brilliance.

The US crossed a total tally of 100 medals, a nation far superior to others as a sporting nation, a country which dominates in all fields.

In the 1968 Olympics, Russia had fifty golds, the US thirty-three, East Germany twenty, West Germany thirteen and Japan came fifth with thirteen golds. By 2000, in the Olympics held at Sydney, the US was at the top, with thirty-seven golds and was followed by Russia (thirty-two) and China (twenty-eight). Australia, the host nation, came fourth with sixteen golds and Great Britain was tenth with eleven. In all the post-colonial Olympics starting from 1960, the top ten have been same, only changing positions a bit here and there. China has been the outlier country.

Since 1980 or so, however, China went on a drastic and phenomenal development path which shocked a disbelieving world. By the Beijing Olympics of 2008, China was top of the tally.

To look at China's rise as a sporting nation is also to look at the nation's rise as an economic power. In the 1960 Olympics, China performed like India, finishing with just one silver. In 1968, nothing had changed. By the 2000 Sydney Olympics, China had touched twenty-eight gold medals and in Beijing with the obvious advantages of being the host nation, China got fifty-one gold medals and pushed the US for the first time in forty years to the second place. By the turn of the century, China had become an economic superpower. China's GDP in 2006 was only $ 2.6 trillion (India is at $2.6 trillion in 2019) and by 2016 had touched an unimaginable $9.4 trillion. During the same period it made its greatest advances in almost every Olympic sport. Its growth as a sporting nation has not been paralleled.

It might also surprise us that two of the most well-known sporting nations we admire, mostly due to its soccer stars—Brazil and Argentina—are Olympic laggards as well. Argentina excels in several sports, including football, tennis, volleyball, basketball. In Rio it had super teams in soccer, volleyball, basketball, tennis, beach volleyball, both in men's and women's disciplines, and most reached the semi-finals. Brazil had the same achievement. Unlike India, both are sporting nations that produced legends whom we all admire and follow—but what was Argentina's medal standing in 2016? It was ranked at the twenty-seventh spot, with a medal count of three golds, one silver and zero bronze, while Brazil—despite being the host nation—finished thirteenth with a mediocre tally of seven, six and six. The reason is that both these developing countries which excel in many team games are laggards in individual athletic and swimming events (which account for the maximum medals) and do not match up with the top nations in sports technology, infrastructure and management. In other words, they are not rich nations.

Let us look at another advanced economy and an underpopulated country. Australia got twenty-nine medals in Rio (eight golds) but slumped from its Athens tally of seventeen gold medals to the tenth position. In Athens and the earlier Sydney Olympics, Australia was in the fourth position. Nicole Jeffery writing in *The Weekend Australian*, 21 January 2018, attributed this to a lack of spending on sports in an article with a hyped-up heading, 'Death of a Dream'. This, despite the fact that Australia for a long time has been among the top ten. Australia is a sport-obsessed nation, which spends most of its time outdoors and so has been spending large amounts to be among the top three in almost every sport. Such an obsession has not gripped emerging nations yet, all of them making just casual allocations with no definite plan.

'The disconnect between the longstanding ambition of sports chiefs to stay among the top five Olympic nations and the resources placed at their command is growing,' Jeffery lamented. She pointed out that Britain has hugely increased its Olympic spending while Australia's has declined. Though there is no direct indication, this slowdown could also be because the Australian economy (AUS $1.6 trillion or US $1.3 trillion) contracted by about 0.5 per cent in 2015. But Australia is a lean and mean nation with a population of just 22 million, over 10 million less than the population of India's small but advanced state of Kerala. So the share of the national pie for sport will remain massive despite the contraction of the economy.

Here is the core high performance funding in 2014–15 of advanced nations (minus corporate funding) according to *The Australian* (in US$ millions). This is the amount for four years on preparations for the Olympics.

UK	334 Second rank after the US in Rio
Germany	275 Fifth rank
Japan	155 Sixth rank
France	384 Seventh rank
South Korea	155 Eighth rank
Italy	189 Ninth rank
Australia	198 Tenth rank

There is nothing much to lament about, as Jeffery does, considering that Australia is poised to move into the top five again—since it can easily dominate swimming, and now is becoming a powerhouse in athletics as well, all due to well-planned programmes, much like in China. Of course, all this goes in tandem with national desire.

According to the data-based analysis website IndiaSpend.com, 'There appears to be a direct correlation between money spent by the UK and Olympic medals won. With a funding of 5 million pounds for the Atlanta Olympics, where it won a single gold medal and finished thirty-sixth, the UK finished second at Rio, its best after a century (it was first in 1908) with twenty-seven gold medals.' Here is a chart showing the increase in the UK's spending on sport and its medal tally at the Olympics from 1996 to 2016:

Two Decades, UK Olympic Spending Fifty-Fold

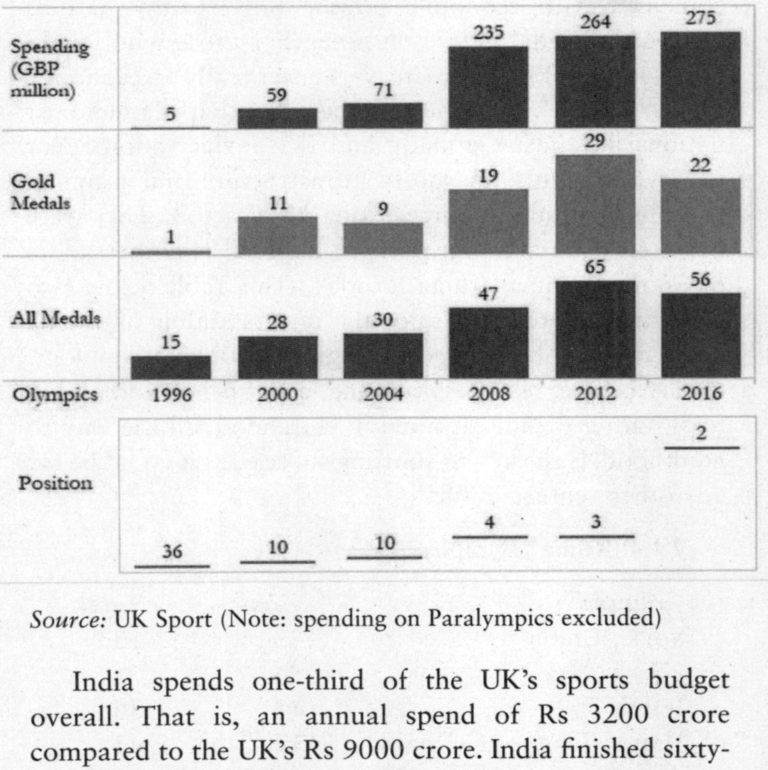

Source: UK Sport (Note: spending on Paralympics excluded)

India spends one-third of the UK's sports budget overall. That is, an annual spend of Rs 3200 crore compared to the UK's Rs 9000 crore. India finished sixty-seventh to the UK's second, though this classification is based on gold medals and not on overall potential. For this we have to look at the fourth or fifth place finishes. India achieved four fourth place finishes, all of which could have been gold actually if focused training and top-level strategies had been adopted. Many top-level athletes in India plateau out because of lack of spending and management.

To buttress my argument, here is a general list of the medal tally of most of the Olympics since 1960, but includes only gold medals and totals to avoid the clutter. For more than half a century, the medal tally eerily coincided with economic power. Top wealthy nations topped the medal tally each time. (For those who would point out that East Germany was never really an economic 'power house', we must remember that Communist nations like East Germany and the Soviet Union spent massive amounts on sports infrastructure and training, perhaps diverting resources from other sectors. They were obsessed with creating sports champions as ambassadors of Communism, as China is today.) This Table below also gives the lie to the rather popular understanding of genetic pool nations being sporting giants. Only technology, infrastructure, relentless training, cash spends and ability to sustain a dream captured in childhood, all the way to adulthood, is the key to sporting success, as it could be for any other venture in life.

1960 Rome Olympics:

Country	*Gold*	*Total*
Soviet Union	43	103
US	34	71
Italy	13	36
United Team of Germany	12	42
Australia	8	22
UK	2	20
France	0	5
China	0	1

1964 Tokyo Olympics:

US	36	90
Soviet Union	30	96
Japan	16	29
United Team of Germany	10	50
Italy	10	27
India	1	1

1968 Mexico Olympics:

US	45	107
Soviet Union	29	91
Japan	11	25
Hungary	10	32
East Germany	9	25
China	0	1
India	0	1

1976 Montreal Olympics:

Soviet Union	49	125
East Germany	40	90
US	34	94
West Germany	10	39
Japan	9	25
UK	3	13

2000 Sydney Olympics

US	37	93
Russia	32	89
China	28	58
Australia	16	56
Germany	13	56
UK	11	28
Japan	5	18
Kenya	2	7

2008 Beijing Olympics:

China	51	100
US	36	110
Russia	23	73
UK	19	47
Australia	14	46
Kenya	6	14
Singapore	1	1

2012 London Olympics:

US	46	104
China	38	91
UK	29	65
Russia	19	68
Korea	13	30
Germany	11	44
France	11	35
Australia	8	35

*

Actually, individual brilliance is what lights up the Olympics, not the superiority of one country. Such countries reach the top since they are collectives of individual brilliance. There were six athletes of incredible brilliance who helped the US bag twenty-eight medals in Rio—Michael Phelps, Swimming, six medals; Katie Ledecky, Swimming, five; Simone Biles, Gymnastics, five, Simone Manuel, Swimming, four; Madeline Dirado, Swimming, four; Nathan Adrian, Swimming, four. This is an amazing number of medals. How long will any non-Olympic nation take to reach the win of twenty-eight medals by six athletes?

To take an athlete to the Olympic-winning level

needs minute planning and the availability of facilities. Some athletes manage to emerge through the rings of inefficiencies that proliferate in poorer economies. An example from Rio is Katinka Hosszu of Hungary who won four swimming medals, more than India did overall.

A newspaper report in *Mint*[32] wonders whether it is better to concentrate on a smaller number of games (maybe swimming and gymnastics?) to increase the medal haul. The point here is that every country does not have traditional strengths in all sports. For India to suddenly produce a Phelps or a Hosszu will be a miracle. Some Indian athletes have tried to escape the Indian environment with all its inefficiencies by transplanting themselves in the US. That is what most global aspiring athletes do. Ideally this should work, although it takes time. It has worked miracles in tennis for many East European nations.

The statistics in the report in *Mint* show that 21.5 per cent of US athletes in Rio won gold medals, 24.8 among Chinese athletes, while for India it was minus 1.7 per cent.

India is the worst performing country in sports in the world per capita. This goes against the theory presented here on economic might and medals. But, as I've mentioned earlier, it is per capita income of a country that is the real marker of its wealth, India may have a high GDP but it is a poor country. There are other factors. Roughly, India's economic growth really began only just over a decade back. Many of Asia's small economies, which came to be called Southeast Asian Tigers (such as Singapore, Malaysia, South Korea, Indonesia, Taiwan) have mostly had double-digit growth for two to three

---

32 Dipti Jain, 'Rio Olympics: How countries performed', *Mint*, 24 August 2016.

decades before they became 'Tigers'. It is difficult for India to have double-digit growth (China also grew at below double digits for many years) so changes at the grassroots will take time, more so since India carries the burden of huge poverty. Despite a respectable GDP, people living below the poverty line in India are estimated to be over 250 million, ten times Australia's population. The GDP is not the be-all and end-all of a nation's prosperity, since such a number does not consider other major economic factors.

Also, as I have pointed out elsewhere, the mismanagement of sport by Indian sports federations is the primary cause of the abysmal state of sport in India. There is a clause in the Olympic charter banning the interference of the government in sports management and this comes to the aid of mismanaged federations. The government and sports federations are involved in a bruising war to overhaul the sports management in the country. Though sport has been slow to start, the explosion of sporting leagues in India is a good sign. It shows how private money can change sport and how sport has to grow outside the narrow purview of federation-conducted events like the Nationals.

Even now the per capita spending on sports in India is a pathetic Rs 8; the massive population clearly has been a drag on India's attempt to emerge as a sports power. Paradoxically, though, a huge population presents India with the chance to harvest so-called genetic pools and some efforts were made in this direction by starting separate sports schemes for tribal people, which took off well, but died out due to lack of support. Due to the complex issues involved it is likely to take at least two decades before India will be among the major medal-winning nations.

When other countries were poised at $2 trillion GDP (India's GDP in 2014) they performed better than India has, according to an analysis by the *Times of India*.[33] When the US was at the same mark in 1977 it won 15.3 per cent of the total medals in Montreal (thirty-four gold; ninety-four total). China at the $2 trillion mark, just after 2004, won 6.8 per cent of the medals. India, however, finished with 0.6 per cent of medals in 2014.

The wealthy countries dominate not only because they can spend huge amounts on sport. They also dominate because they can manage things better, plan for the long term, strategize better, use modern technology and employ better coaches to buttress their ambition. The reasons why they became wealthy nations in the first place are also the reasons why they dominate in the Olympics and most sport. It is not a fluke that the US women's football (soccer, not American football) team won the World Cup in 2019. Football is a relatively new sport in the US but even here they dominate due to the planning, management, and of course, money spent on sport and the well-entrenched national desire to dominate in every field.

*

Small economies have not yet created any stir in the Olympics, the exceptions being Kenya and Jamaica, which have specific strengths. The reason, of course, is they do not have the resources, infrastructure and as smaller nations, have other more pressing concerns. Small countries that are developed also face the same problem. Singapore is an example—despite being an ideal state with an enviable record in nation building, the third-ranked nation in the world on per capita GDP, a major

---

33 *Times of India*, 1 March 2016.

global financial and service sector hub, with no apparent lack of facilities, Singapore has not made any headway in sport—that is, except for the achievement of Joseph Schooling who got a gold in the 100-metre butterfly race in Rio when he defeated his hero, Michael Phelps, no less. Singapore's strengths are in table tennis and badminton, but an Olympic medal seems distant. The reason could be lack of national will and its comparatively low GDP of above $300 billion, which would make sport a lower priority for national spending. There is also no evidence of any specific traditional strengths, despite a huge percentage of the Chinese population, and no geographical advantage like say, Kenya's Rift Valley. And of course, its frighteningly low population of just over 5 million (compared to Hong Kong's 7 million) could be the main problem. One possible way for Singapore to emerge as a sporting nation is to invite medal-winning sportsmen from poorer countries to take up residence there like Qatar, for instance, is doing. Let's not forget, thirty-six migrants were among Britain's Olympic medal-winners in London 2012!

Evidence suggests that everything has to be huge for a country to become an Olympic power: economy (*both* GDP and per capita income), population, geographic size, ambition, strategy, infrastructure. This also shows that physical superiority is as much a rare phenomenon as intellectual superiority is. Only the US, UK, Germany, France and China combine both.

*

Just as the rise of China as a sporting and economic power can be used to explain the link between wealth and sporting superiority, the economic decline of Japan during the last one decade and more can be used to further look at how national wealth affects sporting ambition. Japan has been among the top ten or nearby since 1960. It came third in the Tokyo Olympics, 1964, with sixteen golds after being in the eighth rank in Rome in 1960 (four golds, eighteen total), demonstrating that Japan was rising up from the debris of the Second World War to assert itself as an economic and sporting power. In 1968, in Mexico, it came fifth with thirteen golds and retained the same position in 1976. In Sydney, 2000, however, it had slumped to the fifteenth position with five golds and a total of eighteen. By the time of the 1996 Games held in Atlanta, Japan was beginning to go into a recession, which was a contributory factor for its lowest ranking in many years, when it won just three golds and a total of fourteen.

Economists call the 1990s Japan's 'lost decade' as recession (negative growth in three successive quarters by the textbook) set in. In the 1990s Japan's GDP grew by only 1.5 per cent and this continued to the next decade in one of the most disastrous recessionary cycles happening to an advanced country. Japan was the second largest economy from the 1970s till the slump hit. In a way, China's rise was inversely proportional to Japan's slump. In the 1960s, Japan grew by 10 per cent, by 5 per cent in the 1970s and 4 per cent in the 1980s. In one quarter of 2009, Japan touched a record low of minus 4 per cent even as China zoomed away. For some time in the decade starting 2000, Japan showed signs of coming out of recession, but again in 2014, there was a contraction.

More alarmingly, Japan's birth rate has been falling for over a decade and its population is predicted to fall below 100 million by 2048. The country has lost 40 million people in the last fifty years.[34] Japan's trade war with

---

[34] *The Times*, June 2019.

South Korea and China has added to its problems with exports plummeting and debt spiralling out of control.

Individual brilliance can always rise above such economic hardships. The rise of Kei Nishikori as a tennis powerhouse is an instance. But games like tennis are insulated against problems of a particular country, and Nishikori anyway trained and is based in the US, even though there was a Japanese programme to spot geniuses in sport. Similar is the case with some Japanese athletes. Whether Japan can reclaim lost ground and become a super Olympic power in the near future is open to question. The country did bounce back to finish sixth with twelve gold medals in Rio, 2016, so maybe it has found ways of funding sporting activity again and the hosting of the 2020 (postponed to 2021) Olympics will be the final indication of how much a nation emerging from recession can spend on sport.

Various commentators have alluded to the link between economic and sporting superiority, but few have actually gone into the details of it because there is no final truth in this theory and there can always be exceptions. But overall, there can be little doubt about the link between economic superiority and sporting superiority.

*

Fareed Zakaria, international affairs commentator, wrote in the *Washington Post* of August 2016, about the overriding superiority of the US in the Olympics: 'Then there is the US—decentralized, unplanned, chaotic, with a government everyone loves to hate. Yet it's the undisputed champ. Why? Partly because US public policy actually works quite well and has encouraged excellence in many sports. Mostly it is the reflection of the American spirit which celebrates individualism, embraces diversity and relentlessly pushes for excellence. And that spirit is even more important than winning.'

Commenting on another pathetic show by India in 2016, Zakaria commented: 'India's underperformance might be one more reflection of an enduring feature of the Indian landscape: private excellence but public incompetence. Governance in India works very badly.

'But there is more to it than that. India does not bring the unified nationalist fervour that China brings to these global competitions. Perhaps because of India's diversity, perhaps for other reasons, but it is difficult to imagine the country uniting as China did for the Beijing Olympics.

'Poverty is the easy explanation. India is still a very poor country per capita. But India's per capita GDP is what China's was in 2000. That year China won 58 medals (with 28 golds) about 30 times as many as India won this summer.'

According to US government estimates, India will be the third largest economy by 2030, barring catastrophes. The Coronavirus pandemic is a global catastrophe and so this projection is unlikely to come near fruition. In the case of India, no imagined catastrophe can be ruled out, but roughly the GDP in trillion dollars for the projected top five for 2030 is as follows:

US	23.9
China	18.8
India	7.3
Japan	6.5
Germany	4.3
UK	3.8

This clearly shows that already developed nations may plateau out in sport, just as their economies may. This is also because the population of many such developed nations is too low to sustain any major level of growth, according to economists like Ruchir Sharma—he says that to sustain growth at present levels, Germany needs a million migrant population every year till 2030.

But as we've noted, India does not fit into the economic might-to-medal theory. This is because the enviable growth of India is only about ten years old though the basis of it was laid in 1991, when the markets opened up and the economy was gradually reformed. India had an average of 8 per cent growth for eight years and then around seven. If it sustains this growth for two decades, then the sporting scene will benefit enormously. India's GDP calculation, however, has been disputed by some economists.

Private initiative has already changed the Indian sporting scene, following up on the brilliantly conceived Indian Premier League (IPL) cricket. Every sport in India now has a league with international participation. Sport (international sport and big leagues) has a huge TV viewership in India, making such leagues viable and lucrative—sponsorship of the Indian cricket team is pegged at a base price of Rs 2.2 crore per match it plays and the IPL will rank among the top ten sporting events in the world soon. Everything revolves around cricket in India but the ripple effect has embraced other sport, including soccer, badminton, even wrestling, which has its own league.

Private initiative is turning around the way sport has been run in India. All this has a direct relation to the 7 per cent or so growth in the Indian economy, which is a huge growth, considering the size of the economy. That is why sport has moved into the business pages of Indian newspapers.

People in business have also ventured into the arena of sport. For instance, industrialist Vita Dani is in the sports business as a co-owner of the professional football Indian Super League (ISL) team and the Chennaiyin Football Club (CFC), while her husband, Jalaj Dani, the owner of Asian Paints, has rolled out an ambitious plan to revive table tennis in India over ten years. 'We have a comprehensive plan for both grounds up as well as top down growth of TT in India. We have made a commitment of investing Rs 100 crore in ten years for the sport,' Dani said.

In the eastern state of Jharkhand which has traditionally produced well-known hockey players, an international effort is on to nurture the area's strength in hockey, initiated by the Collectives for Integrated Livelihood Initiatives (Clnl) run by the Tata Trusts in collaboration with a hockey academy run by the Dutch great Floris Bovelander, who was a member of the Dutch hockey team that won the gold at the 1997 Olympics in Atlanta.

The idea is to train coaches in Jharkhand who in turn will coach children in various districts. Dutch coaches from Bovelander's academy come every six weeks to train the state's coaches. The thinking here is to introduce young players to the European style of playing, according to former Indian player Sandeep Singh, who is among the trainers. Bovelander said, 'This initiative teaches a lot of life skills through hockey, but in the end for talented players there should be a place where they are able to get the most of out of themselves. The academy will give players that opportunity.'[35]

Such schemes are bound to show some results. The problem with being based in remote districts is that the

[35] Dhiman Sarkar, 'Here, hockey means hope for a better life', *Hindustan Times*, 19 February 2017.

children have, at some point, to take a call between playing hockey in the hope of a future reward or plunge into rural employment for immediate benefits, even from low-paying jobs. Such schemes also face the issue of commitment, aspiration and goal-setting. Often, the atmosphere at home can be negative. Parents struggle day to day, difficult choices have to be made: to let a child study or take her or him out of school, not to treat a particular disease, take loans from local sharks who then keep them in bondage for long years, which child to favour and which to neglect. So schemes like Clnl's need to have social backing. This can happen if the children are taken out of their environment and put into hostels or maybe better schools in urban areas. This, too, is being tried in some states.

At some point in a child's nurturing, at the suitable age, the child has to show ambition. If three years of intensive coaching have had no effect on the child's aspiration levels, it is a bad sign. The sooner the child displays ambition, talks of doing better, has adopted personal icons, the better. Children who go through training as a ritual with their minds not in it will drop out or have to be dropped.

The 2 Ms are important here: Money and Management. Earlier there was little money and no management. Now in many sports in India, professional management practices are falling into place. This happens in all sectors when the economy is growing. I am not talking about a coach, but a manager who can plot a career minutely and draw up an entire ecosystem around the promising athlete. Various sports scientists are also needed. In addition, the coaches' dream has to coincide with that of the players, like in the case of badminton coach Pullela Gopichand who has alone produced about ten world rankers in—an awesome achievement. Gopichand's drive, focus and unrelenting ambition cannot be matched by many coaches or managers. In fact, India may have lost more athletes than it created over the last decade due to lack of management.

The cricket league, IPL, also changed everything in cricket. Now teams have managers to look into every aspect of a team's functioning. Cricket teams also have coaches for bowling, specializing separately for spinners and quickies. Batting managers, communication managers, logistics and kit managers and many other people plan for the teams. This is very important because till recently we could see Indian teams arriving without kits, without baggage, without planned travel and other such rookie errors.

The link between a country, its economy and sporting glory can almost always be replicated in the life of individual athletes as well. The environment and the geography are most crucial. Which is why so-called talented youngsters are uprooted from their 'dark' environment and taken to the city, or places where neon lights of hope shine, where the big guys are and where dreams are born and sustained.

Just like a country's sports programme needs constant infusion of money, so does an athlete who is trying to fulfil his dream. Such infusions mostly have no logic, are mostly unjustifiable and an accountant's nightmare. Yet, once you capture or appropriate a dream and make it your own, you need the money, more than anything else.

After money comes management. For Olympic medals, the athlete has to be put into a bubble of excellence, firewalled from mediocrity. In that bubble will be top strategists, top coaches, top managers and economists. Look at the world's best managed company,

Amazon.[36] Most teams at Amazon are hermetic entities and the required expertise is embedded in each group. In one recent year, Amazon hired 150 economists with doctorates. The undying search for excellence and ideas in top companies must be inculcated into sports teams and individual athletes. 'Bezos has argued that if humans "think long term, we can accomplish things we wouldn't otherwise accomplish,"' says the *Atlantic* article.

In low-performing teams, societies or nations there is never any long-term planning. Nor is there any search for excellence. Whatever happens in terms of medals for India and other low performers comes by accident or individual pursuit. The problem with such individual pursuit is that it dies out with one or two medals. There is no institutional memory to help carry on such achievements.

For long we said it was the lack of 'killer instinct', a favourite phrase of Indian sports journalists throughout the non-performing decades. That is too facile an explanation.

India's Olympic travails also comprise the history of great athletes who hit a wall, since they found no space to grow. Being an Olympian itself was an incredible truth for most of them so they gave up after their first Olympics.

Desire and ambition are the two medals which most Indian athletes should have worn, if not the medal itself.

---

[36] Franklin Foer, 'Jeff Bezos's Master Plan', *The Atlantic*, 10 October 2019.

CHAPTER FOUR

The Sports Index: The Role of the Mind, Memory and Strategy

One of the purposes of this book is to figure out why some athletes do not make it. Why do some tennis players languish below the fiftieth rank mark forever, despite having all the shots in the game and some fantastic victories that were showpieces of endurance, desire and the willingness to embrace victory? Why are some highly rated athletes unable to make it to the National Basketball Association's (NBA's) top league or to the Olympic podium? The history of sport is also the history of failure. At some point in their evolution, hundreds of top-class athletes and other sportsmen just wither away or plateau out at their prime or while moving towards their prime. Why does this happen?

A lack of adequate and focused practice, the tendency to give up without relentless struggle, the easy decline into a state of helplessness and dejection are all known. Another factor often ignored is that the athlete may be in the wrong game. He may have the right build, the right level of stamina, the purposefulness that characterizes champions—but if he is in the wrong game, he may not have the right mental skills to strategize.

To understand this phenomenon, I've put together an index based on what I call the S5 factors: Speed, Strength, Stamina, Skill, Strategy. These are the major ingredients in any sport. Different sports need different quantities of the S5 factors. For instance, in chess you don't need physical strength or physical speed (being fit always helps) but you need speed of thinking. What does a particular sport require and what do you have in you as an athlete in that sport?

The five factors, separately or in unison, form the basis of any sport or game. Games which have each of these factors in abundance are the most popular games in the world: tennis, soccer, basketball, followed by cricket and athletics. Each game needs a different mix of these factors. Even if just one of these factors is negative in an athlete, he may not be able to come out tops.

Coaches have said that all these factors are important. Each coach has his own take on how these factors work and some of them have worked out detailed texts on the make-up of athletes. We need to look at these five factors individually to help us understand the mental aspect of a game and if an athlete needs any strategizing skills, for instance.

Once these crucial ingredients are looked at separately, it will help us get a fix on the role these factors play in various sports.

Speed: Running like hell

Speed helps in every sport. It is always seen as something one is born with, which is not true. Speed, like strength, has to be acquired by starting early in life, though some genetic factors, such as long limbs, height, right muscle construction and so on contribute to success. The stories of top runners teach us that they ran a lot in their childhood, thus creating the required bodily strength. Speed is the mark of a champion. In one way or the other it is present in every sport as a winning factor. Our natural urge to run is what created sport. In all sports, speed is a must. In sprints, just speed will do even if your stamina is low. However, in long-distance running, speed is less important than stamina, which is vital. Soccer and basketball are classic examples where a player with a better speed is a better player overall. There is no point in being a forward in football with awesome dribbling and controlling skills with the ball if you run like an overfed hippo.

I found the best way to observe the sports index phenomenon was to watch the Indian Super League soccer matches for three years closely from the stands. This league, like other global soccer leagues, has people from all parts of the world participating. For me, it was further proof that Indian soccer suffers because most Indian players are deficient in stamina, strength and speed while top-class in the skill department. Often one could see the African, European or Latin American players outrun and overrun the Indians. In the case of fast Indian wingers, they could not sustain that speed for a length of time. Speedy Indian wingers, such as Udanta Singh, could outrun many Spanish, Nigerian or Jamaican midfielders or defenders but then, once inside the box they always ran out of ideas. Stamina failed them, they lacked energy and presence of mind.

American tennis coach and former tennis player Brad Gilbert[37] in *Winning Ugly* says that American tennis star Michael Chang was among the fastest of top tennis players. I had the opportunity to talk to Chang in Melbourne

---

[37] Brad Gilbert and Steve Jamison, *Winning Ugly: Mental Warfare in Tennis—Lessons from a Master*, Simon and Schuster, 1994.

about Kei Nishikori's strategy as he was the latter's coach. Humble and always willing to share his thoughts, Chang impressed me as a man who has the right ingredients for a coach and can take full credit for Nishikori's rise. According to Brad Gilbert, much of the challenge Chang posed for his opponents as a player came from his speed. This is with special reference to speed in tennis.

Gilbert writes:[38] 'Occasionally you face an opponent who's extremely quick. They get to drop shots. They cover lobs. Shots that pull them off the court are no problem. They are like waterbugs. They skitter all over the place and have you trying harder and harder to hit a shot they can't reach. Forget it. They'll get to everything. And by the time you've hit that one winner (and one may be all you'll get) you've committed lots of unforced errors.

'Michael Chang had that kind of speed. I'll force him way wide on his forehand and come in behind. He'll run it down and make a return. I'll be coming on and hit a volley wide to his backhand and start licking my chops. No way can [... anyone] get there in time to do anything with it. Chang will get there. He will make a shot. He will beat me with a passing shot. Tremendous speed and coverage. Very quick.'

One of the most qualified people to talk about speed and fitness is Pierre Paganini, Roger Federer's trainer. 'You should never forget that you have to use this (fitness drills) on a tennis court, not on the road or in the pool. So you have to create a link between the speed and the athletic way it's used on the court. Nine times out of ten on the court, the speed is on the first three steps and then you are playing the tennis ball. So you need to train to be particularly strong in the first three steps,' Paganini told *New York Times*.

---

[38] Ibid.

'When you judge speed in tennis, you have to judge it differently than you judge a 100-metre runner. You have to judge a great deal the reaction time and how well the speed is coordinated. It's not only important to move fast. You have to move right and with the nature of the sport. You have to move fast and right for a long time in a match,' he said.

So those who end up as also-rans in any sport could be lacking in speed, though they look fit and skilled otherwise. They are in a sport due to certain accidents and coincidences and they play out their role, that's it. Their focus, ambition and understanding of the game's intricacies also play a role in their failure.

Speed, like most other physical qualities, is developed when young. Such a youngster has then to be entrusted to a coach who can fine-tune his or her running. A good example is of how Asafa Powell was turned into a world-class sprinter by Stephen Francis, the legendary coach of Jamaica's Maximum Velocity and Power (MVP) club.[39] Powell was eighteen years old when he joined the MVP. At the Boys and Girls Athletics Championship in Jamaica, the schools' championship simply known as 'Champs' in 2000, Powell came third in the first round of the 100-metre race in a not too impressive 11.45 seconds. A year later he reached the 100-metre final in 10.77 seconds but false-started.

'Francis didn't see Powell's talent (nobody did) but he did see his potential. His technique was so ragged: "I used to lean way back. My arms weren't going up, my knees were going too high; everything was wrong," Powell had said.' Francis believed improvements were possible in every department.

[39] Richard Moore, *The Bolt Supremacy: Inside Jamaica's Sprint Factory*, Yellow Jersey, 2015.

Did Asafa have the so far invisible sporting gene or the sprint gene? Francis had some reasons to believe so. 'Asafa was the youngest of six boys born to William and Cislyn Powell, both pastors in the Redemption National Church of God. His parents had been decent sprinters, his father running 10.2 for the 100 yards, his mother 11.4, but the talent seemed to have passed to another of their sons, Donovan, who was eleven years Asafa's senior. Donovan's personal best for 100 metres was 10.07 in 1995.'

Asafa began working with Francis. The increase in his speed was phenomenal, making us wonder whether he really had the sprint gene in him. Three months later, he clocked 10.50. In the Commonwealth Games in Manchester, it became 10.26 and he finished fifth. In 2003, a few months after two of his brothers died (one shot by a mugger in New York, the other of a heart attack) he went below 10 to 9.99. Then he won the National title at 9.91.

Asafa was speed itself. While many believe that the genetic factor played a major role in his case, there is no doubt that Asafa came up due to Johnson's mentoring in the world-famous club where he could run with the fastest in Jamaica.

Stamina: Hell bent

All sportsmen need stamina, not just long-distance runners or heavyweight boxers. The biggest fear of a tennis player on the verge of a fifth set win is whether his muscles and lungs will hold out. The soccer player at half-time will tell himself that the pace of the game is too fast and they need to slow down a bit if the team has to hold out and not weaken so as to give away goals in the last five minutes.

Endurance is stamina plus the strength of the mind. It is the mind that wills itself to overcome the stock of stamina that the body has. Stamina cannot be measured (unlike speed and strength) and is mostly attribution. Long-distance runners are believed to have stamina due to the lungs' ability to take in more oxygen. Now ultra-marathoners have stretched the limits of the traditional understanding of stamina. Alex Hutchinson[40] says this about ultra-marathoner Diane Van Deren: 'Hampered by poor short-term memory, she doesn't dwell on the effort already expended.' She would say, 'I could be out running for two weeks but if someone told me it was day one of a race, I'd be like, "Great, let's get started!"'

Hutchinson explains that while running, '... she had no choice but to focus on the immediate tasks of forward motion, taking one more step and then another. Semi-oblivious to the passage of time, she is also free of the cognitive challenge—the shackles perhaps of pacing herself. She is all hare and no tortoise—which Aesopian morality aside, has its advantage.' Van Deren had undergone a brain surgery to cure her of seizures but that itself could have given her a different way to bear pain, according to some scientists.

So, stamina is that effort beyond all understanding: to keep going.

It is a quality that is required in all sport, in various degrees. A person who has an 'immense store of stamina' as sports reporters often say, is also a person with the mental strength to keep going. Among the theories that touch upon this aspect are those by scientists like Samuele Marcora or Timothy Noakes, both of whom credited the brain with control over the body and ultimately, over fatigue, endurance and stamina. Both had a brain-centred view of physical endurance.

---

[40] Alex Hutchinson, *Endure: Mind, Body, and the Curiously Elastic Limits of Human Performance*, HarperCollins, 2018.

According to Marcora the decision to speed up, slow down or quit is always voluntary, forced on you by the failure of your muscles. Fatigue, in other words, resides in the brain—an insight that is as relevant to motorcyclists as to marathoners. But the decisions that the brain takes can be forced on one by an intolerably high sense of effort. They can be influenced by factors that one is not consciously aware of. If the brain could be trained to become more accustomed to fatigue, then it would adapt to the tasks of staying in the race, so to say.

Noakes's study of long-distance races in the modern era showed that the strategy was basically the same. A quick start, steady pace and then the final burst. Of the sixty-six world records in the 5000 and 10,000 metres, the last kilometre was either the fastest of the race or the second fastest (behind the opening kilometre).

Noakes[41] propounded the theory that the brain is the 'central governor' of all aspects of endurance, stamina and so on, that the brain alone sets and enforces the limits we encounter during prolonged exercise. By 'central governor', Noakes meant that the brain decides whether to slow you down or to let you increase your speed. By acting so, the brain prevents a total collapse of the body. The race may have its rules, but the brain decides. Noakes suggested that the limits of exercise are not limited by the muscles themselves and also that the brain decides 'how much muscle is recruited at a given effort level.' In other words, whatever our limits are, something must prevent us from exceeding them too much. And that something, he reasoned, must be the brain.

In this abstract from his study Noakes says: 'Two popular models hold that performance during exercise is

---

[41] Timothy Noakes, 'The Central Governor Model of Exercise Regulation Applied to the Marathon', *Sports Medicine*, 2007.

limited by chemical factors acting either in the exercising muscles or in the brain producing either "peripheral" or "central' fatigue", respectively. A common feature of both models is that neither allows humans to "anticipate" what will happen in the future and modify their exercise response accordingly. The peripheral fatigue model predicts that exercise terminates only after there has been catastrophic failure in one or more body systems and only when all the available motor units in the active muscles have been activated. The marathon race provides evidence that human athletes race "in anticipation" by setting a variable pace at the start, dependent in part on the environmental conditions and the expected difficulty of the course, with the capacity to increase that pace near the finish. Marathoners also finish such races without evidence for a catastrophic failure of homeostasis characterized by the development of a state of absolute fatigue in which all the available motor units in their active muscles are recruited. These findings are best explained by the action of a central (brain) neural control that regulates performance in the marathon "in anticipation" specifically to prevent biological harm.'

This rather 'moral' role of the brain in Noakes's theory can be questioned. It suggests that the brain knows what is best for you and so adjusts the activity of muscle fibres and thus the speed, so that you do not die of running. If at all the brain is a central governor and plays a 'moral' role in recruiting and doling out more or less power to the muscles according to the situation, how does this moral function of the brain not kick in when a depressant is about to commit suicide by jumping in front of a train? Surely the central governor can freeze the muscles at the crucial second and prevent a leap just as it does in recruiting muscle fibre for more endurance during a race?

If the brain can play an active role in helping you preserve energy or let you know when to start the final kick in the home run of the 5000-metre race, surely it can prevent you from jumping in front of a train. This proposition may sound an extreme way of countering a long-accepted theory, but an imagined moral role of the brain is difficult to prove completely and beyond reasonable doubt and cynicism.

Around this 'central governor' proposition, there can be larger philosophical questions. There is you and you are the brain. There is no other thinking organ in the body. So where can the distinction be made between you as a person trying to do something, and you as a person having a certain brain which takes certain decisions outside 'your' purview? So whose decision is it to slower your run in the middle phase and quicken it during the last phase or the home run? Who is slowing me down while I want to run? Does exhaustion have a deeper mind guiding it?

Various scientists have questioned Noakes's theories but without doubt he was in the last three decades at the forefront of understanding endurance, sporting achievement and in finding out why winning and losing have scientific explanations. Noakes has run seventy marathons, mostly in the effort to find out about endurance and sporting achievement. Noakes has been a scientist in the true sense of the term, pushing the limits of our understanding inch by inch. His larger question of why we strive for endurance and suffer pain has to be understood and admired.

There is emerging evidence of genetic mutations that could help certain types of athletes. One strong example is that of Eero Mäntyrant of Finland, who won three Olympic medals in cross-country skiing. He had a rare gene mutation which, explains David Epstein, '... spurred his bone marrow to wildly overproduce red blood cells. Red cells convey oxygen to the muscles and the more you have, the better your endurance. That's why some endurance athletes—most prominently the controversial Lance Armstrong—inject erythropoietin (EPO), the hormone that cues your bone marrow to produce red blood cells.'[42] So rare genetically endowed athletes cannot be fully ruled out, though how does an athlete know that he has more red blood cells, unless he is tested for that purpose? Also, now such athletes come under the scrutiny of drug-testing panels and it is impossible to explain that excess of red blood cells came naturally and not with chemical help. This is the reason why arguments of genetic mutation are difficult to pass muster now.

Strength: Fight like hell

All sport has its origins in the exaggerated notions of the male muscle and its mighty potential. There is nothing that the male muscle cannot do. It can even fell empires. Only those with superhuman bodies were expected to be supersportsmen. While waifish women are objects of adoration by women and men alike, the man had to be a muscled specimen. Others were derelict objects who were fragile and meant to be derided and scorned. It was in our culture to celebrate the well-built male body. Today that culture has become a global industry of gyms and steroid supplements, apart from movie franchises. To be insufficiently macho is to feel inadequate, a feeling of shame one carries through life. Most sport was for long an expression of the ability to be strong. Now, of course, skilled sport has given new meanings to the notion of strength.

---

[42] David Epstein, 'Magic Blood and Carbon-Fibre legs at the Brave New Olympics, *Scientific American*, 5 August 2016.

The belief in the strength of the male body had early beginnings. The central idea of all Greek culture was the concept of 'arete', a unity of body, mind and soul.[43] 'In fact, the gymnasia, where Greeks trained their bodies, 'were also the sites of the era's three major philosophical traditions.' The arrival of Christianity was a body blow to this culture. The emphasis turned to a spiritual culture. Christ wasn't a muscled man, though images of the naked Christ, Michelangelo's 'Pieta', for example, show him with well-formed abs, abdominal muscles, as well.

Bodybuilding emerged as a major vocation in the twentieth century. German philosopher Peter Sloterdijk said, '... the trend towards bodybuilding is itself an expression of the spirit of capitalism ... the inner connection between the worlds of practice and work, of perfection and production.'

A strong body is a fit body and all sport encourages sportsmen to spend time in the gym. A cricketer or a tennis player is also a weightlifter in his off-hours. Endurance, however, is a different ball game.

The celebration of most sport could have its origins in the celebration of the male body and its ability to help win wars and boost the collective national ego. US presidents almost always invited heavyweight champs to the White House for photo-ops. It is no surprise that Nazi Germany chose the muscular boxer Max Schmeling as the symbol of the Aryan physique, apart from intellectual superiority.

India was not far behind and the bodybuilding culture existed in many areas, especially Bengal, as we have seen. Being of superior physical strength was itself considered

---

[43] Michael Ian Black, 'Book Review' of William Giraldi's *The Hero's Body*, published by Liveright Publishing, *New York Times*, 8 August 2016.

a matter for celebration and many such people sought global acclaim. Among them were those like the 'Indian Hercules', Professor Ramamurthy Naidu,[44] 'whose displays of physical strength and endurance enchanted princes and plebeians alike' during the second decade of the twentieth century. Also, Indian wrestlers toured the West during those days, flexing their muscles for adoring fans. The Indian wrestling tradition springs directly from the macho culture, which was also part of some religious traditions. Legendary Indian wrestler Dara Singh who never wrestled in official events was nevertheless considered India's strongest man for many years and apocryphal tales were woven around his strength. Young children who didn't drink enough milk were fed imagined stories of how milk helped Dara Singh build his strength.

Among the many sports in which bodily strength plays a crucial role is rowing. Daniel James Brown[45] captures the struggle and pain of the body which only the strongest of men are capable of: 'But the faster the boat goes, the harder it is to row well. The enormously complicated sequence of movements, each of which an oarsman must execute with exquisite precision, becomes exponentially more difficult to perform as a stroke rate increases. Rowing of a beat of thirty-six is vastly more challenging than rowing at a beat of twenty-six. As the tempo accelerates, the penalty of a miscue becomes more severe the opportunity for disaster even greater … Beautiful and effective rowing often mean painful rowing …'

In rowing, or for that matter, swimming, one can see

[44] Prashant Kidambi, *Cricket Country: An Indian Odyssey in the Age of Empire*, Oxford University Press, 2019.

[45] Daniel James Brown, *The Boys in the Boat: An Epic Journey to the Heart of Hitler's Berlin*, Pan, 2014.

the importance of strength. A rower's or a swimmer's body is everyone's dream. Strength is concentrated in the crucial (upper) part of the body. When pain courses through the body, it is strength that overcomes it. All the S5 factors play a role in rowing, though strength is foremost because if one man in an eight-man racing shell or rowing boat gives up even a wee bit, the team is gone for good, since the rhythm of rowing is affected and the timing goes haywire. So all the rowers in the team call up the last resources of strength if at all there is any left in their bodies.

'Rain pelted their bare beards and shoulders. Their oars slapped against wind-tossed waves, sending up plumes of icy spray that blew back into the faces and stung their eyes. Their hands grew so numb that they could never be sure they had a proper hold on their oars ... Their aching muscles cramped up the moment they stopped moving them. And they dropped like flies,' writes Brown.

But in sport, the magic is that the stronger man, even in a weight category sport like wrestling or boxing, doesn't always win. Strength can always be nullified by any other of the S5 elements. One of Cassius Clay's (Muhammad Ali's) early fights was against the stronger Argentinian Alejandro Lavorante in the Los Angeles Sports Arena. An amazing description of a Clay fight by his latest biographer Jonathan Eig gives us an understanding of raw power, speed and unbelievable strength.[46] 'Clay came out jabbing against his bigger, stronger opponent and needed only about two minutes to open a cut under Lavorante's left eye. In the second round, Clay threw so many punches that Lavorante scarcely had time to hit

[46] Eig, *Ali: A Life*.

back. One of Clay's punches—a straight right hand—landed flush on the Argentinian's jaw and wobbled the big man's leg. In the fifth, another right hand flattened the left side of Lavorante's face. Lavoranate fell hard. When the wounded boxer staggered to his feet, Clay threw a furious left hook and knocked him back down. Lavorante fell so suddenly his head bounced off the top rope and came to rest on the bottom strand, as if it were a pillow. The referee, concerned for the fallen boxer's condition, didn't even count him out. He waved his hands in the air, declaring the match over. Two months later, Lavorante fought again, got knocked out again and slipped into a coma from which he never woke.'

The brutality of boxing is the stuff of legend. For example, after heavyweight boxer Wayne Bethea was beaten to smithereens by Sonny Liston in 1958, his support staff had to remove seven teeth from his mouthpiece.

Strength often leaves evidence behind.

Skill: Dancing like hell

It can generally be explained that skill dominates any game played with a racquet or bat or stick or any appendage. Soccer and basketball too require high skill but it has to be combined with high levels of the other S5 factors. Asian countries, where the strong, muscled physique is generally below European or African standards, dominate in games like badminton and cricket that require skill. High skill can neutralize any deficiency like an unathletic body, lack of speed and no real strength. Tennis, cricket and soccer, among others, are high-skill games. For a long time, the Indian cricket team was unfit, lethargic and paid no attention to athleticism or fitness. But even a totally unfit Indian team won the World Cup in 1983. That team was marked by a languorous ease on the field, a lazy approach to fielding and slow bowlers masquerading as medium pacers—but it won through certain skill sets. One of the medium pace bowlers in that team was Mohinder Amarnath whose run-up was so slow that a batsman could catch a wink or two waiting for the ball—yet he took three wickets in the World Cup finals and was also selected as 'Man of the Match' in both the semi-finals and finals of the World Cup.

A person with high skills in playing a game like tennis, can easily outmanoeuvre a giant who serves as many aces as he wants. In tennis, skill is all. Skill can be explained as expertise in all the strokes, a mighty one-handed backhand that lands always on the corner of the other court or just kisses the lines. Skill can also be the ability to rush to the net at the right time, playing the correct shot at the right time and so forth. Such a player can easily neutralize a player who is fast, has huge strength and stamina and is the tallest man on earth. Skill is the ability which a human being acquires through hard work, to produce something of high or even incredible value, using an instrument made for the purpose. A weaver who produces a magnificent tapestry using a loom is as highly skilled as a tennis player making an incredible backhand. Skill cannot be taught. It is acquired. A driver becomes skilled only after he drives for many years with the intention to become highly skilled and has a willingness to learn.

In high-skilled games, coaches and managers play a big role. This is why in sports like soccer and tennis, managers and coaches are as well-known as the players themselves. Many players give all the credit for their rise to their coaches. All top tennis players travel with their coaches even though there is nothing about the game the players themselves do not know. At the Association of Tennis Professionals (ATP) events and Grand Slams, a box is reserved for the 'team' of the player. This is because skill has to be constantly nurtured, and new skill sets developed. Also in such games, strategy is important. The coach has to know the opponents' games as much as he knows his own player's game. Even players at the highest level of a skill game can be heard saying that their performance has improved due to, for example, a minor correction in the grip, or for a cricket player in his stance. These are not perceivable changes but are hidden to the outside world and even to the opponents.

Cricket is a high-skilled game with much fine-tuning, which continues even after the player has attained the status of being invincible. So you can hear India's captain Virat Kohli saying that he has made some adjustments to his stance or a bowler saying that he had developed the in-swinging yorker. Some bowlers in their run-up hide the ball in their non-bowling hand to prevent the batsman from seeing the shining side of the ball. If a batsman knows which side is the shining one (the other is scruffed and not polished by the hands), it will help him decide which way the ball is going to swing—it's always to the side away from the shining side.

Many top players are aware that they need to have the skills to make up for their lack of physical prowess. Listen to Stephen Curry of the Golden State Warriors in the NBA, on why height is not the be-all and end-all in basketball. He underlines the fact that if you are highly skilled, other details do not matter: 'It's about being skilled. Obviously, I'm not the most physically dominant person out there. I'm 6'3", 185 pounds soaking wet and you try to just be able to do a lot of different things on the court. Being able to dribble with both hands, being able to shoot the ball from inside and outside, holding your own at the defensive end and you've got to have heart.' Curry here has just explained skill.

Tennis star Novak Djokovic expressed similar sentiments about skill and physical attributes. Djokovic replied to a question about what his greatest strength is from a *Times of India* reporter:[47] 'It's a little bit of everything that completes it. Tennis is a complex sport, you cannot only focus on one element of your game and not work on anything else. The definition of the word strong is changing. When I mean strong, I don't mean you have to have big muscles and serve big. I think being strong is using the potential of your whole body, a combination of flexibility, agility, coordination, all muscle fibres being activated. My game is more flexibility and recovery, energy supply and endurance. It serves me well when playing best-of-five in Grand Slams. That kind of approach allows me to play at a high level for a longer time. Movement is important as a set up to every shot you are executing. My game is based from the baseline, so I try to work the defence and the offence and the transition from one to another as well. Not so much just power, but accuracy, efficiency and precision which is what I am strong at.'

Here Djokovic is trying to explain skill, but he is a bit dismissive of strength and power. All top-ranked people in high-skilled games will have the same ideas of what it means to be at the top.

But a wrestler who loses is most likely to say that though his strategy was right, the opponent was stronger than him.

Memory: Remembering hell

A subset of skill is memory. They are twins, which is why I am including it as part of skill because they are

[47] *Times of India*, 24 February 2016.

connected irretrievably. Skill cannot exist without a good memory; for example, to know which shot to hit when. It is my suggestion that memory plays a crucial factor in high-skill games. All top achievers in any field have incredible memories anyway. Most top players in tennis and cricket have memories like chess players are expected to have. Chess is fully based on memory and thus physical parameters play no part in the game apart from the fact that the player is fit and not running a 104-degree temperature. Both long-term and short-term memory play a part in any athlete's rise. It is from the recesses of memory that a player plays a particular shot and if he/she has forgotten the shots he/she played in matches years ago, a player cannot progress. But that never happens. Even a top player coming back from a one-year injury lay-off can easily get back to his top ranking because of memory. He can play a smash or a forehand the way he used to even if with not as much efficacy. Novak Djokovic is a perfect example.

I followed the careers of many top sportsmen to figure out if they indeed have amazing memories. It turned out that all of them did. This is easily evident when they speak of battles long ago with the precision and confidence of a surgeon.

Of Norwegian chess prodigy and World No. 1, Magnus Carlsen, it is said that he can look at an opening once and remember it for ever. So also Indian Grandmaster and former world champ, Viswanathan Anand who, like other Grandmasters, can tell you the name of the match and the year after just glancing once at a chess diagram. Anand astounds us with his memory. Here in this interview published in chess.com, he talks in great details about the brain and memory. The first part of the interview which appeared in 2017, shows him toying with the interviewer's memory as if memory is a game of chess. The interviewer was Spanish chess player and coach Luis Fernandez Siles, known as Luison to Spanish chess fans.

Luison: Years ago, when we first met, you were famous for how quickly you played your games, that impressed me a lot in that Linares tournament I visited in 1992 or 1993 …

Anand: 1991, actually.

L: Ah! 1991, then. I trust your memory much more than mine. But it was really impressive how fast you played …

A: Yes, when I was young I got used to playing that way and I always did, that was my pace. Then I understood that that could cost me many points, if in some specific important moments I didn't stop and think deeply … Now I'm more balanced, I don't play as fast … But I don't get in time trouble in all games either.

L: I remember once someone walked into the chess club saying that you'd lost a game on time to Kamsky [Gata Kamsky, Soviet-born American Grandmaster] **…**

A: Yes, in 1995 …

L: Everyone thought it was a joke. Was that when you started changing and thinking longer?

A: No, no. It didn't happen at a specific moment. In that same tournament of Linares'91, in the third round I lost an absolutely won game, a computer today would tell you I had an advantage of +3 or +4 … and I lost because I didn't stop to think.

L: Who was your opponent?

A: Beljavsky [Alexander Beljavsky, Ukrainian and Slovenian chess player]. With experience, you gradually change … But my evolution didn't happen at a specific moment.

Later in the interview, when asked about the mental benefits of teaching chess in schools, Anand said: 'Chess is a very beneficial activity for anyone, not only in schools, but in schools its effects will be seen in academic results, in memory, in concentration, in the ability to organize information, all those are benefits that can be obtained from chess. But those benefits can be obtained at any age. One of the most important things that are being talked about lately is how to keep the brain active.'

Anand here sums up the importance of what he calls 'organizing information' in the brain. This is crucial not only to chess but to every game. Tennis and basketball players also need to 'organize information' that helps them to play the right shots, make the right moves, anticipate the right moment to go for a winner and the rest of it. In chess, this organization is most important. When a move is made, Anand will know about at least three occasions of what his opponent did in such a situation. So Anand has his alternative moves ready. To have alternative moves ready is essential to every high-skilled sport.

The crucial factor is memory. That part of the brain is developed in many champions through some activity in childhood like playing chess, reading or skill games or storytelling.

Chess stalwarts have shown their precocity when very young. For anyone who wants to see precocity and future greatness, such kids are a treat to study. Bernard Taper,[48] in a profile of American Grandmaster Bobby Fischer, lined up this aspect of chess greatness: 'Young Fischer took to the game of chess from the time the moves were first explained to him. That was when he was six and his teacher was his elder sister Joan. Before that, his only hint

[48] Bernard Taper, 'Prodigy', *New Yorker*, 7 September 1957.

of precocity has been his authoritative war with jigsaw puzzles. He entered his first tournament at the age of nine and has twice won the US Junior Chess championships. He also won the Lessing J. Rosenwald tournament, for a game so inspired that it was hailed on the cover of *Chess Review* as "the game of the century".'

Here Fischer shows some similarity with Carlsen in the immediacy and urgency to win, and not to lose any match—the greed to win even matches that are not of much significance is noteworthy. This shows that winning is just not a cultivated faculty but something more inherent. Fischer burst into tears every time he lost a game during his boyhood days.

Strangely, prodigies such as Fischer or Carlsen or Anand never exhibited any extraordinary strength in academics despite amazing intelligence and memory power. Such intelligence also resulted in restlessness in studies and children like this flit from book to book or subject to subject with some inborn tendency for hyperactivity. This could also be a restlessness of the mind in that difficult search for a niche in which to settle down and flower. In the case of these children, the niche was chess and the search ended there.

'Though school tests have shown him to have generally superior intelligence, he does no better than average in his studies, displaying little interest in most of the subjects taught and being restless in class. His teachers are amazed when they hear of his chess victories—not so much at his revealing mental powers that they hadn't suspected as at his being able to sit still for the five hours a tournament game may last. "In my class Bobby couldn't sit still for five *minutes*," one of them [Fischer's teachers] said.'

His mother Regina Fischer is quoted as saying that she tried her best to keep Bobby away from chess. 'For four years I tried everything I knew to discourage him but it was hopeless.'

'She told us that almost every evening her son was to be found at the Manhattan Chess Club ... a venerable institution, with an imposing number of champions. "Sometimes I have to go there at midnight to haul him out of the place," she says.'

This is another indication of the importance of practice even in high-skilled games.

What is the type of memory you need in order to win? In chess, your memory also needs to be sequential: you must remember moves in sequence, what the opponent played one after the other in his match five years back. Even soon after I come out of a movie theatre, I cannot recall the sequences of the plot, while I can remember all the dramatic scenes or visuals. That is not much help when narrating the story to a friend!

To closely follow superstars in any high-skilled sport is also to be amazed at their memory. Roger Federer, when talking to the *Guardian* in July 2016, recalled his match against Pete Sampras in the fourth round of Wimbledon in 2001 with such precision and clarity, it makes us understand why he is such a great player. He recalled this while talking about why he breaks down after crucial tennis matches: 'I saved a break point and ended up winning 7-5 in the fifth with the forehand down-the-line winner, got to my knees and broke down again. I'm like, "Are you crazy? What is wrong with you?"'

But skill is uppermost. Simon Briggs, *The Telegraph*'s tennis correspondent, wrote in 2010: 'Federer is the multiskilled fox of tennis—to use Isaiah Berlin's famous analogy—while Sampras, Agassi and even Rafael Nadal are all hedgehogs who only have one trick, excellent though that trick might be.'

Federer also remembered why and how he cried the first time in his career. That happened fifteen years back from the time he was talking. He was playing for Switzerland in the Davis Cup against the US in 2001. 'We beat the Americans in my home city, where I used to be a ball boy. When I finally won the match, I was so exhausted and happy, I broke down crying. And I was like "what is this emotion?" I didn't realize I had it in me.'

A Reuters report, a curtain-raiser to the Wimbledon final of 2016, commented: 'Since Andy Murray's memory is as razor-sharp as his service returns, he will not have forgotten the parting shot he received from Milos Raonic [Canadian tennis player] when they last played.'

Here is Rahul Dravid, former captain of the Indian cricket team, after his retirement, recalling a past series with great precision in an interview to *Wisden India*:

Wisden: In that way, Australia must have been the tour from hell. You went there with the best intentions, the best preparation, and it all went badly. What went wrong?

Dravid: I think Australia was disappointing. In England I felt we had quite a few injuries and I just felt we weren't necessarily as well-prepared as we were in Australia. Australia, I thought we went there with the best of intentions, the guys cared. They played better, they pitched the ball up, we had some opportunities in the first Test. We didn't grab them. We had them at some 210 for 6 and then they got 320 and we were about 220 for 2, and Sachin got out that evening and I got out next morning. Having said that, you have got to give them credit. They bowled well, pitched the ball up, they swung the ball.'

Dravid remembers what the score was when he got out in the morning as well.

There are many such instances, but here I have to look at Sachin Tendulkar's memory. There is nothing he has forgotten about himself, his game, his scores and what happened during the match. It could be the result of a massive self-obsession, of living in a world that radiated from himself. It could be true that for such people nothing else matters, so complete is their faith and single-mindedness about what they did. Is that why they remember everything they ever did?

In Tendulkar's case it is a bit numbing as well to figure out how deep his memory is. Here is an interview from *Wisden* where he recollects what happened twenty-five years earlier as if it was yesterday. This interview was about his century at the Perth cricket ground, during his first tour when he was just eighteen. Replaying matches from videos and then analysing your game, for instance, figuring out what you actually should have done in a particular moment in that game, is also a way of improving your performance.

Wisden: When you went to Australia, you were fairly established as an Indian cricketer. You had made a hundred in England as an eighteen-year-old. What expectations did you have when you went out to Australia?

Tendulkar: You know, I had actually grown up watching all those ODI [One Day International] matches and that picture was there in front of me. I knew that it was going to be a challenging series but I was prepared for that. I was just excited to be there. And I felt that if I could get runs and come back having done something nice, it would lay a solid foundation. Because everyone knew that if one performed well in England, West Indies and Australia, at that time, then the whole world stood up and took notice of your performance.

The confidence was there that I could go out and score

a Test hundred. I felt it was a big moment, because how many eighteen-year-olds get to play in Australia at such a competitive level? They had a phenomenal bowling attack in that series—[Craig] McDermott, Merv Hughes, Bruce Reid, Paul Reiffel and Mike Whitney. [Shane] Warne and Peter Taylor were the spinners, and in between, Mark Waugh and Steve Waugh also bowled. Tom Moody would bowl a little bit. Allan Border also rolled his arm over a couple of times. The kind of surfaces we played on were pretty lively, and it was a learning experience for me to play some quality fast bowling, attacking and aggressive.

Not surprisingly, here Tendulkar says that even before he went to Australia he had the history of that place and many innings clear in his mind. He was in the zone even before he trod on the pitches there.

It is from the recesses of memory that notes are played, strokes are recreated, a dilemma confronted and solved, hypnotic suggestions made, a wrong righted. Memory provides one with a huge canvas on which to work. It is a past incident that gives one the confidence to tackle it anew. Memory allows you to replay things over and over—for instance, that incredible run ten years ago, that sliced backhand in the collegiate finals. It is also possible that memory starts fading after one is forty years old and from then onwards it is a slow, gradual fade away. This is also one reason why sportsmen, despite being fit, quit the sport at or before that age.

Life's worst tragedy is losing one's memory. If you have watched elderly people in the family or friends slowly but surely slipping into amnesia, you know what I mean. Their eyes cannot focus and they are constantly searching for meanings in what they see. What they see makes no sense because memory is everything.

Achievement in any field comes with practising memory development from a young age. Australian writer Gerald Murnane,[49] is an eccentric recluse who lives in the remote town of Goroke, in the state of Victoria. His novels and short stories are introspective, sometimes esoteric essays and memory, and forgetfulness is a major concern in most of his writings. One such story is 'Precious Bane'.[50] In his mind, he sees a man standing before a wall of bookshelves, gazing at the spine of the last remaining copy of a novel composed forty years earlier. The man has read the book, but he's struggling to remember a single detail from the text, anything, a line, an image. (This is a favourite exercise of the real-life Murnane.) An odd five-page digression follows, in which the narrator imagines the human brain as a Carthusian monastery, with monks in charge of preserving memories. Eventually, he returns to the imagined future reader, who has failed to recall anything from what is, of course, the narrator's book: 'The man fills his glass again and goes on sipping some costly poison of the twenty-first century. He does not understand the importance of his forgetfulness, but I understand it. I know that no one now remembers anything of my writing.'

Murnane has a lifelong fascination with memory and he struggled and exercised all his life to develop and then sustain his memory. Everything is organized and catalogued in his remote house. The *NYT* profile said: 'Murnane pulled out a list of agenda items he wished to discuss (during the interview). The list has been organised, I soon realised in such a way that we would move in a counter-clockwise direction around the room, stopping at

---

[49] Mark Binelli, 'Is the Next Nobel Laureate in Literature Tending Bar in a Dusty Australian Town?' *New York Times*, 27 March 2018.

[50] *New York Times*, 1 April 2018.

various points to discuss objects of particular significance. One of the first items he point out, a poster covered with the racing colours of every jockey who had won the Melbourne Cup from its inception in 1861 until 2008, turned out to be part of his daily routine of memory exercises, which he compared to the offices or hourly prayers performed by the Catholic priests …

'From the poster and clutching his hand behind his back he told me to pick a year. I offered 1970. "Nineteen Seventy," Murnane said. "That horse was Baghdad Note. Emerald green with white striped sleeve and cap." Mondays he said he recited the entire list in order. Tuesdays he went backwards. Other days involved skipping around the poster in ways I didn't quite follow …

'After that he did the same with the fifty states of America and then recited passages in Hungarian, a language he'd learned at fifty-six …' *The New York Times* concluded that Murnane was Nobel Prize material.

From childhood, Nobel Laureate V.S.Naipaul practiced his 'memory drill after every meeting trying to remember words, gestures and expressions in correct sequence to arrive at an understanding of the people I had been with and the true meaning of what had been said.'

All sportsmen while developing their biceps must think of the brain as well. Like Naipaul or Murnane and many others, they must drill some muscle into their mind. Just as the physique needs exercises to keep the muscles toned and performing, so does the brain. Few athletes and coaches give thought to this aspect though all of them talk about the 'mental game' without knowing what they are looking for.

The day after he won his first and only US Open in September 1968, American tennis player Arthur Ashe was photographed by John Zimmerman in the New York subway holding a folded copy of *New York Times* and leaning against a pillar unnoticed, solving the crossword puzzle.[51] Ashe was, of course, a rarity in sport. Intellectual and well-read, he worked relentlessly for the cause of African-Americans and researched and wrote a three-volume *book A Hard Road to Glory: A History of the African-American Athlete*, on the Blacks in American sport towards the end of this life. The point is that a vibrant, curious intellectual attitude and mind is essential for any player to achieve and retain world standings.

High memory, acquired through deliberate mental exercises or through unconscious exercises like reading, memorizing lessons and so on, and the resultant rise in intelligence, awareness, strategic and analytic powers, is a crucial aspect in the creation of a champion. Those who fail despite having physical qualities, are surely lacking in memory or its offshoot: tactics and the ability to 'see' a game when they are playing.

Memory can be developed from a younger age and retained through various mental exercises. This lack of a 'razor-sharp' memory and related mental skills could be one reason why failure is so rampant in sport. This could also be the reason why a person ranked twenty-fifth in tennis is unable to break into the Top Ten or Top Five despite having all the strokes, crucial upset victories over top seeds, the physique and the attitude as well as expert trainers. 'Lack of consistency' is the much-touted argument when the careers of such players are discussed. But how can such lack of consistency be explained? Why should a player ranked twenty-fifth lose out on crucial points? What makes him inconsistent even for a brief moment during a tense match?

---

[51] Maurice Berger, 'The Quiet Heroism of Arthur Ashe', *New York Times*, 18 September 2018.

According to a research report published in *The Daily Mail*,[52] top athletes and racing drivers think faster and more accurately than the average person when under pressure. The study found that their memory performance was 20 per cent better and their mental processing was 10 per cent more rapid than that of others.

Trying to understand the mind and the working of the brain is a continuing and never-ending effort. A *Newsweek*[53] report, 'Why Winners Win', attempted to figure out why athletes triumph or fail, the focal point of this study as well. The article by Nick Summers was strap-lined, 'The New Science of Triumph in Sports, Business and Life'. A box by Sharon Begley within this article explains in detail which part of the brain controls a game or an athlete's response to it: 'The movements of elite athletes are beautiful to watch. But what goes on inside their heads? The best players learn their moves by encoding whole sequences in the cerebellum through intensive practice—and then in game situations, activate them without conscious thought. To return a serve for instance, a tennis player uses her thalamus to focus on her opponent, while the prefrontal cortex quashes distractions. Visual information from the occipital lobe activates the unconscious motor program in the basal ganglia which passes instruction to the posterior parietal cortex (which calls up automatic movements) and the pre-motor cortex (a staging ground for complex movements). The pre-motor transmits commands to the motor cortex, which orders muscle movements. Swing!'

All these complex movements (most of which are still not proved beyond doubt) come from the recesses of memory. Which part of the brain is involved in the act of

---

[52] *Daily Mail*, 17 October 2016.

[53] *Newsweek*, 18 July 2011.

recreating something is almost fully known now, as the report above shows.

What we are getting at here is what American tennis player and coach Brad Gilbert told Andre Agassi who was losing matches despite being phenomenally gifted: 'With your talent, if you are fifty per cent game-wise, but ninety per cent head-wise, you are going to win. But if you are ninety-five per cent game-wise and fifty per cent head-wise you are going to lose, lose, lose.' Here 'head-wise' stands for memory and all that goes with it, the accumulation of skill and the incredible fast recall that helps find a solution to stop a slide and thus reclaim a match.

As we know, Gilbert turned Agassi's career around. He made him use his head more often. It helped that Agassi had the head. If he didn't have the memory power, he may not have had succeeded, according to the *Newsweek* report.

The 'head-wise' here is actually memory. Also strategy, of course. Memory (and not muscle memory as is popularly believed) is what in a split second tells you what shot to hit, what not to, whether to approach the net or not. At crucial moments you are told what to do. That's memory. Whether the actual decision is taken in the motor cortex or elsewhere is a matter of detail.

Even if you are playing a game ten years after you laid off, the shots, the movement in court, an easy familiarity with the surroundings of the court present themselves with some clarity. Your mind has laid it out before you. It's memory. Memory gives you clarity. When a player is in 'The Zone' (discussed in the next section) he is illuminated by clarity of mind. In that state of mind, his body just follows the commands. This is the stage which many experts have seen in Roger Federer. 'RF, a graceful legend who treats the court like his canvas,' as a *Time* report of September 2011 says.

All this happens because the brain stands at the peak of the evolutionary process and is the most complex organism that exists. Even today most details of how the brain functions is unknown to man. But even what is known is enough for us to understand why we, the Homo sapiens, dominate the world. Our brains are the biggest. For comparison, take the emu, the biggest bird, but with a brain that weighs as much as an AA battery. 'Were there a bird with a brain the size of a grapefruit it would probably rule the world,' says neuroscientist Suzana Herculano-Houzel who collects brains of all creatures and studies their physical nature.[54]

Just to understand why our memory is almost like a computer chip, remember that the cranium is spacious enough to house trillions of brain cells, 100 billion electrically active neurons and ten to fifty times. according to Herculano-Houzel. We have to marvel at the complexity of this creature that resides within our heads. Look at what the cerebral cortex does. Most such tasks are completely essential to even athletes whose sole task in life is to improve his physical performance. A champion's brain, just like his body, would have been trained, mostly unconsciously, to take on various tasks that will eventually propel him to the top.

'The cerebral cortex is the difference between impulse and insight, between reflex and reflection. It is essential for voluntary muscle control, sensory perceptions, abstract thinking, memory and language. Perhaps most profound, the cerebral cortex allows us to create and inhabit a simulation of the world as it is, was and might be; an inner theatre that we can alter at will. The cortex receives a copy of everything else that happens in the brain,'

---

[54] Ferris Jabr, 'To Unlock the Brain's Mysteries, Puree It', *New York Times*, 16 December 2017.

Herculano-Houzel says. 'And this copy, while technically unnecessary, adds immense complexity and flexibility to our cognition. You can combine and compare information. You can start to find patterns and make predictions. The cortex liberates you from the present. It gives you the ability to look at yourself and think.'

Sportsmen are generally regarded as muscular morons, but at least for high-skill games like tennis, soccer and cricket, this epithet will not stick. Most of the task the cerebral cortex does is what most sportsmen need. They all have developed various aspects of an intellectual being, memory being prime.

The Zone: One hell of a time

When the mind and the body come together, there is sublimity. That is when a player enters 'The Zone'. The perfection of the goal-scorer, the timing of the long-distance runner, the burst of the sprinter, and that down-the line shot, which kisses the lines and swings away from the desperate opponent on the other side, whose helpless hands are stretched like the wings of a condor, is what sublimity is all about. That is what we go to watch. That is why we play. To reach that rarefied realm, and dictate terms from there, is the epitome of all sport.

Some sportsmen have managed to explain what 'The Zone' means. Some say they remain calm, some say they were 'in the zone'. Others say they could do no wrong on that particular day. Here is what Spanish golfer Sergio Garcia said after he won the Augusta Masters in April 2017, 'Even at (hole) 13 I felt calm. It was the calmest I ever felt at a major championship on a Sunday. Even the bogeys did not bother me. And when we got on the greens, I knew I could make a par ... I could do some good things and still maybe catch Justin [Justin Rose, the English professional golfer].'

He also went on to explain in this interview[55] what he meant by being calm and the mental space he inhabited prior to the much-sought-after victory, his first major title in seventy-four starts and his nineteenth Masters appearance. His career best in the Majors till his 2017 victory was a fourth-place finish in 2004. Twelve years later, he won it. His is also a story of ceaseless ambition and self-belief—though his swing or putt is over in a flash, his mind has the endurance of a marathon runner. When he won Augusta, it was the mental game that he won. 'Not letting things get to me that used to get to me in the past has been a big step forward for me, I'm not going to lie. I didn't always feel that way and not at Augusta, because I started to feel uncomfortable here. But I came to be at peace with it. I accepted what I needed to change. I feel perfectly at home now.'

The report of his victory in the match in the *New York Times* reflects what Garcia himself felt: 'Garcia's mind was uncluttered as he and Rose (who finished second) signed for their closing three under 69 ... then headed to the 18th hole for the play off. Maybe he felt Ballesteros's [Spanish golfer Seve Ballesteros, who was a great influence on Garcia] presence all week, but Garcia, 37, said he felt serene.'

Serenity, clarity, calmness. When a player is in 'The Zone', he is in a place where there is an aura that doesn't vanish. He sees everything in his mind like the blooming drifts of daffodils that Wordsworth saw. There are no clouds of confusion, no cataracted views of possibilities. There appears an inner strength that comes after warding off all thoughts of vulnerabilities and the player is possessed of just the clarion call from his mind to go

[55] Bill Pennington, 'Same Old Sergio Writes a New Script', *New York Times*, 9 April 2017.

ahead. It is the coming together of the mind and body which everyone wants to achieve.

Through sport literature we can trace the glee of the victor who has just returned from 'The Zone'. Always for them, there are not enough words to describe their performance and how they managed to transcend the body and mind and go into another world.

Brazil's soccer immortal Pelé (full name, Edson Arantes do Nascimento) talks of the 'strange calmness' he experienced during the 1958 World Cup final against Sweden. 'It was a type of euphoria. I felt I could run all day without tiring, that I could dribble through any of their team or all of them, that I could almost pass through them physically. I felt I could not be hurt. I have felt confident many times (before) without that strange feeling of invincibility.'

Novak Djokovic, after effortlessly winning the semi-final against the strangely inconsistent Frenchman Lucas Pouille in the Australian Open of 2019, which I watched from the press box, commented later while talking to the press: 'You are driven by some force that takes over you and you feel divine.' Djokovic did not expect the easy nature of his straight sets victory and so the 'divine' aspect might have been an overstatement. But watching the match was certainly a divine experience.

Sometimes it needs fiction to capture the aura of 'The Zone', because it is often indescribable. Thom Jones in his immortal short story 'The Pugilist at Rest' tries to figure out this deep mental clarity which everyone tries to get at. Jones describes the left temporal epilepsy of Russian novelist Fyodor Dostovesky: 'The peculiar and most distinctive thing about his epilepsy was that in the split second before his fit—in the aura which is in fact officially a part of the attack ... Dostovesky experienced a sense of felicity, of ecstatic well-being, unlike anything an ordinary mortal could hope to imagine. It was the experience of sartori. Not the nickel-and-dime sartori of Abraham Marlaw but the Supreme. He said he wouldn't trade ten years of his life for the feeling and I, who had it, too would have to agree. I can't explain it, I don't understand it—it became very slippery and elusive when it gets any distance on you—but I have felt it down to the core of my being …'

Those who have tried to explain what it is to be in 'The Zone' are often lost for words. Yannick Nézet-Séguin,[56] conductor of the Metropolitan Opera, New York, talked of the first time he conducted an orchestra—in a former church, performing Bach's St John's Passion, when he was just twenty-one. He was so overcome, he said, he could feel himself floating up the chapel's ceiling. 'I felt as if I was levitating.'

So for some, 'The Zone' (experienced during a public performance of art, music or sport), can be an other-worldly experience, though the reality is much closer to earth.

Among sportsmen-writers, the topmost intellectual is English cricketer and opening batsman, Mike Brearley, who has made a name for himself as a psychoanalyst, after having led England. He is among those who have tried to understand the mystery of being in 'The Zone', in his book *On Form* published in 2017. His philosophy also veers towards the Timothy Gallwey theory of the conscious self being allowed to take a side seat while the subconscious steers one through. Gallwey, an American tennis player and author, laid down a new methodology for coaching and developing excellence by what he

[56] Dan Bilefsky, 'He Wanted to Be Pope. He Settled for Conducting the Metropolitan Opera', *New York Times*, 13 December 2019.

calls 'The Inner Game'. Brearley's descriptions are most reliable, considering that he went through it and then sifted the experience through the ultraviolet filter of his intellect. Here are some instances narrated by Brearley.

In the 1976 Test series in India when Tony Grieg was leading England, Brearley went out to open the innings in the first Delhi Test, at a time when he was in full form, just coming up after a double century in Poona (Pune). 'The pitch was flat, hard and dry. The day was dreamily hazy with that veiled sunlight so common on winter mornings in northern India. The crowd, smaller than at most Indian Test grounds in those days, but still substantial, felt mistily distant, almost unreal. After two or three overs, a large yellow-and-brown butterfly settled by the stumps at the non-striker's end, basking. I could attend to the butterfly and to the bowling with equally detached interest.'

Here Brearley[57] was in the same zone as Sachin Tendulkar or Sunil Gavaskar for whom even the scoreboard did not matter and the crowd could have been hazily distant or even non-existent. In such cases, the player is in his own place where external elements have no entry—even the crowd is somewhere far and safely away.

We tend to personify form; like 'lady Luck', she may be more than a lover. These deities have power over us just as death and disease seek us out. But form is not simply in the lap of the gods—it is not simple, a matter of which side of the bed we got out that morning, so how far can we control our form? Can we harness it, make it work for us, or is it a wild horse, never to be tamed? This is what Brearley says about 'form'.

---

[57] Mike Brearley, *On Form*, Little, Brown, 2017.

Is form the same as being in 'The Zone'? One is the product of the other; therefore, they are most likely one and the same animal. Form, however, can create self-confidence in a player. Form lasts a while, for perhaps an entire season. 'The Zone' is an elusive being, which appears in the dark like a ghost in white and leads you along out of misery. But being in 'The Zone' is equivalent to being unconquerable. It is a state of mind while being in form and is proof of sporting skill, sporting strength, stamina and speed, depending on which sport it is. 'Form is not a matter of the moment. It takes time to assess. Nor is it a matter of total ease. We have to struggle through hard times, not all of them down to our own shortcomings. Form is sometimes a matter of solidity and imperviousness, like a great oak in a storm; at other times it is more aptly pictured as a capacity to bend and sway before the win like the bamboo that survives the hurricane because of its flexibility,' Brearley writes.

The American sports expert, trainer and agent, Tim S. Grover, who wrote *Relentless: From Good to Great to Unstoppable*, about the secrets of sporting excellence, has this take of being in 'The Zone'. This is about an incident when the American basketball player of the NBA, Kobe Bryant, flew 2000 miles in his plane just to spend an hour with Grover to talk about the pressures he faced after being injured. 'How do you prevent that panic from turning into a total collapse? Sometimes you need to step away and get back to that calm, cool place where you're in total control. Could my player have called me to fly to wherever he was? Sure, that happens every season with different guys. They know if they need me I'm there. But in this case, the player knew he needed space and he was willing to risk the consequence if he got caught leaving the team.

'"Forget about losing," I tell him, looking for that "click" behind the eyes when you know the guy gets it. "Forget about trying, because if you're just trying, then losing is still an option. You want to be the best? Then you ignore the pain and the exhaustion and the pressure to please everyone else."'

Grover goes into great detail about being in 'The Zone' while emphasizing the role of the mind in a winner's life. Most experts agree that to be in 'The Zone' is to be cut off from the conscious mind and feed off the subconscious, as retired oncologist and former tennis player Mulki Radhakrishna Shetty told me in Bengaluru as we watched the India–Uzbekistan Davis Cup tie in 2014. Grover says something almost similar: 'But once a Cleaner [a sort of total player in Grover's mind] steps into the Zone, he's detached from everything on the outside. Whatever else is going on—personal, business, anything—it can't affect him until he's ready to return. That, by definition, is the Zone. No fear, no intrusion. Total concentration. You are not thinking, because thinking turns your thoughts on to everything and the Zone is about the opposite, turning your thoughts off to everything except the task at hand. Thinking takes you away: The Zone keeps you where you need to be. That's your safe haven; you go inside that space and nothing can touch you, nothing can hurt you, no one can call you or text you or hassle you or bother you. The headaches will still be there when you're done, but you have to get to that place where you control time and space, and nothing controls you.'

There is an impression that those who reside or ascend to 'The Zone' during matches are those who possess the killer instinct. For many decades, Indian sportsmen were, for instance, derided with the cliched journalistic comment that they lacked the killer instinct. It meant that they could not hit winners when it mattered, missed golden chances to score during the dying minutes, and just could not deliver the killer punch when it mattered. Or that they lacked ambition. This, in turn, was subconsciously attributed to some hidden nature of people of the Indian cultural ethos, who lacked the ability to fight back till the end, an attribute quite often seen in the Pakistani cricket team, for instance. Is all this true?

Tim Grover, who has worked with many top American athletes and basketballers, feels that a human being has a dark side and it is this dark side that gives him or her the ability to deliver the killer punch. Softies do not possess this. Grover goes to the extent of saying that American golfer Tiger Woods should not have publicly apologized for his personal behaviour that caused the sex scandal when news broke of his various extramarital affairs, because that part was his dark side and some such qualities are required in order to be a winner. Once the scandal broke, his career too deteriorated, since his dark side too vanished.

'You want to see a guy in the Zone, watch videos of Tiger before the scandal; he'd walk onto that course as if it were built for him, and if you got in his way, God help you. All the experts loved talking about his mental toughness, how his father trained him by intentionally dropping clubs and moving the cart during the back swing, how his mother's laughter got him to get out there and "kill them, take their heart." Raised to be in the Zone, said the analysts ... Once the story came out, his career began to deteriorate in every way conceivable,' Grover writes.

It is difficult to agree on this 'dark side' theory because the softest of men have become world champions too. Here there is a confusion between the dark side of human nature with the killer instinct. An intention to deliver a killer punch, either in the boxing ring or the tennis court cannot by any yardstick be stacked up with the moral deficiencies that we possess. Nor is a criminal record essential if you have to deliver a killer punch or a killer drive.

Among those who can talk authoritatively about being in 'The Zone' is Paddy Upton,[58] the mental conditioning coach of the world-conquering Indian cricket team and also cricket coach of the Indian Premier League (IPL) team, Rajasthan Royals. Upton is among the many sport theoreticians who have emerged out of South Africa and have helped change many sport, the world over. In South Africa, people tend to think differently and bravely and so have opened new paths, especially in sport, quite in contrast to India where everything is the holy textbook and thinking is always linear, conservative and follows the straight and narrow. His book on mental conditioning and his philosophy of coaching is worth understanding, though in some aspects he goes overboard.

'What we do know is that athletes in the zone report having laser-like focus, an intense yet effortless present-moment awareness, with an accompanying effortless execution of skill at the highest level of their ability. The athlete is totally absorbed in a state of undistracted concentration on the task at hand. There is no thinking. Time is distorted, in that it passes so quickly, yet things seem to happen in slow motion. Instinct and intuition are heightened as players merge with their environment, somehow seeming to know what will happen next. It leads to individuals being the best version of themselves delivering their best performances, with ease and flow and it leaves them on a height afterwards.'

---

[58] Paddy Upton, *The Barefoot Coach*, Westland, 2019.

Upton goes into even more detail about 'The Zone'. He expounds on the underlying mechanisms of 'The Zone' with a few points that agree with my perception of it, which I quote below.

* The focus is external (what's happening out there); the athlete is focused on the task at hand, such as a batsman focusing on the ball or a bowler on their target.

* 'The Zone' happens when someone is optimally challenged by the task.

* The reality is that very few athletes are able to access this state at will. 'The Zone' mostly just 'happens' generally when most of these and other favourable factors happen to align on a particular day.

After his 6-0, 6-2, 6-2 defeat of Pouille in Australia, Djokovic was asked: 'How often do you have a match like tonight where as you said, from the first point to the last you did everything you wanted and then some. How are those nights?'

He replied, 'Considering the occasion and circumstances and playing semi-finals here, this is definitely one of the best matches I've played on the Rod Laver Arena in my career ...

'Yeah, you just happen to be in that zone that we all strive for. Every professional athlete wants to be in "The Zone", where everything flows so effortlessly and you are executing automatically everything you are intending to execute. You don't ... think too much. I guess you are driven by some force that takes over you and you feel divine, you feel like in a different dimension. It's quite an awesome feeling that we all try to reach and stay in ....

'It's an individual sport, so everything really depends on you, how you emotionally cope with these things. Sometimes you feel more anxious, nervous because who is across the net, occasion or maybe something tenses up in your body and you are not striking the ball as smoothly.'

To be in 'The Zone' is an eternal wish of every player who has plunged into the stormy waters of a sporting career. Few reach the shores of triumph, fewer still reach that garden of immortality flush with fruits. The search for this other state of the mind (and body) has been ongoing. It has been part of a human being's search to understand the ethereal, to scale the unsurmountable, reside in places without the limitations of mortal life. Without any fear of defeat.

You are not in 'The Zone' as soon as the match starts. It needs effort. You are half tired, have started hitting some winners, your mind is egging you on, the focus is perfect, the orange lights of the approaching evening can be seen far ahead. No distraction, the crowd is non-existent, the plane flying overhead did not fall into your ken—you and your mind have decided to win. The body is willing too as with every shot, new power flows through your veins. Your mind is on top of the game.

Paradise: Far from hell

Parallel to this search for an ethereal state of the mind, 'The Zone' where the body and mind are in perfect sync, where the physical segues into the mental and the player makes no wrong move, can be seen as a person's search for the ethereal land, a sort of paradise where the earth behaves in perfect consonance or symphony with entire nature and the humans that inhabit it. Such a search for a paradise within earth, can be seen to be similar to the search of a heavenly state of mind and body to which we ascribe sporting success, nay, excellence. Such perfect states first existed in the imagination before they were actually discovered in physical form.

Or is 'The Zone' a facile way of branding a state of the unachievable? Are we just intuiting? Are we trying to fill an empty space with some light and knowledge? One thing for sure is that this elevated mental state does not happen all the time. It is a 'high' for which the player has to work hard.

Adventurers who roamed the world too, often found themselves in a world of intense clarity. In literature, poetry especially, we can find such a search for lands which resembled this imagined paradise. Such a paradise was often imagined before we reached there. Throughout the centuries it was pinned to the polar region, which has evoked tremendous interest among writers. Polar literature makes for amazing reading. Just like the Everest books.

In the article 'Polar Expressed', in *The New Yorker*,[59] Kathryn Schulz looked at the history of polar literature. Among the early imagined places in the Arctic was Hyperborea. This mythical place, as a physical land, was reflective of a human's yearning for a paradise on earth, where the body itself could be transcended and everything worked in unison, where the mind and the body could be in a cosmic dance. Like in 'The Zone'.

Schulz writes about one such imagined region of the Arctic in literature, 'That name was Hyperborea: the region beyond the kingdom of Boreas, god of the north wind. Somewhere above his frozen domain, the Greeks believed, lay a land of peace and plenty, home to fertile soils, warm breezes, and the oldest, wisest, gentlest race on earth. "Neither disease nor bitter old age is mixed/in their sacred blood,' the poet Pindar wrote of the Hyperboreans in the fifth century BCE. "Far from labour and battle they live."'

Here where disease, old age and other debilitating things did not exist is 'The Zone' of sports that we

[59] Kathryn Schulz, 'Polar Expressed', *The New Yorker*, 24 April 2017.

all crave for. To create a space, physical, metaphysical, metaphorical, mental. In that space all higher desires can be met. Sporting glory is just one of them.

Be it the Arctic or Antarctic, the snowy vastness offered many challenges to humans. Many made it their life challenge to conquer the Antarctic or to walk across it. Anglo-Irish explorer Ernest Shackleton's story of his expedition into the Antarctic in 1894 is a classic in human ambition, endurance and strength. Henry Worsley, a retired British army officer, enamoured all his life by the Shackleton expedition, mounted his own expedition to walk across the South Pole from one end to another with no aid. After disaster stuck his ship, the aptly named *Endurance*, Shackleton finally managed to reach Elephant Island. Later he wrote that he and his men in the course of their journey had 'pierced the veneer of outside things' and 'reached the naked soul of man'.

Polar expeditions like Shackleton's or Worsley's are driven by the human mind. Such journeys make little sense due to the impossibilities of taking on a continent of ice. Often such journeys resemble careers of sportsmen too. It is a daily fight against odds, one defeat following another, and everywhere there is desolation. But many sportsmen soldier on, the body and mind mysteriously egging them on to continue playing. This is the same feeling that captures long-distance runners. Shackleton had prescribed various qualities that his expedition members should have. 'First, optimism; second, patience; third, physical endurance; fourth, idealism; fifth and last, courage.'

Shackleton's book, *South: The Story of Shackleton's Last Expedition (1914–1917)*, is the most amazing story of human endurance and ambition. The expedition wasn't sport but it embodied all that sport stands for. The questions of 'Why sport?' or 'Why climb the Everest?' or 'Why go to the South Pole?' have no logical answer. If the Everest was conquered 'Because it was there', as mountaineer George Mallory famously said, so is sport played because it can be played. All such attempts were aimed at stretching the limits of human understanding and endurance.

Are those who lose out, those who do not have the mental faculty or the desire to reach 'The Zone' at all in any game, unable to ascend this region of utter calmness where the snow and frost of self-doubt are banished at will?

So does 'The Zone' actually exist or it is a projection of imagined states of mind, just as there were imagined lands which 'the gentle races of the earth' inhabited?

Among various experts who have come close to explaining what that different or the 'imagined' elevated state of mind can be, is Timothy Gallwey,[60] who divides the mind into two for the limited purpose of analysing an athlete's mental side. Self One is the conscious and Self Two is the unconscious aspect, so to say. The domination of Self Two is what makes the mind of the player tick, make him do the right things on court and then ultimately, takes him to victory.

'To still the mind one must learn to put it somewhere. It cannot just be let go; it must be focused. If peak performance is a function of a still mind then we are led to the question of where and how to focus it.

'As one achieves focus, the mind quiets. As the mind is kept in the present, it becomes calm. Focus means keeping the mind now and here. Relaxed concentration is the supreme art because no art can be achieved without

---

[60] Timothy Gallwey, *The Inner Game of Tennis: The Ultimate Guide to the Mental Side of Peak Performance*, Pan, 2014.

it, while with it, much can be achieved. One cannot reach the limit of one's potential in tennis or any endeavour without learning it …'

Gallwey's solution to learning how to focus is to watch the ball. What he means is not just to watch the ball coming at you but to go to the next level and watch its seam as it spins. This will make the player see the ball better. Here he draws the difference between watching the ball and 'discovering' something more in its movement and its trajectory.

Coaches and experts may have other ways of explaining this phenomenon of being in 'The Zone'. Gilles Muller's upset of Rafael Nadal in the fourth round of Wimbledon in 2017 with the fifth set going to 15-13 is another example. Here was a thirty-four-year-old sixteenth seed, generally considered a journeyman, up against the marauding Nadal fresh from the French Open victory and also impatient to finish off this minor hurdle and cross over to his appointed place in the quarter finals.

Muller took the first two sets, then Nadal took the next two and the fifth threatened to go all the way to overtake the five-hour-thirty-one-minute-long 2012 Marin Cilic versus Sam Querrey match or even the eleven-hour-five-minute John Isner versus Nicolas Mahut match in 2010, both at Wimbledon. Muller from the very beginning was seeing the ball clearly and was tying Nadal up in knots with his serves, which were swinging wildly. This gave Muller the chance to take Nadal out wide and then move up to finish off the desperate return in the classic serve-and-volley style. This was the general pattern of the game.

How could Muller dictate terms to Nadal? The reason was that on that day he was in 'The Zone'. His face showed it—he could see everything clearly. He had the answers, he was ready for the long rallies and was up for finishing the match up with a volley. Now to do all this with Nadal is not easy because if a player moved to the net, he could effortlessly pass him to stymie his ambitions right there.

Here is the Reuters report on the fag end of the epic struggle: 'When Nadal broke early in the third though, it signalled a shift in momentum that took the match to a deciding set in which logic suggested the Spaniard would dominate.

'Muller had other ideas. Nadal was forced to save two match points, one with an ace, at 4-5, then two more again at 9-10, the first with a steadfast volley after moving Muller around the court. Muller came under fire at 6-6, saving a break point and fought off four break points in an absorbing 18th game.

'After 32 holds of serve someone had to give up and surprisingly it was Nadal.'

On any other day Nadal would have swallowed Muller. But on that Manic Monday, that Monday when the world stops to watch sports giants assert their supremacy once again as if by rote, Muller was in 'The Zone'. The mental inhibitions that stymied him during his seventeen years on the tour fell apart. Though that mist of nearly two decades of struggle and failure, it was obvious that Muller could see a world beyond where everything was crystal clear and clear waters flowed. He had put his mind somewhere at a place where his self-doubts vanished. His groundstrokes were so perfectly timed that crackling sounds echoed. His mind had reached the Arctic Zone. Was there a chattering beast inside Muller or was it a comforting angel?

Once drained of all strength and your mind tells you to go on, what are the colliding thoughts within the mind? Does one tell you to give up the fight and the other to keep it going? To go wide with the serve or put one more down the T? It could be due to those colliding thoughts that made Muller lose four match points against Nadal. And still won.

What could Muller say after this titanic match, a classic in graphite-era tennis? He was as humble as could be expected from someone who is quite friendly with failure and near-wins. 'I really did well in the first two sets, then Rafa stepped it up. It was a big battle. When I had the last two match points, I thought I just had to give it a shot. Somehow in the end I made it.'

When Rafa hit the last shot long, Muller stood there, disbelief writ large on his face.

Two days later Venus Williams reached the final. She often talks like a philosopher, a hidden pain lurking beneath her pioneering role as a woman sportsperson. She described what it means to her to win and what happens on court. She was in 'The Zone' of course: 'Even though there is entertainment for the players, it is complete and pure focus. You don't see anything or hear anything except the ball and what's going on in your head. That wave is finally a moment of "I can enjoy this" before I go off the court.'

Is memory instinct?

Many players are termed players of instinct. They are mostly left alone by coaches and managers who make little effort to rein them in.

Where does this instinct come from? The instinct to rush in, move away, stay at the far post, try a bicycle kick? It is mostly memory, while instinct is the process of trying out something you have tried elsewhere or have been practising secretly. To lob the ball over the opponent's head and swerve past him to collect the lobbed ball is instinct. We can also call it memory because this visual imagery was stored in the deep mind of the player when he practised hard during his street soccer days or just for fun. Store a visual image in the ganglia and it will pop up in the most opportune moments—then we the fans, have an image, a story, an anecdote that we will talk about for ever.

Quick thinking is often termed as instinct. In a whirr, a top player can change the course of the game with an unseen or unexpected move. He would have at some point played this in his mind. Everywhere in sport, the mind is often talked about. What about boxing which is seen as a mere physical sport in which the stronger man wins? Cassius Clay's younger brother Rudy was also a boxer and fought in as many tournaments as his brother but was no match for his brother.[61] 'My mind was not as quick as his. Boxing is a thinking man's game,' Rudy consoled himself.

In the 2017 Premiership League of football clubs, midfielder Emre Can of Liverpool scored with an incredible bicycle kick. This is what he had to say about it later to *Sunday Times*: 'The first thing in my mind was "I will head the ball" and then the ball was a little bit behind me and then I just had one option to finish which was the bicycle kick. Of course, it can go wrong. The ball can go off your foot to the corner flag. I don't practice bicycle kicks but you have some picture in your head and it's just instinct. I've never scored a goal like that (as a professional) but I did it once when I was fourteen or fifteen playing for Eintracht Frankfurt. It was in the last minute, a winning goal. When it went in, I went crazy.'

In many cases, conservative coaches kill instinct and

---

[61] Eig, *Ali: A Life*.

instead, force the player to go by the textbook. It's ideal not to kill it. Because a player is what he is in his mind—and what controls that is what we call memory. If a player has no memory—visual, textual, or mostly from his own practice—he is unlikely to carry it out in the field. Even Can here remembered that he had tried the bicycle kick once. Anyone who suffers even a minor memory loss will be unable to survive as a player, even if he is physically fit.

This is evident if a player tries to cut out a shot or a move which he had learnt in his youth. To unlearn a shot, a particular way of doing the forehand for instance, is a tough ask, though a change of grip is possible. A basketball coach who tells his student to cut out the long ranger but instead to try driving in, may not find it easy to change his ward's 'instinct'. When he is on court and when he is near the range, his mind tells him to shoot.

This is also the reason why many players can be heard saying that they do not like playing as a withdrawn forward, preferring to be upfront. To play upfront is the instinct, a habit, a liking cultivated from younger days. In that position the player can do certain things that he likes.

The question of whether memory is what formulates or provides instinct has been a matter of conjecture, though here we can see that it's somewhat the same. Some studies have come close to figuring out that elite competitors have faster memories and thus quicker decision-taking abilities. All this goes into recognizing that an elite athlete has a better instinct than an average competitor.

A study reported by the University College, London's Institute of Cognitive Neuroscience,[62] said: 'Elite athletes perform tasks that many of us could never comprehend but what is fascinating is their mindset when tackling

[62] *Daily Mail*, 17 October 2016.

such challenges.' Everything points towards the crucial and decisive role that the mind of the superior athlete plays in keeping him at the top.

'When some decisions can be the difference between success and failure, it is perhaps unsurprising that the study showed that athletes were consistently several seconds faster when performing their tasks.

'A few seconds or a few per cent may not sound much but this is a long time in sport and is the difference between winning and losing.'

The study included racing drivers and skydivers, who perhaps have to take the quickest decision in all sport, apart from top sportsmen. The study found that their memory performance was 20 per cent better and the speed of their mental procession was 10 per cent more rapid.

According to the report, the aim of the study was to test the theory that because of their training, elite competitors have an enhanced ability to handle intense situations and emotions. This and other studies confirm the role of the mind, speed of decision-making and memory itself in keeping a top athlete at the top position.

However, I disagree with certain theories that associate champions with superior mental faculties other than memory, which can vary from person to person.

In an article in *The Age*,[63] Michael Gleeson, quoting research, suggests that champion tennis players can predict what an opponent is going to do next. 'He (Djokovic) like other elite players intuitively knows sooner than other players where the serve is going. Average players react to the ball [by] leaving the racquet. The best players don't. They know before the ball hits the (opponent's) racquet

---

[63] Michael Gleeson, 'Why Champions Seem to Have More Time', *The Age*, Melbourne, 27 January 2019.

where the serve is going to go. On an average, it is a third of a second before the ball hits the racquet.'

These findings were arrived at after conducting tests like the Temporal Occlusion Test at the Victoria University by Damian Farrow who in 2019 was professor of skill acquisition at the university.

While this finding could be the outcome of laboratory tests, if we look at champion players we see that most of them are as vulnerable to certain shots by their opponents as average players are. It is difficult to believe that Djokovic and other top players can foresee where a serve is going to go, one-third of a second faster. In that case it will be impossible for their opponents to fire aces or score points of their own service, since this theory argues that it is an inbuilt faculty. No champion player has claimed this faculty exists in them. In fact, most of them say they are quite average on many fronts.

When Nadal was interviewed after he defeated American tennis player Frances Tiafoe in straight sets in the Australian Open of 2019, he said of Tiafoe's game: 'Yeah, he's quick. He has a strong forehand. It is difficult to read his game sometimes. He can go to the net. He can sometimes slice.' Why is it difficult for Nadal to read a lower-ranked opponent's game? The reason is that he has no innate faculty as claimed by this research. Champions too make an inordinate number of unforced errors, such as letting opponents serve out points with aces.

This theory doesn't hold and only adds to the many unsubstantiated theories that make an understanding of sport complicated, unreal and obtuse. Such theories are mostly the result of the imagination running riot. In this case it goes something like this: If a player can return serves so well, then he must have an inborn ability to foresee where the serve is going to land.

Strategy: Plan like hell

As we have seen, the mind plays a big part in a player's rise. I have pointed out that it is memory that is crucial. There are other aspects like analytic power, a bit of neurosis and the ability to be always on edge, making you pounce on every chance that comes your way. Many players have nervous tics (Djokovic), involuntary spasms (Aussie cricketer, Steve Smith) and compulsive habits (the most famous being Nadal). All this points to a state of mind that is a bit above or divergent from the normal sedate mind.

If memory has a role to play, then it means that there are patterns to a person's play. On particular occasions, a player repeats what he did earlier. New evidence suggests that not all things we know are remembered for long and that the brain moves 'useless' memory into the dustbin of forgetfulness. A memory becomes useless when it is not recalled either by association or links, whether accidentally during a casual chat or directly when an occasion arises.

In an article in *The Verge*[64] titled 'Are You Forgetful? That's Just Your Brain Erasing Useless Memories', Angela Chan writes: 'Most of us think perfect memory means never forgetting actually helps us navigating a world that is random and ever-changing.'

Blake Richards of the University of Toronto who studies theoretical links between Artificial Intelligence and neuroscience says: 'So it makes sense that our brains would makes us forget outdated, irrelevant info that might confuse us or information that leads us astray. Still the brain actually spends energy making us forget

---

[64] Angela Chan, 'Are You Forgetful? That's Just Your Brain Erasing Useless Memories', *The Verge*, 21 June 2017.

by generating new neurons.' Such an argument might be difficult to accept at its face value, considering the amount of junk memory that we recollect every minute of our lives without any provocation. Episodic memory (actual happenings) are, according to this theory, more quickly forgotten than general knowledge (semantic knowledge).

This is easiest to track in a sport like tennis than in a team game like soccer. Tennis Australia's Game Insight Group has done exactly that. Dr Machar Reid who heads this group, brings out a mind-boggling analysis of a player's patterns and behaviour on court after the analysis of his or her games. Each player's on-court habits and patterns are different. They can differ vastly in case of siblings as well, as this analysis of Serena and Venus Williams, who reached the final of the 2017 Australian Open, shows. While measuring a player's performance in the biggest moments or most important points of a match (called clutch points or clutch moments) as relative to their opponent, Reid and his team concluded the following about their performance in 2017 Australian Open. This analysis came before the final match, trying to predict which way the match would go.

Serena's overall clutch performance has been down three percentage points against her long-term average but that can be explained at least in part, by the fact her road to the final has been pretty clinical. She has really controlled most of her matches from start to finish.

If we look at the historical data for Serena, in the years where she hasn't gone the distance at the Australian Open, she has steadily fallen away in clutch moments from round one through to her exit.

We look at players changing direction during a point as one element of work rate and Serena loves to control the centre of the court and to make her opponent do all the changing of direction. In this way she is playing in 2017 like she was in 2015—directing traffic, but with a real purpose, as she is hitting her groundstrokes to the centre of the court much more than last year.

Venus has been hitting her forehand and backhand closer to the sideline, which is exactly what she needs to do to get her sister off balance by spreading the court and creating opportunities to make Serena change direction.

We know that the serve will be important in determining who holds the trophy aloft. The preferred first serve for both sisters is up the Ad court. But it's the next shot in the rally where they change tack.

Serena tends to go in behind her opponent, where she wins 70 per cent of the time. Venus goes into the open court.

Venus prefers the T on the deuce court but some of her most successful shots are born from the other side of the serve box.

When Venus serves wide to the deuce court and follows it up with either an angled ball in behind her opponent or deep on the other side, she extraordinarily wins the point 100 per cent of the time. If she adopts this approach to Serena and forces a change of direction, it could pay off.

But if Venus goes for the wide serve, it needs to be executed with the highest quality because any mistake will unleash the power of the Serena forehand and Venus knows that better than anyone one.

Phew! This is how minutely patterns to a player's game are now analysed. This is possible because a player is controlled by her mind and memory. Djokovic cannot suddenly step out on court and play like Federer, though he can replicate all of Federer's shots. The way you play is an addiction. Every player has a graph of consistency and patterns sticking with him through his career. It is here that triumph and failure lie embedded. This is why most players ranked outside the Top Twenty for five years, for instance, mostly remain there all their lives. They are in a plateau from which they find no escape. They have everything they need to win. Yet they don't. They get titles off and on but they do not win enough. They lose to the same opponents, who are higher ranked.

For a closer examination of this phenomenon of the mind playing a big role in a sportsman's life, we have the example of German tennis player Alexander Zverev and his elder brother Mischa. Alexander (twenty years old in 2017) learnt the game from his brother but overtook him in the rankings and is well positioned to be in the Top Ten for a long run. Such examples help us understand the role that genes play in a sportsman's life. Since they have the same genes, why is it that the elder brother was overtaken by the younger (like in the case of Williams sisters?) Their father Alexander Zverev Sr was a tennis player who competed for the Soviet Union, having appeared in the Wimbledon championships twice without going anywhere. We see in the history of the sport that failed or underachieving sportsmen relive their career through their children with a sort of vengeance—Alexander Jr has already won more games than his father could even dream of.

Alexander broke into the Top 100 in 2015. He lost the first two finals he reached and then won all the next four finals. He told the *Independent*: 'My success has a lot to do with Mischa. He was the one who always used to practice with me when I was little, when I was a junior.'

What is deficient in Mischa that he hasn't been able to rise like his younger brother? The reason could easily lie in the way he practiced during his early years, the mental aspect of his game, his memory power and the various ways in which his mind sees the game, works in pressure situations. How easily can he climb to 'The Zone', for instance. Can we see the burning desire in his piercing looks?

In many cases of siblings being in the same sport, we see that if the younger fellow gets past the elder, he still gives credit to the elder brother and believes that he is better in ranking just by fluke and his elder brother will make it. This is similar to what Alexander thinks about his brother—but it will not be a surprise if the younger one defeats the elder if they were to meet in a match. While Mischa raised the level of his game to beat Andy Murray, he fell in the next round in the 2017 Australian Open.

Is Mischa in the wrong game, going by the S5 analysis? Well, Alexander says that he himself had the option of picking any game in which he excelled as a young boy—hockey, soccer and tennis. Alexander's success lies in the fact that at a crucial stage he chose the game that fit him to a T. 'When I was growing up, I played a lot of sports. There was a time when I was playing field hockey, tennis and soccer at the same time. I was actually quite good at all these sports. My field hockey team was the German field hockey champion and the football team was the Hamburg champion. To focus on tennis was my decision.' If Alexander had stuck with soccer, would he have made the same impact? At six foot four he was clearly more suited to tennis, though at the time he took the decision. he would have been shorter.

Mischa's problem has affected many tennis players—being unable to break open the door to the top room. If we look at those who have won junior majors, most of them have faded away. Between mastering the junior level and trying to play with the big boys, a large majority of them fade away. That can be seen in the history of every game. In the entire nearly 100-year-old history of the Australian Open, only twelve players have won both the junior and senior titles. This is roughly the pattern in other Grand Slams as well. What is the reason? Obviously, it's because many players peak only after their junior age, maybe at eighteen or twenty. It's a slow, long climb.

Ken Rosewall, former world-ranking Australian tennis player, has a good record in carrying on his junior form in the Australian Open. He won the junior titles in 1950 and 1952, and won the seniors in the next years—1953, 1955, 1971 and 1972, a career stretching to more than twenty years. After 1985, when junior winner, the Swedish Stefan Edberg, won the seniors as well, no junior winner has won the senior title in Melbourne. The reason clearly is that in the memory and mental sphere (strategy, focus, ability to enter 'The Zone'), they have been outgunned by others who never did well in the juniors or gathered pace slowly but surely as they moved into their late teens.

This chapter tried to show that any player, to succeed well, needs to be in the right game. Many fail because they are not in the right game. There is no point if a skilled mind wastes time in a strength-sport and so on. Many sportsmen seem to naturally select their game. Some do this after trial and error, as Alexander Zverev did.

If finally, each game can be scientifically classified as what type of S5 game it is, then a player's ability can be related to it and it will make it easier for youngsters to choose—and then go on to become champions. Otherwise they will end up singing a variation of 'The Summer of '69' by Bryan Adams:

'Me and some guys from school
Had a ball and bat and played real hard
Sweat all day to sunset, but lost real bad.
I should have known, we'd never get far.'

CHAPTER FIVE

Tennis: The Most Evolved Game

How do all the existing theories, postulations, the contraindications pan out in each sport? Can we conclude that in one sport, genetic influence works and in another just practice and sumptuous learning? In a skilled sport, does practice play any big part? These are the perplexing questions which we have to dive into to figure out the basic question of this book: why do some people excel and others just fade away?

I will analyse some representative games and put forward certain arguments. Tennis comes first because it is perhaps the most advanced of sport, due to the high levels of skill and strategy and also because it is an individual game, where the player fights alone. At one level, the game is full of grace and ballet-dancing dexterity, but on the other hand, it can plummet into muscular crassness. The game can make the devil surface, quite without warning. It's the only sport where the player thrashes his racquet to smithereens in an inexplicable show of self-destruction and anger.

A game with such visible muscle on court, has an imposed serenity when the game is on. No one is allowed to move, squeak or sneeze when a match is on and woe betide anyone who, when a game is in progress, as much as expresses his anxiety over a shot that skims the net, or even lets out a noisy burp helped by the afternoon beer. So, it's an anti-sport where the ancient notion of crowds baying for blood is completely neutralized. In chess too, silence is required but that is a mental game where followers are also lost in thought.

Badminton is similar to tennis in many ways with the field of play divided by a net and a similar racquet used, though the tennis ball and the shuttlecock hit in badminton are very different. Badminton is perhaps a more decent game than tennis, the many errors that a player makes are accepted with quiet dignity, the loser and winner letting out just occasional squeaks and unlike tennis, there is no fuss about spectator movement or noise. In fact, the screams of the spectators from a neighbouring badminton court can easily distract a player on the verge of a silken touch at the net, when even a minor wobble of the wrist can destroy the point.

Tennis, despite being the most evolved sport in terms of skill sets, is still a club sport and not a street sport, which means that the underprivileged class is kept away, thus depriving the game itself of the huge population coming from labour classes and thus more muscular. For the young Black boy in the streets of Harlem or far away Colombia, tennis is not an option. 'To what purpose would poor Black boys learn tennis? [Jake] LaMotta, [Floyd] Patterson, ['Sonny'] Liston, Hector Camacho, Mike Tyson—all learned to box in captivity so to speak,' writes Joyce Carol Oates in her spectacular book *On Boxing*. The relation between boxing and deprivation has been acknowledged, but in tennis it is almost the other way around—affluence or at least, admission in an expensive school in a city in an advanced society, is almost a necessity for a future tennis player. Till as late as the mid-1960s, it was difficult for Blacks to get entry into US tennis tournaments, so well entrenched was racism in the game.

The first Black to win the US Open was in 1968 was Arthur Ashe who also won the Australian Open and Wimbledon in 1975. Althea Gibson won the women's title in Wimbledon in 1957 and the US Open in 1958. Then we had to wait for the Williams sisters, Venus in 1994 as a professional player and Serena in 1995, to come along.

Tennis thus remains a predominantly white sport and an exclusivist sport. So if any sporting achievement is credited (wrongly) to racial or genetic roots, there may seem to be enough reason for it. The tennis top line is the complete rebuttal of the 100-metre final line-up in the Olympics or vice versa. Almost all of its Top Fifty ATP ranked players come from the US or Europe or Australia and now South America as well. Most of them are white. The ATP Top 100 has only four or five Blacks, showing how much the game is tilted towards the more financially fortunate nations. But the situation is surely changing for the better, especially with women's tennis being the trendsetter in becoming more inclusive. Tennis is now a truly global sport, though in Africa, it lags behind.

'I submit that tennis is the most beautiful sport there is. And also the most demanding,' wrote American author David Foster Wallace.

The word 'tennis' is derived from 'tenez', French for 'take it', or a challenge thrown from the other side of net. Some form of tennis existed in Shakespearean times, prompting the great bard to dwell on its vicissitudes and sure enough, take a metaphorical leap. In Shakespeare's *Pericles*, the tennis court is compared to the ocean, no less, not that during those times there was the Monte

Carlo clay court by an ocean. According to American writer and editor John Jeremiah Sullivan,[65] it occurs in the part of *Pericles* that scholars now believe was written by a tavern-keeper named George Wilkins. Pericles, the prince of Tyre, has just been tossed half-dead onto the Greek shore and is discovered by three fishermen:

'A man whom both the waters and the wind,
In that vast tennis-court, hath made the ball
For them to play upon, entreats you pity him.'

King Henry's imagined reply at the battle of Agincourt was rendered into verse, probably by the poet-monk John Lydgate, around 1536:

'Some hard tennis balls I have hither brought
Of marble and iron made full round.
I swear by Jesu that me dear bought,
They shall beat the walls to the ground.'

Tennis has held an appeal as a sport for more than a century now. Gerald Marzorati in an article in *New Yorker* reveals that among those who played the game was Leo Tolstoy himself, who took to the game when he was about forty.

'What brought Tolstoy to tennis so late in his life? Or better, what brought him around to tennis? When he was in his forties, he thought tennis was a faddish luxury, a pastime of the new rich, something imported, inauthentic—a child's game enthused about by well-to-do grown-ups who refused to grow up. We know this from Part 6, Chapter 22 of *Anna Karenina*, which he was writing in the 1870s when the modern game of "lawn tennis" was developed and patented by Major Walter Clapton Wingfield, a British army officer.'

Marzorati writes that Wingfield is believed to have

[65] John Jeremiah Sullivan, Introduction to *String Theory: David Foster Wallace on Tennis*, Library of America, 2016.

drawn on a number of sources for his game: the indoor squash-like English game of racquets, 'real tennis' from the court of Henry VIII, *Jeu de paume* from France, a Basque game called pelota, and badminton. Wingfield originally called his game '*sphairistike*' from the ancient Greek for 'skill at playing the ball', but a better example of his marketing savvy was his idea to package racquets, balls, a net and poles in boxed sets suitable for shipping. In 1874, his first year in business, he sent out thousands of sets, one of which—imaginatively—winds up on the 'carefully levelled and rolled croquet-ground' of the house where Tolstoy's Anna, having left her husband and son and shocked Moscow society, has gone to live with her lover, Vronsky. Tolstoy never wrote about the game but at least we know that the game drew big minds, a situation that continues today.

High skill, high focus, high strategy

So tennis has its intellectual outriders who told us what we didn't know about the game and its many warriors. David Foster Wallace who played tennis at the junior level is among the most valued tennis writers who played a big part in elevating the game from the clay surface to higher realms where only poetry can do it justice. Wallace, considered a leading American writer and modern novelist of the present era, killed himself in 2008 after a sustained struggle with depression, during which period he produced great novels. Sports lovers know him for a profile of Roger Federer but an equally competent piece he wrote, 'Derivative Sport in Tornado Ally', was about playing tennis in Central Illinois which was ravaged by high winds, making it impossible to control the ball.

Wallace recollects from his personal experience of playing and also alludes to the near spiritual state of mind, 'The Zone'. This laying bare of tennis as a sport is couched in the overall study of what it meant to play tennis in high winds and in this case, getting lifted up and thrown like a ball by the tornado. In a way, this description of tennis helps us understand the higher reaches of the game and also why it is being argued that tennis is the top sport. The observer and the participant are the same, making it an awesome truth.

'The only time I ever got caught in what might have been an actual one (tornado) was in June'78 on a tennis court at Hessel Park in Champaign, where I was drilling one afternoon with Gill Antitoi [one of Wallace's childhood friends who often played tennis with him]. Though a contemptible and despised tournament opponent, I was a coveted practice partner because I could transfer balls to wherever you wanted them with the mindless constancy of a machine. This particular day it was supposed to rain around suppertime and a couple of times we thought we'd heard the tattered edges of a couple of sirens out west towards Monticello, but Antitoi and I drilled religiously every afternoon that week, trying to prepare for a beastly invitational in Chicago where it was rumoured both [Bruce] Brescia and [Christian] Mees would appear. We were doing butterfly drills—my crosscourt forehand is transferred back down the line to Antitoi's backhand, he crosscourts it to my backhand, I send it down the line to his forehand, four 45 degree angles ...'

In this passage, Wallace was trying to show how the impending storm was never a threat to them as they were, after all, ensconced in the divine activity of playing tennis, till, of course, the tornado lifted both of them and crashed them to the walls.

Well, it is not always the case, but tennis in its ardour

and demand, somehow rises above other sport. Just to master the forehand is one of sport's most hard tasks, maybe close to the Produnova vault (a frontspring followed by a double somersault off the table in three front flips, all in less than three seconds), in gymnastics. I have been trying for twenty years so I know. But I started playing tennis at forty, the age at which nothing new can be learnt or mastered, though wisdom can be gained. The tennis forehand is not a racquet hitting the ball. Agassi came closest to a description of what the forehand is when he wrote what his father-coach told him when he was learning the game: "Brush the ball." Try brushing a ball which is coming at you at speeds above 150 kilometres and you know what we are getting at. What you get is not acrylic on canvas. You get blood on clay.'

The swing and follow through of the forehand and the backhand are in themselves wonderful to watch if you care about the game. Normally, the viewer's eye follows the ball, not the follow through, so you miss the cameo. At the end of the follow through, when the shot has been executed with satisfaction and the ball has landed, the player for a moment strikes the pose of a ballet dancer caught in a pirouette, in some cases both his hands stretched out in the effort of the stroke and balance. Sometimes at the culmination of the backhand swing you can see the face of a player like say, Nadal, contorted in the agony of the execution but we know that the pain is just temporal for soon to follow is the breathlessness of triumph. After a Federer single-handed backhand, his hands are stretched like the wings of a condor catching the thermals. There is a hidden brutality even, the unexpected grunt that escapes, adding to the totality of the act. Here there is no bestiality of the giant who has just dunked the winning basket and hangs on to the hoop in confirmation and crude celebration.

The topspin forehand or the classic tennis forehand has to be mastered before the age of twenty or it's almost impossible to perfect it. The swish of a ball from a Nadal forehand is enough to send a hummingbird to retirement. It is a deadly combination of speed and topspin. If you are spinning a ball like in cricket, you have to sacrifice on speed, which is why spin bowlers are also slow bowlers.

Tennis allows you no such grace or concession. It is like asking the spin bowler to also be the fastest bowler in the team. In cricket it's impossible. A batsman hitting the ball for a six does not have to bother about imparting spin to his shot. Thwack—that's it.

Let's look at the speed of the forehands of the topmost players. Mind you, it's not just about hitting a ball with all your strength.

Average ball speed (statistics of 2018)

Roger Federer	75.8 mph
Rafael Nadal	88.7 mph
Noval Djokovic	78.2 mph
Andy Murray	69.8 mph
Andy Roddick	88.5 mph

The Nadal forehand topspin has been variously measured from 3800 rpm (rotation per minute) to 4800. Federer's backhand slice has more topspin (5300 rpm) but the slice is all topspin and little speed or power. The slice has to be placed well, somewhere near the net but despite its topspin, the slice always delivers below expectation and is used mostly in clay courts. But its execution adds so much grace to the game

Here's Wallace again: '[Michael] Joyce's strongest shot is his forehand, a weapon of near Wagnerian aggression and power. Joyce's forehand is particularly lovely to watch. It's more spare and textbook than [Ivan] Lendl's whip-crack forehand or [Björn] Borg's great swooping loop; by way of decoration there's only a small loop of flourish on the backswing. The stroke itself is completely horizontal, so Joyce can hit through the ball while it is still well out in front of him. As with all the great players, Joyce's side is so emphatically to the net as the ball approaches that his posture is a classic contrapposto.'

Backhand

If the forehand exists at the intersection of muscle and art, the backhand is a miracle. This is the case in all racquet sport. In a backhand, the shoulder has to work the other way, from left to right for a right-hander. Many adopt the two-handed backhand because one hand can be used to control the shot and the other to give the power. The single-handed backhand is too much to ask of one hand, yet it's worth going miles to see this shot delivered by Stanislas Wawrinka or Federer or Dominic Thiem. It is not possible to impart as much topspin to the backhand as one can with the forehand. While playing the backhand, the control is what the players are most bothered about, since they are playing on your wrong side, the right-hander turning to the left and vice versa. The backhand is the attempt to cheat the brain's natural faculty or preference for one side and so involves a lot of unnatural exercise. When Federer plays the shot, he looks away from the court in front, mostly towards the left and in full front towards the left. To execute that shot without looking at the ground in front of him requires a mental map of the opponent's court, I mean the exact length of the court.

It is this spatial faculty of the brain, I believe, that helps a player like Federer execute the one-handed backhand without looking at or without being able to see the court even with the corner of his eye. The length of the court almost to its last inch is recorded in his mind and the shot lands at the far crosscourt corner. In various moments of every sport, blind play is required. But the one-handed backhand with its requirement of timing, the swing to generate the power, the tightness of the wrist which does not let the ball falter in its voyage of destruction, the fabulous follow through with the hands splayed in triumph, all this is asking for too much. Only the forehand can match it. Which is why if there is half a chance, many players run around and convert a potential backhand into a forehand.

Mastering any shot in any game is tough but to have the forehand as a weapon is an achievement that is unparalleled in sport. Getting the spin right on the billiards table is as tough, some may argue, what about pocketing a three-pointer at the hoot? But there is nothing as profound in its physicality as well as skill of the forehand.

With these two weapons, any war should be easy. Mastering such shots is tough. It calls for wasting a decade of your youth when the options to spend your time otherwise are many. But in the minds of some, a minuscule percentage of people in this universe, a thought strikes and stays with them during their teenage years. To be a sportsman. To be a winner. To succeed every day. It's a plunge into the dark.

What we are getting at here are the unknown aspects of a game. By knowing this, we can at least attempt to figure out why a huge majority of talented, hardworking professionals do not make it to the top. Between stragglers and achievers, there is an invisible moat which is impossible to cross. Management gurus call it the glass ceiling.

A grid for success and failure

The point in all this description is to lay a grid for success and failure. Why do many people get lost in the sporting maze, a labyrinth full of traps and impossibilities? What keeps the below 100 rankers going is the belief that they will soon crack it and go zooming up. Many do not achieve this dream, due to faults in strategizing or practice, or lack of desire. India's leading tennis player (in 2019), the left-handed Prajnesh Gunneswaran, struggled in the 200s for a long time. He told me just after he won a International Tennis Federation (ITF) Futures event in the blazing heat of a Trivandrum (Thiruvananthapuram) summer in 2017, that he hoped to touch the 150s' rank soon. 'No chance in hell,' I mumbled to myself then.

How wrong I was! Prajnesh persevered and reached the seventy-fifth rank in 2019 and became India's lead singles player.

To keep winning is tough. Tennis analyst Dan Weston's theory is that a winner is one who has the higher combined percentage of service and return winners. The top guns mostly have a percentage of above 110. 'By this measure Nadal has been hugely impressive on clay in 2017, winning 69.1 per cent of points on serve and 48.3 per cent return points—a combined success total of 117.4 per cent. That (2017 clay court performance) is better than in any of his clay-court seasons except 2012.'

According to the report, Nadal was moving to the top in 2017 on the wings of amazing statistics. An average service speed of 116 mph, one of his highest, he led the ATP in break points saved, and was in the Top Five for break points converted.

By the same theory Federer won 71.1 per cent of points on serve and 39.0 per cent on return on hard courts in 2017 a combined success rating of 110.1 per cent. This is lower than his performance for three previous years.

Another, perhaps better, way to look at a sport is to look at how its stars create and destroy, rise and fall, falter and conquer. In tennis it is possible to come closest to the truth or at least to the brink of the dark hole. The best way to examine this is to look at the number of times Novak Djokovic lost in 2016–17, and why. And also, why a top-ranked player whose ranking dips can always reclaim his rank, if he persists.

Djokovic lost to Czech Jiri Vesely, ranked fifty-fifth in the second round of the Monte Carlo Masters on 14 April 2016, when the score was 6-4, 2-6, 6-4. This was the first time that Jiri Vesely had beaten a Top Ten player. Among the most talented players on the circuit, the Czech is also among the most unpredictable, which is what players who are at around the twenty-fifth to fiftieth rank normally are. My conclusion is that they are not tops in the mind game and lag a bit behind in some aspects of the mind game explained in the previous chapter.

Vesely was among the Top Fifty in 2017 and is the typical player who just cannot find his way to the top, even though he has the game. Match statistics show that he is not lacking in any aspect of the game. However, consistency is not his forte. That is a statement used against many players who never make it to the top—consistency. They win one, lose the next. It is all beyond explanation. They are bereft of mental power and other aspects of memory that we dealt with. I watched Jiri on his comeback trail in 2020, winning an ATP 250 title in Pune. He was slowly getting back his confidence and was serving consistently around 200 mph. It was easy to figure out from what he said that he had various doubts about his abilities. See the comparison of the performances of Vesely and Djokovic.

	Vesely	Djokovic
Aces	4	3
Double faults	4	3
First serve	59%	66%
First serve points won	69%	72%
Second serve points won	61%	45%
Serve points won	66%	63%
Break points saved	25%	63% (5/8)
Service games played	14	14
First serve return won	28%	31%
Second serve return points won	55%	39%
Return points won	37%	34%
Breaks converted	38%	75%
Return games played	14	14
Total points won	50% (84/168)	50% (84/168)

When Djokovic loses a match, it is mostly because of faults in the second serve and maybe a few more unforced errors. In the Vesely match he won the same number of points as Vesely, showing that there is very little decline in performance but a bit of a fall at the crucial juncture of the match. It shows that Djokovic was never in 'The Zone' and his mental stature not at its best due to his concerns about his elbow injury.

In a 2016 match, after beating Grigor Dimitrov of Bulgaria, Djokovic expressed some of this concern. 'I think my game is where it needs to be at the moment. Sure I can play better. I know that but you can't always be 100 per cent.'

Actually, the top players play almost always at 100 per cent. The Top Ten keep winning everywhere, not counting the occasional upsets. If you look at it dispassionately, the ATP tour like similar tours in other sport, is a venue for the winners to keep proving themselves again and again. Only if they lose is there a stirring within the tennis community. Look at what Marin Cilic said before his 2016 Paris Masters match against Djokovic. Cilic had just beaten David Goffin 6-7, 7-6 and was up against Djokovic who has won all the fourteen matches against Cilic. This in itself shows the humanoid nature of victory. It is relentless. 'It's obvious Djokovic likes to play me or if you want to put it differently, I don't like to play him as much. But I'm confident. Every match is a new match.' Cilic won the match, his first against Djokovic.

Djokovic's early losses during 2016–17 while on his comeback from injury had started worrying critics. He lost nine matches since the 2016 Paris Open. Six of the nine defeats came against players ranked outside the Top Ten, when the defeats happened. Sam Querrey (41, at Wimbledon), Juan Martin del Potro (141, at the Rio Olympics), Roberto Batista Agut (19, at the Shanghai Masters), Denis Istomin (117, at the Australian Open, more on that in a later chapter), and two losses to Nick Kyrgios (17,16, at the Mexico and Indian Wells).

What does this signify? There is nothing here to show that Djokovic's game deteriorated during this period due to his rather long injury lay-off. It always takes time to get back to the top spot after an injury or a frustrating and frightening lockdown as in 2020. But invariably, top players get back their spots because embedded in their memory are the strategic skills and the details of shot-making that are required. They don't have to relearn anything because they remember well. But Djokovic panicked. In May 2017, as the defeats continued, Djokovic sacked his entire support staff including his long-time coach. Within a year, however, Djokovic was back at the top and his smiling confident self.

I watched the Australian Open 2017 match where Denis Istomin, the Russian-origin Uzbek tennis player, defeated Djokovic. In any match, where do the flaws of a player lie? Is it in the number of unforced errors which most sports journalists quote in their reports that are the sole reason for defeat? Unforced errors are easy targets for coaches and critics to point out while looking at failure. Djokovic made seventy-one unforced errors in a five-setter of over four and a half hours to Istomin's sixty-one. A difference of ten, which means ten points given away by Djokovic that he actually should not have given away. Of the rest of the seventy-one errors, sixty-one were neutralized by Istomin's own sixty-one unforced errors.

In the 2016 Australian Open, Djokovic made 100 unforced errors (breaking his own record) in his four-hour-thirty-two-minute match against French player Gilles Simon, which Djokovic won. Unforced errors can be neutralized by other positive points. It is not the only criterion for defeat, though it is a major factor.

In serves lie another story of any match. Here, despite Djokovic's fastest serve being 6 kilometres per hour less than that of Istomin, he maintained a higher average fastest serve speed and also a higher average serve speed. This means that Djokovic clearly neutralized the faster speed that Istomin had with his first serves.

Djokovic, of course, made more unforced errors. But then he neutralized that in baseline points and net points won. So there is very little to pinpoint as major or consistent errors on Djokovic's part. It is just that Istomin was in 'The Zone' that he does not often reach.

What did Djokovic do wrong? He played below par, his mind was not right there and he thought that the match against Istomin would be a walk in the park like all second seeds have the right to think. Also, Djokovic was looking completely underweight, forcing a reporter to comment on his 'bean-stalk' legs. The number of unforced errors is also an indication of a lack of total focus and other mental concerns.

After the match, Djokovic was circumspect but did not read too much into the defeat. (But since January 2017, when this match was played, he lost again on clay, ending up with his dismissal of his staff.) After the defeat by Istomin, this is how Djokovic opened up at the press conference held afterwards.

Q: You played Istomin five times before and only lost a set. Did you ever see any of this Denis Istomin before?

Djokovic: Of course I never underestimate any opponent. Doesn't matter which tournament I play on or which round. I try to give the best that I can. Him playing this well, I mean it is amazing. He played obviously above his level. You got to give him credit for that. Many things came together for him today.

Q: In the narrative of your development, we thought that after Doha maybe you put behind a slightly disappointing second half of the season last year. Do you still feel like that?

Djokovic: I started the season very well. Again it's a tennis match. On a given day you can lose. I mean nothing is impossible. There is over a hundred players playing in the main draw. I guess the quality of tennis keeps rising each year. Everybody becomes more professional. I guess they improve. They get better on the court. What can I do? I did try my best till the last shot, but it didn't work.

Q: Is it [the reason] more physical or more mental, even though it's always a mixture between the two? Which side would you choose?

Djokovic: I don't think it was physical. We both looked okay. After four and a half hours, we didn't seem to be tired. Of course, four and a half hours is not easy on the body. But still I don't think that has affected neither me nor my opponent. It was just in the game of tennis. You know one guy beats the other guy. That's all I can say.

In the press conference, Djokovic showed why he is a champion. He refused to dwell on the defeat too much, though it was a debilitating one for his career and almost fell into a pattern in 2016–17. Deep within, he could see some signs of trouble but he gave full credit to his conqueror, Istomin.

For any player coming back from a long lay-off, it takes time, sometimes more than a year to claw back to the top. If the focus and motivation is there the player will get back to the top, mainly because he/she has mastered all the shots earlier and it is all embedded in the mind. There is no other hidden secret to it.

Many tennis experts have come to the conclusion that Djokovic is one of the best returners of serve and this is one major reason for his top position in the game. But experts forget that many players have strong points, but they are not on top because either their strong points are neutralized by their weak points or they are not consistent enough with their strong shots.

'Most of the great returners are not actually reacting to the ball. They are reacting to the position of the server's body, the server's tendencies. The best returners always have the best analytical mind,' Mark Kovacs, sports scientist at the Kovacs Institute, comments on Djokovic's returns.[66]

---

[66] Joe Ward, Bedel Saget and Geoff Macdonald, 'A Look at Novak Djokovic's Mastery of the Tennis Return,' *New York Times*, 1 September 2018; Sean Ingle, 'Rafael Nadal and Roger Federer just keep rolling by', *The Guardian*, 15 May 2017.

About his analytical mind, I am in full agreement. But Kovacs's analysis that Djokovic spreads his leg the widest for a stronger base, nor the way he starts on his return shot needn't necessarily be the USP of his great returns. You can hit a great return even with your feet closer. You have to spot the incoming missile as early as possible. Federer, too, has great returns as do so many other players. Great players are those who do impossible things and exist outside the textbooks.

In the story of the temporary decline of champions, we can spot some aspects of failure.[67] When Scottish tennis player Andy Murray arrived on the scene he was just sixteen, and sent a well-known player to retirement. In his first match on the ATP Challengers Tour in 2003, Andy Murray played the South African Davis Cup veteran, Neville Godwin. Unprepared for Murray's style of play, Godwin suffered what can only be described as a meltdown. As Murray tells it, Godwin tried to hit him with a ball in the middle of the match and then turned his rage inward, babbling to himself things such as, 'I can't believe I am losing to his guy.' After losing in straight sets, Godwin retired from tennis. Murray smiled archly as he retold the story. Asked if his game was engineered to inflict such misery on opponents, his smile widened, 'Well, I hope so.'

Like Godwin, some veteran players, champions and journeymen alike take defeats badly and some of them are convinced that it is the signal to stop.

But those like Istomin are used to failure and yet they plod on. In his more than a decade-long career, Istomin has risen up from near the 1000 ranking all the way up, but finally found the insurmountable hurdle of Rank Fifty or thereabouts, moving between fiftieth and eightieth like

---

[67] *Time* magazine, 28 June 2010.

a pendulum swing of destiny. Off and on, he pops up on international news with an upset win and then settles back into the comfort zone of potential champions who could not make it.

Among the various analyses for the Top Ten players reaching the top, we come across this statement by Craig O'Shannessy, ATP analyst, where he says that the reason for Murray's ascendency to Number One is his drastic improvement on of his second serve.[68] 'At the 2015 Australian Open, Murray's average second serve speed against [Indian player] Yuki Bhambri was a pedestrian 85 miles per hour. In the 2016 first round match against Alexander Zverev his second serve speed averaged 93 mph with the fastest 108 mph.

'Points won on second serve have steadily risen for Murray from 51 per cent won in 2014 now up to 54 per cent in 2016 which puts him thirteenth on tour this year up from twenty-fifth last season.'

Tactical improvements are a must, of course. But in the end, the top players must have the dominating strategy.

Are strength and stamina big winners in tennis? Or is it all strategy?

The intellectual, strategic mind grows with age (till at least forty when memory power stagnates, sagging naturally for everyone, sportsmen and others). That could be the reason why the average age of tennis toppers has increased. In 1992, the average age of Top Ten men's players was twenty-three. At the end of 2016, it was roughly twenty-nine. If one sees that the four top players in the world were in the mid or late thirties (Federer, thirty-eight,

---

[68] Kevin Mitchell, 'Andy Murray's work ethic is behind his rise to No. 1 and he can stay there', *The Guardian*, 21 November 2016.

Nadal, thirty-three, Djokovic and Murray, both thirty-two, in 2019), one can understand how strategic playing, which comes with experience, is crucial to their being on top. In fact, unlike what is commonly believed, thirty is the right age to peak in any sport including, surprisingly, sprints. Even at thirty, sprinters can slice microseconds off their timing for the 100 metres race at below ten seconds, which shows the amazing power of the human body.

Most great mathematical theories have also been produced at around the age of thirty, as Sylvia Nazar, the biographer of John Nash, says in *A Beautiful Mind*, and not by wizened old men in their eighties sitting crouched in book-laden rooms decorated with cobwebs, as is the common perception. So thirty is when Homo sapiens are at their peak, both mentally and physically. In most sport, thirty-five is considered the right age to quit. Some toppers manage to stretch it for two or three years more.

There is no better example of longevity at the highest level in sport than Roger Federer. Of the 128 players in the French Open of 1999, Federer is the only man still playing, even in 2020. In 1999, when he made his debut in Paris, Federer then seventeen, lost to Australian Pat Rafter, 5-7, 6-6, 6-0, 6-2. He lost but he had served notice. 'After the first set, he got the hand of how I played and he like, sliced and diced me,' Federer said of this match twenty years later in 2019, showing off his incredible memory as well.

If a player reaches the top through hard work and a superior strategic mind, he is likely to stay there for some time. Federer himself put it best when he said after his 2017 Wimbledon triumph, 'I dreamed pretty big. I trained really hard, really well and really clever over the years.'

Yet the domination of the tennis Top Three stretching over two decades has astounded all sports critics. There are no clear answers. Remember they are vulnerable in many ways. Rafael Nadal for instance has won more than 100 matches after being a set down.[69] They never give up. Every time they are a set down, they tell themselves that they have achieved success before—they remind themselves of the craft they have mastered.

No Top Ten or Top Twenty-five player has been able to stand up to the might of this Top Three. The head to head numbers are, well, numbing. It is only a player in the Top Ten who will reach a Grand Slam final, with very few exceptions. Djokovic, for example, has played twenty-two of twenty-six Grand Slam finals against players ranked in the Top Five, eighteen of twenty-six against the Top Three and fourteen of twenty-four against the Top Two.

Federer has made 415 Grand Slam appearances, out of which he has won 357 and won twenty titles; Djokovic made 323 appearances for 280 wins and sixteen titles, while Nadal made 309 Grand Slam appearances for 271 wins and nineteen titles. Sometimes, in their triumphant ride through the boulevards of grandeur, there are worrying moments. From twenty-nine to thirty-five, Federer won only one Grand Slam. Yet they work on their game and come back.

Longevity in any field is an achievement in itself. The tennis triumvirate of Federer-Nadal-Djokovic has exhibited this inspiring trait, making us wonder about the frailties that drag us down.[70] 'What separates the long-lasting from the rest is maintaining a good attitude. Set by set, sometimes even point by point matches are strewn with frustration—break points and game points frittered away, set and match points squandered and somehow you

---

[69] October 2019 figures.

[70] Peter De Jonge, 'How Roger Federer Upgraded His Game', *New York Times*, 24 August 2017.

have to see the big picture, recognize how good your life is compared with the average civilian's and matches that seemed over, all but ripped from your grip ... and not go dark. It's harder than it looks.'

Remaining on top is a bit different from reaching there. It's lonely at the top and losing is not an option. Yet the biggies remain there match after match, tournament after tournament, year after year. That is why we get head-to-head results like this:

Novak Djokovic versus Gaël Monfils: 17-0
Roger Federer versus David Ferrer: 17-0
Roger Federer versus Richard Gasquet: 16-2
Roger Federer versus Mikhail Youzhny: 17-0
Ivan Lendl versus Brad Gilbert: 16-0
Roger Federer versus Stan Wawrinka: 22-3

It is beyond average comprehension how Monfils could have lost seventeen times to Djokovic, even though he knows Djokovic's game inside out after all these contests.

Yet, how has Monfils lost so many times to Djokovic? It is completely unfair and unjust. In him we see the perennial puzzle of sport. Why can't such a great player win? He is already a Top Ten player but who can figure out why he cannot get past the Top Three? Writer Ben Austen[71] thought about this puzzle too: 'He is a player who crackles with the possibility that at any instant he may do something beyond the limits of physical laws or human capabilities or merely the respectable convention of tennis.' Monfils, despite being in the Top Ten, has won only ten career titles, despite winning 493 matches overall and has not reached the final of a Grand Slam, while making more than 16 million dollars in prize money alone.

---

[71] Ben Austen, 'Gaël Monfils Hits Monstrous Shots. Why Can't He Win?', *New York Times*, 26 August 2017.

Monfils obviously has a self-confidence problem despite having all the big shots in the game and a forehand described by Austen as a 'big menacing wallop.' Clearly, he doesn't sincerely believe that he can reach the final of a Grand Slam and when confronted by any of the Top Five, he gives up the battle. It seems also that it's a lack of burning desire since he has already made more money that he can ever count. However, perhaps one fine day he will walk into a Grand Slam final and wallop the hell out of the guy at the other side.

A lifetime of persistence almost always works. Grammy-winning singer Billie Eilish and her brother were selected to write and compose the theme song for the 2021 James Bond film, *No Time to Die*. Theme songs for Bond films are the shortest cut to immortality for any musician. After the song was released early in 2020, Eilish told an interviewer, 'Subconsciously and consciously we've been trying to write a Bond theme for our whole lives.' That's how you win too.

Leander Paes, who has survived and played close to three decades on the ATP tour, has this to say about perfection and strategy, 'It's about doing the same things over and over again till you reach an automatic stage of execution. It's about mapping the brain with the patterns that unfold on court till the time the body responds without conscious thought.

'What to do during the twenty seconds between points, what to do during changeovers, what is the ritual when the momentum is with you, how the same changes when it isn't, these are just small components of the whole that makes a tennis player.'

Some of these points that I have drawn out (and widely used) are applicable to most individual games apart from tennis like badminton and squash. A winner must know:

1. What shot to play when.
2. Direction of the shot.
3. When to go for a winner or just play defensively or keep the rally going.
4. Which shot not to play against a particular opponent.
5. To unroll a top power game or wait and slow down the game.
6. New types of drop shots and such variations for these shots. A trick shot.
7. Play out of character to fox the opponent.

But ultimately, there is only so much a player can strategize.

One of the big lessons in match strategy comes from Arthur Ashe who defeated Jimmy Connors in the first Wimbledon all-American final (1975) since 1947. Connors was the favourite after getting past Roscoe Tanner who served at 140 mph.

Ashe was the most intellectual of all tennis players and he had a mind that was moulded into perfection amid the rough, difficult upbringing in a Black neighbourhood and living in a racially discriminating world where he could not play in many tournaments because of his colour. Before the 1975 finals, he discussed the Jimmy Connors game with his friends. They represented some of the best minds in tennis ... while he didn't expect any of them to come up with a perfect plan, he hoped for some sage advice as well as moral support.

As Ashe recalled the scene, 'We broke down Jimmy's game, shot by shot. His major weakness was the low forehand approach shot. Also he liked pace and he loved opening up the court, hitting crosscourt. If you tried to open up the court, he could try to open it wide. I had to go wide on both sides with my serves and keep as many balls as possible down the middle. Keep the ball low. And pray.'

At the end of the strategy session, Ashe had a revolutionary plan in mind, one that involved hitting shots seldom seen on the grass courts at Wimbledon. He later explained what it was: 'I could hit a slice forehand. But sliced forehands were a shot that players used in the 1920s ... we saw it more at the club level on clay courts, than on the tour. But I knew I could use the sliced forehand if I had to. I also had a backhand slice and I made up my mind that slices were going to be my bread and butter shots ... When he served I would chip the ball down the middle and short because the grass was worn down the middle, the ball wasn't going to bounce very high. If he came to the net, I would lob to his backhand side.'

This is how the strategy for an upset win was evolved. When Ashe walked on to the centre court that day, he was possessed of immense clarity and faith. 'I had the strangest feeling that I just could not lose,' he told *World Tennis* magazine later. Ashe's winning score was 6-1, 6-1, 5-7, 6-4.

Ashe's two other matches, the semi-finals and finals of the 1968 US Open, have also become classics both as sport and as literature. John McPhee,[72] analysing the Ashe–Clark Graebner semi-finals and a year later, merged the reportage with the rise and decline of racism in sport in the US and told us of the struggles of Ashe to make it so far. It was Black social history couched as sports reportage, revealing unknown insights into the game as well as the grim stories of the Black struggle, starting with the ship that brought Ashe's ancestors in 1735 and

[72] John McPhee, 'Levels of the Game', *New Yorker*, 7 June 1969.

unloaded them as cheap cargo in Virginia in return for tobacco. One young woman with a number was Ashe's ancestor listed as just 'a Negur girl'.

Notions of race play out in the match report. There is nothing about Ashe's game that Graebner does not know and Ashe says he knows Graebner's game "like a favourite tune". Ashe feels Graebner [also American], plays the way he does because he is a middle-class white conservative. Graebner feels that Ashe plays the way he does because he is black.' McPhee made this perhaps sweeping and unscientific statement about the game: 'A person's tennis game begins with the name and background and comes out through his motor mechanism into shot patterns and characteristics of play. If he is deliberate, he is a deliberate tennis player; and if he is flamboyant, his game probably is too ...'

After a lifetime of hard work, a player walking out to play the fifth set in a Slam is the very apogee of sport. For sheer ardour, endurance and test of persistence there is nothing like a five-setter. His hands touching his hamstring for reassurance, for instance, is a sight worthy of being embedded in your mind for ever. For you, the viewer, has no such quality or desire. Standing in court in the beginning of the fifth set, his mind in 'The Zone', his body almost luminescent with sparkles of sweat reflecting the many stadium lights pouring down into the court past midnight, the tennis player is what we all aspire to be in life too. Last set, last chance, last mistake. It is more than four hours of relentless tennis and the player is alone, with no one to even pat his/her shoulder and mumble, 'No shit shots, understand? Run down every ball, understand?'

The thunderbolts keep coming from the baseline one after another, as the player runs wide to return a crosscourt even though the lungs are about to burst, the sudden sprint to the net to pick a drop. It is unending and cruel. Is sport all about stretching the limits of endurance? Or is it something more? Instead, why can't sport be a pleasant evening activity?

But when you see Nadal from far outside his court, curving in a furiously spun forehand to the edge of the line, you understand that sport is not just endurance. Someone said of Muhammad Ali after a bout in 1966, '… for seven or so minutes, Ali turned boxing into ballet.'[73] In that bout, Ali connected 100 punches, taking only three.

Nadal, Federer, Djokovic and the other toppers in tennis—that's what they do. They connect 100 punches, taking only three. Sitting somewhere high up near the bleachers, we marvel at sport and tennis and endurance and glory. Later, when you have shuffled out of the stadium with the awestruck and beer-smelling hundreds, you see the stars are all up and twinkling happily as if they, too, high up from the grandstand of the cosmos, witnessed history and grand art unfurl.

---

[73] Matthew Syed, 'Muhammad Ali was beautiful, flawed, and courageous—he was definitely the greatest', *The Times*, 25 March 2020.

CHAPTER SIX

Marathons and Sprints: Running Faster and Stronger in the Race Against Time

The final of the 100 metres race at the 2012 London Olympics showed us the incredible possibilities in sprints and what running really means. Such runs amaze us, demonstrating the sheer power of the human body and the relentless ambition that keeps driving the human mind to break the limits of time, a basic concept of sport. The result of the 100 metres race was a template from a futuristic sci-fi movie. It was perhaps the first most audaciously successful attempt by human beings to mock at time and to tell themselves that the human body sees no barriers.

In that searing event, which did not get as much publicity as it should have, the following marvels happened. It was the:

1. First time in history that the top three finished under 9.80 seconds.
2. First time in history that the Top Five finished under 9.90 seconds.
3. First time in history that all four of the fastest men on the earth participated in the same event.

4. First time in history that seven of eight men ran to the finish under ten seconds.
5. First time in history that the fastest timing recorded in the Olympics 100 metres race, did not win a gold.

The race was a whirr that finished in a flash but will last for ever in history and stay in the imagination. Time just stopped and watched. The picture of that finish with lumps of sheer muscle and chiselled bodies lunging for the tape, must be held up everywhere as the stellar example of human beings trying the almost impossible. Just to show that it's possible.

Well, come to think of it, that day in London men ran like cheetahs. Men ran like they were not on their feet but on wings. A group of eight men ran like nowhere else, at any time. Those eight men are why sport exists. This is what each of them clocked—Usain Bolt (Jamaica): 9.63; Yohan Blake (Jamaica): 9.75; Justine Gatlin (USA): 9.79; Tyson Gay (USA): 9.80; Ryan Bailey (USA): 9.88; Churandy Martina (Netherlands): 9.94; Richard Thompson (Trinidad and Tobago): 9.98; Asafa Powell (Jamaica): 11.99 (injured).

The Top Three almost repeated the feat four years later, once more pointing to how certain people on top of their fields can never be toppled. In sporting theory also, this is a lesson. The top ranked will be top ranked and cannot be defeated easily, a lesson that we saw played out in tennis.

In the Rio Olympics, 2016, 100 metres final, the Top Eight clocked—Usain Bolt (Jamaica): 9.81; Justine Gatlin (USA): 9.89; Andre De Grasse (Canada): 9.91; Yohan Blake (Jamaica): 9.93; Akani Simbine (South Africa): 9.94, Ben Youssef Meïté (Côte d'Ivoire) 9.96; Jimmy Vicaut (France): 10.04; Trayvon Bromwell (USA): 10.06.

All those who line up for the 100 metres final have been Blacks—for a long time now—giving rise to various genetic pool theories. Sprints and even middle- and long-distance running bring to the fore the issue of the genetic pool. Only certain types of people, from certain types of places, can do certain types of work (here running) better than all others who are white, brown and so on. Such people, most of them from small nations, also challenge accepted notions of athletic superiority. In future they could overturn the concept I have proposed here of wealthy advanced societies being the most capable of churning out world champions. Many small nations are poor and underdeveloped. Yet they can produce world champions if some factors come into play. What are those factors?

The places from which sprinters (and other Olympic runners) come makes us wonder. These countries or mostly tear-shaped islands strewn across various oceans are not part of any larger discourse in sporting theory. In fact, the line-up in the sprints of the 100 metres is a wake-up call to our sense of geography. We didn't know these countries existed. We didn't know that such people existed—and, of course, we didn't know they could run like the wind. Here is a run-up of such countries and islands where people run the fastest in the world. In the London Olympics, 2012, the line-up in the 100 metres heats show these:

Heat 1: Bolivia, Congo, Guinea-Bissau, Tonga, Bangladesh, Laos, São Tomé and Príncipe.

Heat 2: Suriname, Indonesia, Gabon, Pakistan, Palau, Tuvalu, Marshall Islands.

Heat 3: The Central African Republic, Singapore, the Maldives, British Virgin Islands, the Federal State of Micronesia, Solomon Islands, American Samoa.

Heat 4: Burkina Faso, Mauritius, Saint Vincent and the Grenadines, Malta, Nepal, Kiribati, Cook Islands.

The presence of unknown athletes from unknown states or islands in the heats of the sprints and other running events seems to enhance the theory of genetic pools hidden in remote island nations or regions. This theory finds ready resonance among a majority of sports writers and theorists. This theory gains ground also due to racial bias where Blacks are seen as a physically fit race, good only for hard labour (like running the marathon) while the superior races win in skill sport or dominate in so-called higher activity.

In running events, Africans have been in the forefront, though representing different countries, mostly the UK and the US. This again proves that once potential athletes move to advanced societies (which have hubs of excellence), they can reach the top easily.

The last white man to win an Olympic sprint was Alan Wells in 1980. Of the ten fastest 100-metre timings, eight belong to Jamaicans. It is so tempting to argue that a few East African countries, certain Caribbean islands like Jamaica and Trinidad, and some nations named above are the locations of such genetic pools.

There may be about 1000 athletes in the so-called genetic pool nations, but this does not prove that there is a special gene that makes you run fast, a conclusion that is emphatic. Richard Moore in *The Bolt Supremacy*[74] narrates the efforts that sports scientist Yannis Pitsiladis has put in and his conclusion.

Pitsiladis has blown apart the assumption that Africans have a super gene when it comes to running. Underlying this assumption is the unstated argument,

---

[74] Richard Moore, *The Bolt Supremacy: Inside Jamaica's Sprint Factory*, Yellow Jersey, 2015.

the colonial narrative so to say, that Africans have only physical qualities and not intellectual abilities. Pitsiladis started with Ethiopia and Kenya and collected saliva swabs from athletes. There are about 3,000 Kenyans who make a living by professional running (about 100 in India). The more the number of people engaged in a particular sport, the better the chance for champions to emerge. His conclusion is: '... there is no compelling genetic evidence that there are race-related genes to explain this phenomenon.'

Till then the existing theory about Black assertion in athletics was based on the book *Black Superman* by Patrick Cooper. It stated that the sickle cell trait seen in Africans helped them have a higher percentage of fast-twitch muscles and lower haemoglobin made them ideal candidates for breaking speed records.

My surmise is that African or Black domination in running has more to do with the Ericsson–Pitsiladis theory than anything else. Many Black children are physically active in their childhood to such an extent that their bodies are well primed for an athletic life. Their daily movements (walking and running) of close to 10 kilometres for a long period of their childhood, for instance, puts them at a great advantage when they come into actual athletic training where young kids newly introduced to hectic physical activity stand little chance. Even if they do, they cannot really catch up. Perhaps the greatest modern long-distance runner, the Ethiopian, Haile Gebrselassie, ran 10 kilometres to school and back every day. He was only five feet three inches in height (with very short strides) yet he won two Olympic medals and four world championship medals.

Once when Usain Bolt was late for a sports event, he ran all the way to the stadium. This is not something a white kid in New York would do since he is not trained that way. Impulsive running and physical activity thus has a lot to do with the lead that African children get.

The crucial role, however, comes in early beginnings and systematic work. For this to happen the role of the environment, as stated earlier, is crucial. Then comes the role of the coach. Over and above this natural or physical childhood activity like running with the cows or running to and from school, Jamaica also has the best coaches. As a result, the best sprint coaching school, the Maximizing Velocity and Power (MVP) Track and Field Club is based at the University of Technology, Jamaica. If we look at the history of these clubs, we will know that behind great athletic achievements are not superathletes but supercoaches.

Everything in Jamaica seems geared towards creating sprint champions. Nowhere else can we see a whole society working towards creating the fastest people—the schools, the clubs, the coaches, the annual junior tract events, the agents, the superstars.

It didn't start one fine day when a gene pool started a mysterious stirring. Jamaica had a history of athletic, mostly sprint, superiority from 1948 onwards when it first participated in the Olympics. It was Herb McKenley who started the athletic programme in Kingston, after playing the stellar role in winning Jamaica's gold in the 4x100 metres at the Helsinki Olympics. In 1948, Jamaica's first Olympian, McKenley, had to settle for the silver in the 400 metres after a photo finish with fellow Jamaican, Arthur Wint.

The history of sprints in Jamaica runs pretty deep. The athletics medal table in Helsinki makes for surprising reading. With its population at the time of 1.5 million, Jamaica took the silver in the men's 100 metres, the gold and silver in the 400 and the gold in the 4x100 metres. Wint also claimed a silver in the 800 metres race.

This rich tradition was built on a strong foundation by coaches who were former athletes. McKenley, Dennis Johnson and Glen Mills were maniacal in their search for athletic heights, perfection and their empathy with their wards. Many top coaches have been failed sportsmen, bringing into their job a rare dedication and furious determination to win as coaches after failing as athletes. To win on your own is one thing, but to make someone else win is something else altogether. It is a difficult task, calling for all resources at your command, the psychological underpinnings to a purely physical endeavour, making it a superhuman effort.

Mills, who became known world over as Bolt's coach, considered himself a failure at the age of thirteen. He realized he would never make a career as a sprinter and surrendered himself to fate, so to say. 'I was disappointed that I wasn't able to measure up to the others,' author Richard Moore quotes him as saying. He would go and watch boys training under his school coach Henry MacDonald Messam who saw him hanging around and called him over. 'Come here, little man. I see you here every evening and you are not training any more. Why?' Soon a partnership started and Mills moved fast from doing odd jobs to coaching kids and finally landed Bolt himself. Their partnership was confirmed in October 2004.

Moore captures the early part of the relationship. Bolt had left his first coach, Fitz Coleman, because he was too tough, 'Mills told Bolt they would be working to a three-year plan, aiming to peak at the Beijing Olympics (2008). He arranged for a masseur, Everald Edwards, to work with him; each training session would begin with a session on the table, having his muscles kneaded and manipulated, getting his body ready for punishment. Most importantly, Mills got to know him and would visit him at home if he saw Bolt was down or distracted in training. When that happened, "I'd go quiet," Bolt said, and a visit from Mills would follow. Over a game of dominoes, they would discuss what was on his mind and agree on a course of action; usually the course of action advised by the coach. "I like to help them develop into total human beings," Mills said. "You try to be involved in the rest of their lives as much as they let you." "He is like my second father," [75] Bolt said of Mills before the Beijing Olympics.'

All Jamaican runners give credit to the club system in Jamaica.[76] 'We have great coaches in Jamaica though we don't have a lot of infrastructure,' Yohan Blake, Bolt's running partner and rival, says. Though he believes in the genetic roots of champions, Blake also thinks that the environment and what he calls natural factors play a role in the creating a world winner. 'I think it is natural talent we harness in Jamaica. Ninety-nine per cent of the fast runners, people who are very successful, come from the country—running down the cows. Also the type of food we eat, it's very strong food—yam, banana—it's very pure from the ground. We have programmes where even the college champs and primary champs start at a very young age. And then we transform from here.'

On the face of it, both sprints and long-distance running seem to have very little strategic acumen involved, though speed, stamina, strength are, of course, prerequisites. In sprints the only strategy is on how to run the bends (200 metres, 400 metres) and at which point to go into full throttle. A good start is a prerequisite, of

[75] *The Guardian*, 6 August 2008.

[76] *Hindustan Times*, 4 December 2019.

course. In long-distance running, the use of pacesetters, how fast to go in the early rounds, when to start the final kick, are all part of the strategy. In hurdles you need to fix the number of strides in between hurdles. Everyone uses somewhat similar strategies in running. There is little skill involved in this raw form of athletics—all you need to do is run like hell.

However, economy of movement is very important, which is why all critics scoffed at the running style of Emil Zátopek, Czech long-distance runner, who was known as the 'Czech Locomotive' for his speed—he flailed his arms and showed the intense pain of every breath as he neared the finish, his last rounds always a flurry of arms and writhing, something no coach would allow in these days.

In a study published in May 2017[77] in the *International Journal of Exercise Science*, scientists at the Brigham Young University in Utah set out to closely examine the strides of both expert and inexperienced runners and see what would happen if they tweaked their strides. Volunteers were made to run on a treadmill at whatever speed they chose. For novice runners it was the fastest pace they could maintain for at least twenty minutes. To calculate what they called 'running economy', each volunteer's steps were counted to determine the length of each person's stride. 'Running economy is important. In physiological terms, economy is a measure of physical demand. If one form of moving requires less oxygen than another, it is more economical, less strenuous and easy to maintain.'

When runners modified their strides (lengthening or shortening), their economy generally declined. This shows that instinctive running is the best option. Lengthening or

---

[77] *New York Times*, 4 September 2017.

shortening strides may have negative results. According to Iain Hunter, a professor at the university, these findings indicate our bodies know what they are doing when it comes to choosing running form even without any instruction. 'Our most efficient stride is "built-in",' according to Hunter.

We may marvel at Bolt's lightning speed but there are scientists who believe that Homo sapiens are just pedestrian sprinters while being champion long-distance runners. Daniel Lieberman, professor of human evolutionary biology at Harvard University, says that in relative terms the feats of Jamaicans are utterly normal, whereas elite endurance runners are way above.

'The max sprinting speed of Bolt is around 10 metres/second which is well below the max galloping speed of most mammals. Bolt would be beaten by any dog or even a squirrel. A lion could go twice as fast for much longer. We suck. The truth is a sprinter's man is pathetic. We did not evolve to do it. We are hunters and so what makes us special is our ability to run long distance,' Lieberman says.

In contrast to Bolt, elite marathoners run up to 6 metres per second for 26.2 miles. Lieberman says we have become 'specialized sweaters', pointing to the human ability to get rid of heat via a high density of sweat glands.

What is the difference between a 200-metre runner and a 400-metre one? Stamina, strides or is it just speed? Can a 400-metre runner succeed as a 200-metre runner also? Quite possible, but then striding patterns differ. A 400-metre hurdler and a 110-metre hurdler know the number of strides between hurdles that they have to take and sticks to that. If it goes wrong, the rhythm changes and the runner is likely to step on the hurdle. All this is strategy. But athletics, among all sport, uses the least strategy. Therefore, the skill element in an athlete is minor. There is no higher strategy in athletics, like in soccer or basketball or cricket, which is why there is little need for an athlete to have a high-thinking strategic coach. If an athlete emerges who can run at full gallop from the start of a 1500-metre race, then what is the need for any strategy? Emil Zátopek was a classic example of relentless running and practice.

Not all running is speed. 'The physiology of running can be broken down into three parts. There's the body's fitness: how fast you can get oxygen to the muscles and how fast you can go before lactate accumulates in the blood. Then there's running economy: the efficiency with which you move. And then there's mass: how much you weigh. Multiply fitness by running economy and divide by mass. That's how fast you will go,'[78] writes Nicolas Thomas in an article about running a marathon after forty.

It is a bit difficult to break down running into simple arithmetic but ultimately, running is all about endurance and human will that keeps the muscles moving, overcoming the projected role of the 'central governor', the brain. All that a marathon runner needs is the stamina to last out. No extraordinary skill sets are called for from a marathon runner, nor does he need to have any large memory power to change speed or how to use the elbow to keep out pestilential runners in the pack. The marathon runner can also check his watch to figure out if he is running in keeping with the plan. In case he realizes that he is a bit fast in the first split, he can slow down or ask the pacesetter to slow down a bit.

[78] Nicholas Thomas, 'An Aging Marathoner Tries to Run Fast After 40', Wired.com, 2018.

But there is no doubt that once he shifts into a rhythm most probably after the first couple of kilometres, the top marathon runners move into 'The Zone'. It is the same with any endurance attempt. The runner's mind is in a place where only top athletes, writers or scientists reach. This is what Jack Schumacher, a Swiss writer of the 1930s, wrote about Paavo Nurmi, the Finnish long-distance and middle-distance runner known as the 'Flying Finn'. 'Nurmi and those like him are animals in the forest. They begin to run because of a profound compulsion and because a strange dreamlike landscape called them with its enchanting mysteries. Their awe-inspiring times are a way of giving thanks to Mother Earth.'

Colin O'Brady, American endurance athlete, who became the first man to traverse across Antarctica from coast to coast, recounts how he covered the final 77 miles of the 921-mile solo journey, in a thirty-two-hour final sleepless burst.[79] 'I don't know, something overcame me. I just felt locked in for the last thirty-two hours ... Under intense stress, the line between lucidity and madness can be fuzzy, especially so for someone who had been alone for two months, trekking miles each day while doing battle with raging winds, unseasonal snowfall, white-out visibility and polar temperatures.'

At the end of any endurance effort, the mind would have conquered the body and hence the fuzziness which many such athletes or adventurers have reported. Otherwise, the mind would shut down and the body carry on nevertheless. The marathon is among the most fascinating of sporting events, though it hasn't got its due yet. In its primitive urge, its utter lack of supporting instruments ('just shoes and socks' as a marathoner

---

[79] *New York Times*, 26 December 2018.

said), its ability to give us pride in our own species, the marathon is unmatched. Endurance and human ambition are closely linked. To keep running and not to give up is life's big lesson in every field. We all give up and end up at some point as failures. Not for us the rigours of a long-distance runner, nor can we get attuned to the loneliness of the sport. We need the spark and instant glory of the sprint.

The marathon has legend and history wrapped around it. We know the story of the marathon runner of Athens, Pheidippides of the Greek military who was a day-long runner, running from the battlefield of Marathon to Athens to announce a Greek victory over the Persians, a distance of about 25 miles. We need to know the stories of some great long-distance runners to know how human beings ran from the time they wanted to run. The long distance also makes us wonder why we run till we perish. But here lies the very essence of sport.

By1925, the stern-faced Paavo Nurmi, the son of a carpenter, was being hailed as the greatest long-distance runner ever. *The Real American* newspaper of 1 May 1925 said: 'Paavo Nurmi, the famous Finn whose frail legs and stout heart have made him the most talked about athletic figure in the world today, thrilled a crowd of more than 45,000 persons at the Coliseum in the greatest track and field meet ever staged in America.'

Nurmi ran each race at an even pace, unlike Emil Zátopek who was to emerge soon after, showing that long-distance running could have different strategies. Nurmi ran all the three long races, including the marathon, and won five golds in the 1924 Olympics. Then efforts were made to block him from winning and two long-distance events were held close to each other.

When Emil Zátopek[80] arrived, long-distance running was already a European forte and big runners had already dominated the Olympics. He and his six brothers were often thrashed by their devilish father for little or no reason, so the first running they did was away from their carpenter father. Zátopek's long-suffering mother complained that the geese never put on weight because the young Emil would 'run them ragged' around the fields as soon as he came from school and the geese ran out to welcome the kids back.

Zátopek's is the first recorded case of hectic practice by an athlete. He ran through forests and vales and on the riverside. He had the worst running style possible and with his flailing arms and his wiry limbs pushing him along, his face contorted in pain in the effort of winning, Zátopek was a coach's nightmare. 'Ugly rolling gait and flailing arms, tongue lolling, face contorted,' was an early description of his running style. Yet he kept on winning. The strategy of conserving energy with the minimum of body movement was to come a bit later.

Zátopek is the first sportsman or athlete who taught us the importance of rigorous and what Ericsson would later call, 'deliberate practice'. 'Whoever surpasses my training will also break my records,' Zátopek is quoted as saying by Broadbent in *Endurance*.

In Helsinki in 1952, Zátopek won three golds, for the 5000 and 10000 metres and the marathon. The marathon win was the culmination of the biggest ever long-distance racing odyssey in the Olympics. He won the marathon gold with a timing of 2.23:3.2. His wife Dana, who passed away in 2020, won the javelin gold in Helsinki.

---

[80] Rick Broadbent, *Endurance: The Extraordinary Life and Times of Emil Zátopek*, Bloomsbury, 2016.

The *British Athletics Weekly* commented that Zátopek was an exception to almost every rule of law.

So is the marathon a burden placed on us by one part of the history of Athens? Why run the 42 kilometres (26 miles 385 yards) with such dedication and passion? A tennis player takes a break after every three games, a footballer gets a fifteen-minute break after forty-five minutes of exertion but a marathoner has to keep going for more than two hours with every segment of his body functioning like a Rolls-Royce engine. It is not for the faint-hearted to try. The heart pounds at 160 beats a minute and the body works overtime to power the heart, lungs and legs. The burning and resynthesizing of adenosine triphosphate (the lesser known ATP) creates three times as much heat as it does energy. Lactic acid begins to singe the muscles.

This human madness has had surprising results in testing the limits of endurance. It has given us disproportionate confidence in our own abilities. We think we can keep going. In a 100 years, the marathon timing has been cut by fifty-five minutes (in 10 April 1896, Spiridon Louis of Greece ran 2.58:50 at the Athens Olympics). Since 1998 alone, the marathon timing has been fallen by three minutes and eight seconds, until 2017. Along with the rapid advancement of science, minutes fell off the marathon timing like autumn leaves.

According to journalist Jere Longman,[81] a marathon of 1.59:59 (which Kenyan long-distance runner Eliud Kipchoge ran under controlled conditions, therefore, the record is not recognized) would require a searing pace of four minutes thirty-four seconds per mile, seven seconds faster than the pace of the current world record. It would require 85 to 90 per cent of a runner's maximum aerobic

[81] Jere Longman, 'Man vs. Marathon', *New York Times*, 11 May 2016.

capacity—twice the capacity of an average man—and a sustained heart rate of about 160 to 170 beats per minute. (The typical resting rate is sixty to 100 beats per minute.)

The era of Zátopek and European dominance in running was not to last. In a dramatic shift, unknown people from the part of the world so far dismissed as the dark continent emerged as the best specimens of human endurance. From 1908, the US, European nations and Japan dominated until Abebe Bikila of Ethiopia ran the marathon in a heart-stopping 2.15:16.2 in 1960. From then on, we have seen the emergence of runners from Kenya, Ethiopia and Morocco who have changed the way we thought of ourselves as an animal species. From 1996, the marathon took another leap, so to say, towards the limits of possibilities. Khalid Khannouchi of Morocco who did 2.5:42 at the Chicago marathon, 1999. In 2002 he bettered it to 2.5:38. After Kenya's Paul Tergat touched 2.4:55, the thought of a two-hour marathon gripped the imagination of scientists and coaches and runners worldwide.

Incidentally, no white man has won a major world championship since the 1980s, not counting British track and field sprinter Alan Wells. African domination (East and West) in running is mind-boggling and has sent various scientists and coaches on gene-hunting exercises.

'The marathon is at the highest level, a delicate exercise in expending energy evenly over the entire course, and the fastest times are generally achieved when the second half of the race is run at the same speed (an "even" split) or slightly faster (a negative split) than the first. Sudden rises or dips in pace can kill a record attempt stone dead,' says author Ed Caesar.[82]

---

[82] Ed Caesar, *Two Hours: The Quest to Run the Impossible Marathon*, Simon and Schuster, 2016.

Eliud Kipchoge and the barriers he crossed

The marathon since 2010 has revolved around Kenya's Eliud Kipchoge, just like earlier eras of endurance running were dominated by Abebe Bikila, Zátopek, Nurmi and other Kenyan runners like Paul Tergat. Any game or sport or athletic event needs its superstars not just for the records but to inspire a new generation to take the game forward and to bring down barriers. Kipchoge is just five feet six inches tall and weighed only 115 pounds, a bird of a man who can remain unnoticed in a pizza take-away queue.

He embodies all the scientific theories that this book projects and also practises the mental aspects discussed in these chapters, proving most of the theoretical aspects discussed. I was surprised to learn that he is a prolific note-keeper and early in 2020 tweeted the picture of his new notebook alongside the fifteen or twenty he has already filled up with his strategy and work-out notes and some philosophic musings like motivate+discipline =consistency. 'When you write then you remember,' he told *New York Times'* sports reporter, Scott Cacciola,[83] before the 2018 Berlin marathon where he bettered the world record. Remembering is a vital part of any champion's make-up. If you don't learn from mistakes, you will repeat them.

Kipchoge made his marathon debut in 2013, moving away from track running, with a timing of 2.05.30. Since then he has been undefeated, winning eleven marathons. Earlier, the belief was that an athlete could run only eight marathons in his life; now they run two every year. 'I always tell people that this is a really simple deal. Work

[83] Scott Cacciola, 'Eliud Kipchoge is the Greatest Marathoner, Ever', *New York Times*, 14 September 2018.

hard.' He never went in search of genetic answers to his prowess. He just worked hard.

The man who converted the eager runner was Olympic silver medallist Patrick Sang who conducted sports events in Kapsisiywa where Kipchoge also grew up. Sang gave him work-out programmes which Kipchoge followed religiously. Kipchoge credits Sang with all his achievements. 'When you are young, you always hope that one day you will be somebody. And in that journey, you need someone to hold you by the hand. It does not matter who that person is, so long as they believe that your dreams are valid,' Sang told *New York Times*.

In September 2018, Kipchoge broke the world record in Berlin, the place for world records both in sprints and long-distance running due to the flat course and ideal weather. 'He ran with three pacemakers, but that number dropped to one by 15 kilometres when he reached in 43.88. The final pacemaker Josphat Boit led Kipchoge through halfway in 1.01:06 before dropping out at 25 kilometres, covered in 1.12:24, leaving Kipchoge to run 17 kilometres alone,' *The Times* reported.[84]

'Rather than dip the pace, Kipchoge accelerated. By the time he passed Josphat Boit in 1.55:32, the record looked a certainty. He finished four and a half minutes ahead of second-placed fellow Kenyan Amos Kipruto who finished 2.06:23 with Wilson Kipang a further 25 seconds behind.'

All that remains for Kipchoge is to officially break the two-hour barrier to be elevated to the ranks of the immortals, if at all he isn't already. To look at the man running is to think about sport and its many meanings. To run is a natural instinct. We all run from disaster and

---

[84] Ron Lewis, 'Marathon record ripped to shreds by Kipchoge', *The Times*, 1 September 2018.

the police—but this man and the many around him run to dare destiny. The commercially backed project in which Kipchoge broke the two-hour barrier in Vienna on 11 October 2019, clocking 1.59:40 is an unimaginable effort. Though not an officially sanctioned record, Kipchoge's effort coming just a year after he failed to cross the two-hour barrier (the Nike Breaking2 project) can only be marvelled at. In Vienna, in a route near the Danube, selected for its straightness and the weather conditions, there were forty-one runners to pace him through the 42 kilometres. 'Berlin was about running a world record. Vienna is about running and breaking history, like the first man on the moon,' Kipchoge said after the run. To do a Roger Banister (the British middle-distance athlete, the first to break the four-minute barrier running mile) with the marathon was not even thought about till Kipchoge whose lungs seem to be a machine, came along. At thirty-three, the bird-like man stood at the peak of human endeavour.

It was in 1991, that the idea of a sub-two-hour marathon was first thought of. By that time the barrier was getting nearer with every marathon and was around two hours and six minutes. Michael Joyner, an American physician, published a paper in the *Journal of Applied Physiology* estimating that a perfect athlete could do the marathon in 1.57:58. He had taken into account the Vo2 Max (maximum oxygen an athlete can consume) and the lactate threshold. At that time, it was only a distant possibility. The next twenty years would change the marathon and it was one man who was responsible for this—Kipchoge.

Nike's effort has been to develop a shoe that will propel the long-distance runner. The Nike Vaporfly has an embedded metallic strip that can give a spring to the feet of a runner. Nike's effort, which began seriously in 2015, almost succeeded in the first sub-two-hour effort in a Formula 1 race track in Monza, Italy. Kipchoge crossed the barrier just twenty-five seconds below the aim, but Nike had hit upon the right way to do such runs: with a six-man arrowhead formation of pacesetters moving just in front of the runner.

Before the sub-two-hour run, Pitsiladis believed that the official under-two-hour marathon would ultimately be run near the Dead Sea, which is below sea level and where the oxygen available is 5 per cent more than is available above sea level. This phenomenon is nature's gift to work on for a marathon. 'What excites me is understanding the limits of human performance,' Pitsiladis told Jere Longman of *New York Times*. 'What can man do?'

The Pitsiladis project primarily aims to use science to conquer the two-hour barrier. This includes genetics, biomechanics, running efficiency, race strategy and so on. Nike's main focus is to develop a running shoe which will let the marathoner feel no weight and would give him a good lift at every step. The Nike Zoom Vaporfly Elite shoes have a metal plate embedded in the sole which allow the runner to cut the friction and get a good lift without the need to bend or exert the toes as much as in normal shoes.

If Nike's focus is shoes, Pitsiladis has so far focused on clothing and design. But his idea of a shoe is a coating of film pasted on the feet like a piece of plaster, completely negating the 200- or 300-gram weight of a shoe. He envisages marathon clothing embedded with sensors that detect, body heat, heartbeat, blood pressure and is then projected on to the screen of the car running in front, or something like that. 'We want to bring the race into the living room and have the garments contribute to the outcomes we get,' Pitsiladis told *New York Times*.

Pitsiladis wants to explore training not just at the oxygen-enriched Dead Sea but also at various altitudes, from 5,500 feet to 11,500 or even 13,000 feet. The idea is to provide oxygen during training to see if this could stimulate the body to produce even more red blood cells at higher altitudes—the brain too might adapt to those enervating and hypoxic work-outs, producing faster race results at sea level.

'It's almost the equivalent of running with weights on your feet and then you take the weights off and you can fly,' Pitsiladis says.

In marathons, coaches normally advise that the second half should be run a bit slower till the finishing spurt just to prevent a burnout. But Pitsiladis wants the second split to be run faster since the body is lighter due to loss of liquid.

In the continuing debate between the role of genes and practice, Pitsiladis tends to be neutral. He also runs down the role of Zátopek-like practice and believes there is no need for a long-distance runner to run over 125 kilometres a week. Half the distance would be enough. In keeping with this line of thinking he gives preference to the environment and the history of the location. He believes that the person who finally breaks the two-hour barrier will be 'someone who had grown up in a rural East African village at altitude, enhancing his oxygen-carrying capacity, and who was accustomed to hours of daily activity, like walking or running to school, hauling water and herding cattle.'

There is, however, a larger issue when we discuss the genetic pool or athletic gene. If you are in a skill sport, how does any sporting gene (if it exists) help? Which gene is required to become a football star as opposed to a cricket star? Or is it just enough to be an athlete so that the skill part of the game follows naturally? Carrying this argument forward, is it enough that we fill a football team with eleven well-built guys who can run fast and have a semblance of skill?

A well-known cricket player can never switch to football or any other game at a late stage even if he is genetically endowed. What does the word 'athleticism' encompass? Fast running, weight-lifting capability, high scoring rate from outside the zone colour in basketball, a set-piece expert in football? My reading is that a son of Olympic medal-winning parents may have physical qualities in height and strength but that is a long way off from becoming a medal-winner in Olympics or any sport. It is impossible to believe that the kid of an under-ten-second sprinter will also run the 100-metre race under ten seconds at the age of twenty. Since that is not possible, then it is safe to assume that genes play little part in sporting excellence. You have to earn it with high levels of desire and practice.

If you are genetically endowed, the question to ask is 'For which sport?' Are there different genes for different sport? In future, will there be a discovery of a cricketing gene, or a footballing gene? Never. The reason is that different kinds of sport are human inventions made to suit human frailties. Genes are not.

But genetic factors like height, weight, splayed feet or lung power will go a long way in helping you acquire excellence in a sport. You have to be in the right sport, run the right distance race. To select the right sport is important as I have tried to show, by dividing sport into games of strength, skill, speed and then strategy. Ed Caesar points out that athletes of the Kalenjin tribe of Kenya who dominate long-distance running, are generally skinny, stringy guys. True, but the same type of people can be found elsewhere in other communities as well. Body structure differs drastically even within the same athletic event.

For different athletic events and for different sport, a wide variety of genetic support is required if at all genetics fully contribute to excellence in sport. If a footballer is genetically endowed, what aspect did he get from his father: the dribbling skill, positional play, set-piece skill or just the speed and the body structure? Even if a child is born with endurance genes, what if he does not have the desire to run? Is desire or the urge to win, the willingness to struggle to reach the top also a genetic quality? How does all this come together in the same person?

According to Denis Noble, a philosopher from Oxford University quoted by Caesar, genes are not a blueprint of life, but rather, they work in systems and groups more like a set of organ pipes that can be played. So, we have to assume that Arjun Tendulkar (son of Sachin Tendulkar), who is a left arm fast bowler inherited certain genes that work a certain set of organ pipes within the overall music-playing system of the human body.

If a fast-running son of an Olympic sprinter ends up in cricket, what natural advantage will he have over other cricketers? Very little, in the sense that perhaps he can convert his ones into twos. But a batsman from a non-cricketing family who has style, class, and all the runs due to hard work he put in as a child, is definitely the better cricketer.

Similarly, a criminal's son starts out as a pickpocket, not because there is any gene required to become a thief or a killer. In that house, mostly criminal activity is discussed, so to try to pick a pocket is the natural outcome of growing up in that environment. In a house where the laws of gravity are not discussed, it is natural that the game of lifting is easily the prime theme.

Yet, for a long time running will be seen as a genetic blessing due to Kenyan and African dominance. The other qualities to become a long-distance runner have been explained by the great explorer, Ernest Shackleton. 'First optimism, second patience, third physical endurance, fourth idealism, fifth and last courage,' he said were the qualities required of an explorer. All this is required of most sportsmen too.

When you run the marathon, you are alone with lactic acid coursing in your veins and systems about to shut. You need the courage, the desire and the thought of what brought you here on this beautiful road in a distant land where a few stragglers try to egg you on. When your lungs are about to burst, does glory matter? The truth is that it does—to many.

CHAPTER SEVEN

Boxing: Weights and Measures and Heavy Hits from History

How do we look at a boxing? As a primal brutal sport? That is the perception, but boxing exists much beyond all that at an exalted level. Boxing needs all five of the S factors in equal and good measure: speed, stamina, strength and skill. And strategy.

Speed

Speed here is not speed in running, but in movement of the feet and body and the reflexes to avoid punches, which is extremely crucial. A reaction that is even a split second slow to duck a punch can make all the difference. You can do without speed maybe, but quickness of the feet is a crucial feature in boxing. A combination of speed and skill adds to the strength and stamina of a top boxer.

Champion boxers of all divisions possess these qualities. Through anecdotes from the lives of these legendary champions here we can see how the four elements combine to create the mighty boxer.

Boxing has produced great physical specimens. Naturally. The famous reporters who assembled to see them fight have spent many words on the boxer as a physical specimen, most with sculpted bodies that produce so much of power. Cassius Clay's (Muhammad Ali's) speed overshadowed his size and strength. Dr Ferdie Pacheco who became Clay's physician said, 'In 1961, '62, '63, he was the most perfect physical specimen I had even seen from an artistic and anatomical standpoint even healthwise. You just couldn't improve on the guy. If someone came from another planet and said "Give us your best specimen," you'd give him Ali. Perfectly proportioned, handsome, lightning reflexes and a great mind for sports. Even when he got a cold it went away the next day.'

Boxers are also products of intense training, not just God's gift to mankind. Cassius Clay, as soon as he found his calling, spent all his time in the gym training as a teenager. He loved it and he talked about his training often. But then even at his age he had his calling. He knew that he would be number one—that was his driving force.

A.J. Liebling[85] wrote of Sugar Ray Robinson, who had giant muscles, and about the intense training that he put in. 'The great layer of muscle on the back of Robinson's neck is the outward indication of his persistence. It is the kind that can be developed by endless years of exercise, the sort of exercise no shiftless man will stick with.' He also stated the ultimate truth of all sporting victories: 'A boxer solidly constructed, intelligently directed and soundly motivated is bound to go a long way.' To be solidly constructed, intelligently directed and soundly motivated applies to all sport.

Boxers are seen as languorous, mighty men who just pack power into their punches and watch their opponents

---

[85] A.J. Liebling, *The Sweet Science*, North Point Press, 2004.

crumble. But as important is speed. In one of the Cassius Clay's early professional bouts, his opponent was Charlie Powell. In his inimitable style, Clay predicted that the match would be over in five rounds and later amended it to say it would end in three. At the weigh-in, Powell taunted Clay: 'Fight me, boy! Fight me and I'll kill you!'

Many boxers mean it literally.[86] *Death under the Spotlight: The Manuel Velazquez Collection* documents 2036 deaths in boxing, starting from 1725. Manuel Velazquez, born in 1904, became a boxing abolitionist after his friend, a boxer, was confined for life in a mental hospital from injuries sustained due to boxing. Painstakingly, Velazquez documented boxing deaths over three centuries and campaigned for boxing to be banned. For all such activity, boxing and its many variations, including cage fighting, has only become more brutal since the extraction of blood and the pounding of a human body is still entertainment for human beings.

In the third round of this brutal 1963 fight, Clay pounded Powell with forty unanswered punches, effective in precision and speed. Blood gushed from Powell's left eye and drained into his mouth. None of that blood that flowed into his mouth revived Powell. Finally, from the cumulative effect of all the punches, Powell slid slowly to the canvas, eyes closed, crawling on all fours as the referee counted ten.

Speed and reflex are equally key since it was not one punch that finished off Powell. 'Clay throws punches so easily you don't realize how much they shock you until it's too late.' Clay taught the boxing world the importance of speed in a sport where power and strength were considered the only criterion. All writers who covered

---

[86] Eben Pindyck, 'An Obsessive Chronicle of Deaths in the Ring', *New Yorker*, 22 December 2015.

Clay's events wrote about the way his feet moved and the way his jabs were delivered. Sports journalist Richard Hoffer paid his tribute to Muhammad Ali the week after he died at seventy-four:[87] 'If Muhammad Ali was in his time the most famous person in the world, it was as much a tribute to his talent for provocation as to his boxing. He was a glorious athlete, of course, his white-tassled feet a blur to match his whizzing fists.'

Most of Clay's opponents realized it was too late to react to his whizzing fists. That was the speed with which Clay pummelled. He also moved fast and evaded punches as if he was a video game brought alive with a joystick.

Clay's speed was the result of his sustained practice and he put his speed and strength on show from the very beginning. In the ring it was impossible to catch him. In the definitive *Ali: A Life*, Jonathan Eig writes: 'In his first fight Clay, wearing a white tank top with the number 272 on his back came out of his corner jabbing and dancing, zipping in and out so quickly that his twenty-four-year-old Belgian opponent Yvon Becot, looked like a man trying to hit smoke rings. He punched, missed, looked up to see where Clay had gone and punched and missed again. When Becot poked his head up, Clay popped him with a left jab. In the second round Clay came out slugging and knocked Becot down with a left hook that travelled so quickly that few in the audience would have seen it. Before the second round was over, Becot was too damaged to go on. The referee stopped the bout.'

Ali once said 'The secret of my success is speed. I'm the fastest heavyweight who ever lived.'

Speed, though not very obvious in some sports, is a primary requisite for winners of all games.

---

[87] Richard Hoffer, 'Muhammad Ali 1942–2016', *Sports Illustrated*, Muhammad Ali Special Issue, 13 June 2016.

Stamina/strength

To last even ten rounds in a heavyweight fight is almost impossible. It requires the type of stamina which only a handful of people have. During such a match, the small heart has to pump oxygen through an entire mountainside. When Sugar Ray Robinson fought the heavier-by-20 pounds Joey Maxim in June 1952, the bout went to ten rounds. The referee Ruby Goldstein, a former welterweight in his forties, who had to do a lot of work getting the fighters out of clinches, himself retired at the end of the tenth round. Referee Ray Miller who was around, was summoned to carry the fight beyond the tenth round and he came in with renewed energy, egging on the tiring giants. In the eleventh round, Robinson hoping to finish off this unending nonsense, hit Maxim with a looping right, his speciality, sending Maxim across the ring. But the giant refused to give up and Robinson's legs wouldn't move so that he could amble across and finish the bout with a killer blow. 'Maxim shook his head and went right on fighting in his somnambulistic way,' Liebling wrote.[88]

When Robinson came out for the thirteenth and last round, he moved as if he had gout on his feet. His arms fell on both sides and wouldn't obey his commands. All nerve and motor activity were shutting down. Finally, Robinson swung wildly at Maxim, summoning some energy from unheard of recesses of his body, but missed Maxim completely, like the movements we see in Charlie Chaplin movies, and fell on his face. Maxim waited for him to get up and set him up against the ropes, landing two blows to finish the fight.

One could argue that Sugar Ray Robinson and Joey

---

[88] A.J. Liebling, *The Sweet Science*, North Point Press, 2004.

Maxim lacked stamina but in heavyweight boxing, a fight lasting out thirteen rounds is as difficult to run the marathon wearing jack boots. Thirteen-round heavyweight bouts, like a five-setter, are stories of human endurance at which we can only wonder endlessly. Sugar Ray Robinson was a strong man, with gigantic muscles, but also put in intense training, as Liebling wrote.

Over the years, developments in nutritional science have helped boxers gain or control weight at will and also add strength to their arms and legs in the weeks prior to a bout. In the weeks before a bout, it is all about body conditioning—tactics and strategies only come in to play during the latter part of the training.

British welterweight champion Conor Benn said about his body and his preparations, just before a bout with Czech professional boxer Josef Zahradnik on 20 April 2019:[89] 'I do about eight weeks of training in the lead-up to a fight. It changes throughout in terms of intensity and nutrition. At first it is about getting fit and bringing my weight down as I ease into it. The training intensifies as my weight comes down, but it does get easier as the body adapts ... In the last week the training is light. The sessions are short and sharp, just getting the heart rate higher but not putting the body under any fatigue. All the hard work has already been done, I am not going to get fitter at this stage.

'My physical strength is my big legs. They are like tree trunks. When I am in the later rounds of a fight, I can count on my legs to hold through.

'My hands are of an average size but this is not really an issue. If you can punch, you can punch.

'It is not all about attack, though. It is so important

---

[89] *The Times*, London, 20 April 2019.

to defend my body. Every punch you avoid gives you a longer career. You have to use the gloves as a defence mechanism and protect your head. Repeated punishment through the years to your body does it no good.

'I have got some battle wounds from my career. I have a very big scar on my knuckle and a cut above my right eye. I once broke my jaw and had to get stitches on the inside of my mouth. Boxing is a brutal sport.'

Every sport is, in a way, brutal. A champion has to live the sport day in and day out. Playing any game is not a walk in the park on a spring morning. The life of the player and the sport merge. Often star players are lost after they retire since they have no life outside sport. Boxing shows us that it's not just about what it takes to become a champion boxer but what it takes out of you. After it's over, it doesn't matter if you have legs like tree trunks. They are just a heavy load to carry.

Strategy

What goes round and round in a square ring is strategy. In most sport, skill and strategy are closely aligned for without adequate skill—a range of shots, a range of offensive strokes, a deft way of dribbling—there cannot be a great strategy. In boxing, strategy mostly revolved around how to sap the opponent of all strength. Maxim's manager Dr Kearns told Liebling about the marathon bout with Sugar Ray Robinson: 'I just told Maxim, just keep the fellow moving, moving. Then he will have to clinch and hang on.' It was splendid strategy which worked to the hilt. Robinson's legs gave way.

In boxing, strategy can be everything even though we think it is the might of the blow alone (strength) that matters. To land a right hook in a heavyweight bout is the apogee of art and muscle coming together. That is because the opponent is aware of what is happening; he moves back and then lands a left. In most cases, the basic strategy as we saw in the Robinson fight is to wear the big guy down and then land a punch because it is not easy to land a punch when the menacing opponent is full of beans. He will dodge the oncoming punch and return with a right or left hook that will finish off the bout. To attempt a big hit and miss is in itself a debilitating flaw in boxing. It can throw the hitter out of balance—it means the total waste of precious energy and then it is followed by a counter-punch which will hit the bull's eye or rather the eye itself.

In the obscenely money-spinning $600 million Floyd Mayweather versus Conor McGregor bout of 27 August 2017, Mayweather won in ten rounds against cage fighter Conan McGregor in Las Vegas. McGregor, strangely, was boxing for the first time professionally since he was a regular in the mixed martial arts (MMA) circuit called UFO. In MMA, wrestling, kick-boxing and any act that can cause injury is used, while boxing has strict rules. That a star from the MMA circuit had to be imported to give Mayweather a good fight itself is indication of the paucity of talent and strength in professional boxing in the post-Tyson era.

The Las Vegas fight went to ten rounds despite McGregor's inexperience in the orthodox form of boxing. An MMA bouts lasts only for twenty-five minutes and so Mayweather waited out ten rounds before moving in and battering the tired McGregor, who looked as if a bottle of red dye had been emptied on his face—till the referee moved in to stop the fight. 'Our game plan was to take our time, let him shoot his shots early, then take him down. He's a lot better than I thought he was ... he used different angles. But I was the better man ... It was our game plan to take our time and take him out down the stretch,' Mayweather said after the bout.

These are important strategic positions to take. The reason is that boxing is a sport that can fell you. To tire out your opponent itself is a tiresome task because you need to keep dancing around the ring and moving out of the way of huge punches coming at your face with the surety, arrogance and confidence of a Great White. So to wait out your opponent like Mayweather did is a supreme but risky strategy. But such strategy has to be planned according to the strong points of each boxer. Mayweather had to have the staying power for his coach to come out with this strategy.

In this running commentary from *The Guardian* live blog we can see how well the Mayweather strategy worked.[90] The match can be termed as a win of strategy over strength since it lasted for ten rounds. 'Round nine: Conor has never fought for so long in a single professional fight. Maybe he knows he needs to go for the knockout because he charges out for the start of the round. He appears to have got in a big body blow but he's warned for a low blow. As the fighters are separated, Conor puts in a late blow. With around 90 seconds to go, Conor checks the clock and Floyd gathers himself and comes in for the kill. He's picking the Irishman off at will now and Conor tries to go into the clinch. The rookie's hands are dropping. This could be over soon.

'Round ten: I think Conor needs a KO now to win—but as he tires he's losing any kind of power in his punches. It's his lack of experience at a fight going this long that's really hurting him. And Floyd comes forward—he's rocked by a big right. The Irishman doesn't go down

[90] *The Guardian*, 27 August 2017.

though and continues. But his legs have gone and Floyd goes in for the kill—and the ref stops it.'

It worked according to plan, showing how much of a role good planning and strategy played in such a physical sport.

Ali was dyslexic and a poor reader (like many other heavyweights)—he flopped the military draft test and was classified as below average in IQ. Later, he was reclassified and pronounced mentally fit to be drafted. So how did Ali have the brains to evolve winning strategies? That is the reason the managers of boxers have a huge role to play in their success. In fact the skill, memory and strategy aspects of boxing like in some other sport as well, are fully outsourced. You do the thinking, I do the hitting, I do the playacting. You tell me what to do, bro. All the boxer has to take care of is his strength, speed and stamina. There wouldn't have been a Muhammad Ali or a Mike Tyson without their managers or coaches like Angelo Dundee or Cus D'Amato.

Ali had the help of great boxing minds, starting with Angelo Dundee. But he always had the right strategy. In the 1974 Zaire fight against George Foreman, some of this was on show. When he landed in Zaire, Africa, for the first time, the crowds started chanting 'Ali bomaye (Ali kill him)!' But as Richard Hoffer writes: 'Ali seemed incapable of killing Foreman, though, and indeed appeared in mortal prelim himself. Yet he invented a stunning strategy which demanded he accept Foreman's heavy hands as he sagged back into the ropes. Later christened "rope-a-dope", the game plan at first appeared suicidal but then as Foreman grew arm-weary, brilliant. Although Ali suffered the kind of punishment that can take years to fully manifest itself, the tactic did result in an amazing victory, when he took Foreman out in the eighth round.' So everywhere in boxing we see the clinching role of strategy.

We can also see the clinching role of the coach/manager in a boxer's life. Mike Tyson draws out this relationship beautifully in his autobiography *Undisputed Truth*. Tyson was created by Cus d'Amato. Outside of Cus D'Amato, Tyson was nobody.

Tyson's ghosted *Undisputed Truth* is a major work in many respects, not just in sports writing. His shocking candour, his ability to lay bare the skeletons in his cupboard, shames us. We see life in moral terms and try to fit into various such moral slots. Tyson had no such hypocrisy or values. The autobiography in Tyson's hands is catharsis itself, the book being coated with the terrible yet strangely shimmering sludge of dark life. But in that muck, we see nuggets of humanity, of struggle, we feel the weight of odds stacked against a poor boy, then the larger lessons of life. The book frightens us with details of the low life, all the more powerful because it is the account of a man who lived it and rose above it.

Cus d' Amato was a coach like no other. He took Tyson to his house and his wife Camille and told her, here's your son. Under their parentage Tyson evolved as a boxer, went up and often, down in life but managed to cling on—then he became the world champion.

At the beginning of his professional career, Cus had taken Tyson to major boxing arenas around the country to show his ward what his stage was, the stage where his life had to be made by destroying others. He advised, 'Make this your home, know this arena, know this place with your eyes closed. You are going to live here for long time. So get comfortable.' Tyson did.

To get comfortable in various arenas is a major factor in any sport. In the player's mind the arena, its dimensions, its treacherous gutters, its unseen elevations, must be clearly drawn up. In sport like tennis or badminton, the length and breadth of the court must be carved into memory, so that the player can whip the backhand without looking. Like Federer or Wawrinka. Like any great coach, Cus knew this well. And Tyson, sure enough, made the ring his home.

Boxing as a great sport and a lesson about life

The boxer in the ring has many matters at stake—in fact, much more than that of any sportsmen tense and ready for the starting whistle. The boxer's very life is at stake. If he doesn't die then and there, there is a chance of him carrying away life-threatening injuries to his head.

The difference for the boxer is that loss, humiliation, shame are only part of the risk—physical injury, even death, awaits as well. One is punished for one's failure as Franz Kafka, the visionary novelist, imagined one might be punished for one's sins, 'the sentence etched into flesh, killing even as it pronounces judgement,' as Joyce Carol Oates wrote.[91, 92]

Boxers carry weights much beyond the category they fight in. They carry the weight of superior masculinity and hence, expectations. They carry the weight of having to pummel others to submission, by their blood-soaked victory they are symbolic of the victory of the cause they represent, be it that of Black assertion or of Nazi superiority or sometimes replaying the David–Goliath myth. Against all odds somehow, they have to bear the burden of being philosophers over and above being sportsmen, and more than ever they have to show they conquered adverse circumstances before they could land on the ring. Most of the top boxers were born into deprivation and almost all Black heavyweight champions were uneducated. They

---

[91] *The Guardian*, 27 August 2017.

[92] Joyce Carol Oates, *On Boxing*, Harper Perennial Modern Classics, 2006.

got big cheques but a large majority of boxers did not even know how to sign. For example, Sonny Liston's wife had to tell him how much his latest cheque was worth. To shake off all the darkness that surrounded their lives and then to go on and conquer the world, is a monumental achievement.

Overcoming drugs, disease, death, jail and its brutality, the many write-offs he has experienced, the boxer arrives on the sporting scene. Here too, he has to overcome the negatives both physically and then metaphorically, because in many ways he is a morality fable. This is the mighty task of a boxer, never so much that of a footballer. Many of history's greatest boxers, such as Jack Dempsey, learnt their craft in jail or on the streets.

Boxers mostly have been adversity's boys. Having overcome all that, having pulled themselves back from the brink, they come to the ring to play out their life stories all over again. Boxers had their causes and like Muhammad Ali, who rejected the draft saying, 'I ain't got no quarrel with them Viet Cong. They don't call me nigger,' most boxers had ethnic, nationalistic, or racist scores to settle and of course, they themselves were life's big stories.

A boxing victory is often final—because the opponent has been felled. Counted out. Humiliated. Left wiping the blood oozing out of his nose and eyebrows. And from that haze of humiliation and blood, the defeated boxer begs for another fight, like Mike Tyson once did in the evening of his career. It was out of such brutality that the world's most written-about sport evolved.

'For decades boxing had been a central spectacle in America, and because it is so stripped-down, one-on-one, a battle with hands and not balls or pads or racquets, the metaphors of struggle, of racial struggle most of all, came easily,' writes David Remnick[93] in his seminal biography of Muhammad Ali.

Heavyweight boxing always got banner headlines and on the day of the match the eveningers sold out, the next day's tabloids were sticky with red ink. Most US Presidents watched matches, putting aside more pressing matters of state. The winner of the heavyweight title (mostly American) was always a guest at the White House, though some have scored a political point and refused to go.

The large mental and metaphorical canvas on which boxing as a sport existed drew some of the world's greatest writers, novelists and journalists to the sport. Boxing from the beginning of the twentieth century was a metaphor of life's biggest and basic intention: to fell the opponent. That is what drew novelists, biographers, Pulitzer winners to the preparatory camp of fighters. Writer James Baldwin, known for his essays on the situation of Blacks in the US, and American novelist Norman Mailer covered the Sonny Liston–Floyd Patterson fight in 1962 (Liston dropped Patterson in 1962 and again in the rematch in '63). Baldwin was not a boxing expert, but he came anyway, with a commission.

David Remnick recalls the incredible collection of great writers who covered the Joe Louis–Floyd Patterson encounter. 'The literary undercard of the Patterson–Louis fight in Chicago featured the meeting of Norman Mailer and James Baldwin who was on assignment for *Nugget*. A.J. Liebling (who was covering the event for *The New Yorker*) apparently did not care for the presence of visiting novelists. 'The press gatherings before this fight sometimes resembled those highly intellectual pourparlers

---

[93] David Remnick, *King of the World: Muhammad Ali and the Rise of an American Hero*, Vintage, 1999.

on a Mediterranean island. Placed before typewriters, the accumulated novelists could have produced a copy of *The Paris Review* in forty-two minutes.'

Journalism's fascination with boxing or a version (prize ring) of it started from 1700 when *The Times* started carrying reports on fights in the ring. But boxing, though the most physical sport with no obvious mental or skill to it, was written up over the years by eccentrics and literary stalwarts and thus came to occupy a seminal position in the consciousness of the Anglophone world.

This fascination can be seen in the immortal publications devoted to the sport. Of these *The Ring* and Pierce Egan's *Boxiana: or, Sketches of Ancient and Modern Pugilism,* are referred to fondly by Oates who thinks such publications played pivotal roles in making boxing central to American sport and macho culture, something similar to the 'pehelwan' or wrestler culture in India. Oates pays awesome tribute to *The Ring*, a magazine founded in 1922 by Nat Fleischer. 'The Ring's Hall of Fame corresponds to the pantheon of saints elected by the Vatican except it is in fact more finely calibrated, its saints arranged under various groupings and subgroupings and its balloting highly complex past, present and a hypothesized future are tirelessly examined and in which one finds articles on such subjects as "The Greatest Disappointments in Ring History", "The Greatest Mismatches", "The Greatest Left Hooks", "When a Good Little Man Did Defeat a Good Big Man".'

In classic boxing bouts there was blood, pain and humiliation. There was an overflow of adjectives and phrases and top novelists. Boxing has contributed the most to English phraseology. Writers of politics, disasters, change of governments, inauguration of presidents, all borrowed heavily from boxing, which apart from everything else had a ready supply of metaphors, imagery, similes and adjectives.

Boxing history is studded with matches that held the world in awe. The Max Schmeling–Joe Louis rematch in 1938 was proof of everything that boxing stands for. From long-time editor David Margolick's description, it would seem that the world had stopped that night of 22 June 1938. Time had stopped too. The richest in the world were there, the best writers in the world were present. It had the largest radio audience in history. It was a macho world and 'No Ladies Admitted' were printed on all press passes, though women watched from the bleachers. Hitler listened to the commentary on the fight from his retreat in Bavaria.

A German reporter was wonderstruck: 'The stadium (Madison Square Garden) lay in an unreal grey haze,' looking like 'the open greedy jaws of an antediluvian beast.'

Clem McCarthy, the greatest boxing commentator on NBC's coast-to coast network, Canada to Honolulu, was understated but grand: 'Good evening, ladies and gentlemen, the two principals in the greatest bout in a generation are in the ring.'

The German commentator Arno Helmis had no such restraint. It was 3 a.m. in Germany, Helmis's voice crackling through, clearly from a febrile mind: 'The moment has finally come ... This isn't a stadium anymore. This is an overflowing feverish melting pot full of passions let loose and if one should throw a match I am sure the whole stadium with all its people will be blown up ...'

The world's top English writers summoned imagery, similes from mythology and history and adjectives from the street flowed in equal measure. To Ernest Hemingway, for instance, Louis seemed, '... nervous and jumpy as a doped race horse.' He got it wrong

After all the global fuss, the bout lasted a minute and Joe Louis took his revenge. Germany cut out the radio commentary as soon as Max Schmeling was out for the count.

McCarthy's description recreated by Margolick will suffice for the one minute brutality of pure strength and beauty: 'And Schmeling is down! Schmeling is down. The count is four.' McCarthy tried capturing it all but even a rapid-fire delivery honed at hundreds of racetracks, he could not keep up; no horse had ever done so much so fast. It was the crowd's muffled, dense, thunderous roars, and not what McCarthy blurted out a millisecond later, that told the story. 'With each blow you imagined Louis saying: So I fouled you eh? Boom! ... So you gave me a beating I'll never forget eh? ... Boom!' Joe Williams wrote. Black America could now exhale. 'Laughter roared through the land like the mighty Niagara breaking though a cardboard dike,' Frank Marshall Davis wrote. So startling was what was unfolding at the stadium that not everyone knew how to react. To Richard Wright, it was all 'so stunning that even cheering was out of place.'

Schmeling got up four times, each attempt lasting only an instant. 'Another powerful combination sent him to his knees. A red drool dribbled from his lips and forced a crimson beard of bubbles on his chin,' wrote Austen Lake of the *Boston Evening American*.

McCarthy was breathlessly counting the hooks: 'Right and left to the head! A left to the jaw! A right to the head! And Donovan (referee) is watching closely. Louis measures him. Right to the body! A left hook to the jaw! And Schmeling is down!'

Louis's final right to the face, seemed 'to smash it like a baseball bat would an apple,' according to *Herald Tribune*'s Casswell Adams.

His trainer, Max Machon, slapped Schmeling's face to bring him back into the real world from hell where he had been dispatched for one full minute. When the German boxer asked, 'What was the matter?', Machon told him it was over.

Their first match in 1936 had lasted twelve rounds. That match was the victory of strategy. Schmeling had noticed a flaw in Louis—that he let down his left hand. Before the rematch Louis had set this right—and the result was the one-round defeat.

Yet for all their bombast and build, heavyweight fighters are as scared of defeat and humiliation as anyone of us. It is a fear that a tennis player does not have to carry. Thom Jones's immortal anti-war short story 'The Pugilist at Rest', is about a Vietnam veteran who was a champion boxer as well. Before one of his fights, the protagonist recounts. 'Jack Dempsey [Australian heavyweight champion] used to get so scared before his fights that he sometimes wet his pants. But look what he did to [American heavyweight champion, Jess] Willard and [Argentine] Luis Firpo, the Wild Bull of the Pampas. It was something close to homicide. What is courage? What is cowardice?'

'I got over the first scare and saw that I was quite other than that which I had known myself to be. Hey Baby [the story's narrator had fractured the skull of a fellow recruit with the butt of his gun; the recruit was called Hey Baby because he wrote a letter to his girlfriend beginning with "Hey Baby"] proved only my warm-up act. There was a reservoir of malice, poison and vicious sadism in my soul and it poured forth freely in the jungle and rice paddies of Vietnam …

'I pulled three tours. I wanted some payback for Jorgenson [the narrator's friend who was bullied by Hey

Baby]. I grieved for Lance Corporal Hanes [a Marine who was killed in Vietnam]. I grieved for myself and what I had lost. I committed unspeakable crimes and got medals for it.'

Jones tries to examine the link between violence and boxing. 'The Pugilist' is definitely one of the best Vietnam stories written, not necessarily a boxing classic. The description of an ambush is so real that we feel that our guts too are spilling out and there is blood around our feet. Jones himself didn't fight in Vietnam in real life. But he takes us there into the vortex of violence and killing. The pugilist is one who has seen violence ... monasteries are not known to have produced boxers.

Fat City written in 1969 by Leonard Gardner is a candidate for one of the best novels ever written. For some reason it remains forgotten, even though it is classic about two boxers who are doomed to fail from the start, a novel that haunts you. Ernie Munger and Billy Tully are sports' big heroes in a way because they never made it and finish their lives, beaten and bruised. Here, boxing is a metaphor for the defeated, a fable that warns us about the inevitability of defeat in life—one day, you will fail.

Gardner was an amateur boxer himself and he transplants his trauma and defeats into the novel like no one has. The descriptions of failure and the yearning for a win are gut-wrenching. The pain of failure adds to sport's attraction. Gardner takes us to the other side of boxing where life, boxing, poverty, struggle, destiny and that unending quest for a quiet family life are all linked. He also knows best what a coach goes through. There is defeat, failure, humiliation that makes boxing so inhuman, yet so daunting a sport. The coach and the boxer, the sport's undividable pair, feed on the dregs. Each bout is a battle for survival. Poverty is just beyond the ropes, but inside the ring, fame and fortune awaits.

What awaits is also the ultimate humiliation of lying spreadeagled on the mat like a forgotten sculpture, or being on all fours unable to get up as the referee counts the death knell or just waves his hand not even bothering to complete the count. Here is one such fictional bout in the eyes of Gardner.

'At the bell, (coach) Ruben was standing behind Ernie just outside the ropes, facing a short Negro with bulging arms and a Mohawk haircut. Then, sitting on the ring steps beside Babe, their heads on the level of Ernie's dancing feet, Ernie's new gold-trimmed white robe still over his arm, Ruben experienced the first waning of confidence. He saw in the Negro's opening blow a power that was undeniable, that was extraordinary. It was a wide hook slung to the stomach under Ernie's jab; and as instantaneous strategic adjustments were occurring in Ruben's mind, Ernie was struck under the heart with a right of resounding force. Ruben then felt a foreboding. Though Ernie manoeuvred with a degree of skill, there was an aspect of futility in it all. When he reached out with both gloves to block a left, Ruben's hand went into his sweater pocket for the ammonia vial and a right swing landed with an awesome slam on the lean point of Ernie's chin. He went down sideways along the ropes, toppling stiffly in the road and hit the canvas on his back, his head striking the floor, followed by his feet. His eyes stared momentarily, then closed as his body went rigid.'

Ernie survives this and other defeats, travelling on Greyhound buses to a few bouts here and there. He never makes it out of Stanton, California, doing farm labour for a living.

Fat City takes us through the pathos and tragedy of a sportsman's life. Staring at you is the impossibility of achieving. The coach and his many students go through it. Ruben experiences the same dread after Ernie was knocked out to near death. 'But now under the ring lights Ruben experiences the same dread, as he massaged Ernie's arms with unhurried hands, his face distressed but not frantic, he felt the hopeless folly that was his life.'

On the fiftieth anniversary of his novel, Gardner told *Paris Review*[94] that he was an amateur boxer but his life was full of boxing stories told by his father. His vision of being a novelist was not to write about the comfortable life of professors and children (typical of Indian English novels). His metier was the rough side of life. 'I was interested in the rougher side of life. There's something about struggling people, poor people, that's dramatic. Struggle is dramatic ... A boxer can get killed any time he enters a ring. And also, I grew up with an ex-boxer father who talked about boxing all the time. It was a world I got very interested in.'

'Part of the thrill of boxing is the chance to watch a fighter find a way to endure the unendurable,' writes Kelefa Sanneh.[95] Sanneh wrote this after the controversial Tyson Fury versus Deontay Wilder heavyweight match on 1 December 2018, which ended in a draw after twelve rounds. In the rematch I February 2020, Fury, the British heavyweight champion, dropped Wilder, the American heavyweight champion, in the seventh round. Fury is a classic case of a boxer who lives in the intersect between clarity and darkness and his story would 'even stretch Hollywood's credulity'. Fury belonged to a gypsy family and called himself the Gypsy King.[96] A giant of a man at

---

[94] David Lida, '*Fat City*, Fifty Years Later: An Interview with Leonard Gardner', *Paris Review*, 6 February 2019.

[95] Kelefa Sanneh, 'Tyson Fury and Adonis Stevenson: A Shocking Night of Boxing', *New Yorker*, 2 December 2018.

[96] Decca Aitkenhead, 'Tyson Fury Interview: The Boxer on Fighting Depression and His Inner Demons', *The Times*, 10 November 2019.

six feet nine inches, his 'wingspan' or reach is seven feet. At his premature birth, his father predicted that he would grow up to be a seven-foot world heavyweight champion and named him after Mike Tyson.

Like all top rankers in sport, Fury started early, joining an amateur boxing club at fourteen, though he had dropped out of school at ten to help his dad. His first opponent took one look at the even then tall Fury at six feet five inches and fled. Fury went on win the British, Irish, European, Commonwealth belts. He defeated the Ukranian giant Wladimir Klitschko in 2015. Then for two years he plunged into depression; alcohol and cocaine followed and he lost his mind. Later, he pulled himself up, shed 63 kilograms, and started fighting again in one of the incredible stories of sporting comebacks.

It is difficult to believe that boxers like Fury can surmount inner demons and physical punishment to such an unimaginable level and then get out to fight again. Like other champions, 'winning a world title was all he'd ever wanted.' The fear of defeat haunted the great heavyweights, obviously because a knockdown is complete humiliation. Some fighters, such as like Floyd Patterson, carried a wig with them so that they could escape from the arena unnoticed after a defeat.

Ali was always aware of impending failure. The fear of losing almost possessed him. The boasting was part of the effort to get rid of such phobias. On the eve of his first fight with Sonny Liston in 1964, Ali, then Cassius Clay, wrote a first person account.[97] It ended like this: 'Folks ask me what I'll do if I beat Liston and what I'll do if I don't, but I don't have the answer yet. I'm not too worried. I think I can make it in something else the same

[97] Cassius Clay, 'I'm a Little Special', *Sports Illustrated*, 24 February 1964.

way I've made it in boxing. If things go wrong in the fight, I'll just wait a while. Summertime comes, flowers start blooming, little birds start flying and you wake up, get up and get out. You change with the times.'

It was good for sport that Ali did not have to change. Boxing and the world changed. That was because Ali battered down so many walls, and took on bigger historical opponents: America itself, the senselessness of war, the pomposity of Christianity as an imperial religion and the perennial evil of racism itself. Ali stays with us because he won all these bouts and cleared the way for a brighter future in this badly riven world.

CHAPTER EIGHT

The Coach, His Ambition, His Follies and His Champion

In sport, there will be champions and superstars. And in the champion's shadow can always be found a coach, sometimes brash, often self-effacing, but always helping his ward climb his personal Everest.

Personal coaches must become part of the champion's life and ambition. Strategies to become a world champion cannot be drawn up over a cup of tea. It is a tiring procedure full of wrong moves. That is why a coach needs to be at the side of the player and live in close proximity with his protégé. The coach is not a visiting professor who makes periodic visits to gauge the progress of his students left alone for weeks to do assignments. The personal coach is a permanent prop that offers solace, defends shortcomings, throws light on the dark recesses of deficiency of the opponent, manufactures energy drinks (Agassi's coach), searches for cures for various ailments in far-off lands, puts a hand around his champion after a last-gasp loss, and in the hour of triumph sits back and watches his boy hold the trophy as the streamers fall all around him. He is a mother.

A champion is an industry in himself and needs skilled staff. Like a car taking shape in an assembly line, the champion has to be fitted and kitted out with many things.

How do we gain insight about the coach–player relationship? I have taken the words of well-known French tennis coach Patrick Mouratoglou, coach of Serena Williams for a long time, and also part-time coach of the emerging Greek god Stefanos Tsitsipas. These detailed and surprisingly candid Q&As recorded at the Australian Open 2019 press conference shine light on the mind of a top-level coach. These words also reflect what I have been trying to get at, to emphasize the constant effort that goes into keeping players in their top mental and physical condition. A top player has to be kept in a bubble where she or he breathes only the rarefied air that champions breathe.

Mouratoglou: A constant by the side of a champion

Exhibiting childish candour mixed with a deep insight into the mind of a champion like Serena Williams are the characteristics of Mouratoglou. The faith in and dependence that Mouratoglou and Serena have on each other is complete. Both give each other everything they can. This is what goes into the making of a champion. Mouratoglou also runs an academy in Paris and coaches other top players too, but he is with Serena during the major events.

Q: It's now been many years that you have been working with this incredible champion and incredible woman (Serena), a cultural icon as well. Can you share what you have really learned from her as an athlete and also as a person.

A: It's difficult to summarize it in a few words. She just—I mean, when you start this job, you have an idea of what a champion is in terms of mindset and she just comes from that 100 per cent. She comes from that, I mean champions. I'm talking about her, but she doesn't think like the other players.

I have worked with a lot of players in my life. I have a tennis academy as you know. I have worked with thousands of players and there is only one Serena in terms of mindset.

You become who you are, how you think and a champion's champion—I mean there are a few things that champions do or think that are different from other people. I always tell this story. You know—Roland Garros has always been a difficult tournament for her in the past and when we started 2012, she just lost in the first round. And after she started to win Grand Slams again she won Wimbledon, the US Open, the Olympic gold … she told me she was struggling to win Roland Garros. Last time she won it I think was in 2002 and we were in 2013 when she started to talk to me about that.

We made a plan and she worked incredibly hard to win this one and she won it in 2013. So eleven years after. After the trophy ceremony she went to stretch and she told me 'Come with me I'm stretching. After two minutes she turned to me and said 'Now we have to win Wimbledon.' She already forgot it (Paris win). She was chasing something for eleven years, not two minutes, ten minutes after she was already focusing on the next goal. That's different. There are guys who win one tournament and they celebrate for fifteen years (*laughter*).

Q: Why do you think your relationship with Serena endures? Because a lot of players keep changing coaches.

Is it just that she won so many Slams with you? Is there some kind of dynamic about both your personalities?

A: I think there are several things. First of all, she's a very loyal person. She's incredibly loyal. I think she is also very responsible. Like she doesn't blame others for her problems. She loses a match, she doesn't say it's my fault. Even though I think it is my fault too. But this is me with myself.

She would never blame me. She takes everything on her. Because she's strong enough and courageous enough and confident enough to be able to look at herself and say, I failed. Not that many people do that. It's easier to put it on somebody else. She does not do that.

So that's already two main reasons. It's her personality.

Maybe also—and I think also we have a very strong relationship. I think we trust each other. We have been very successful. It counts too. And I think it's refreshing also to see that when there are problems, the first reaction of the player is not to say, Okay I'll get rid of the coach, it's going to be better. It's not going to be better. It's not about that. It's about the connection and the trust.

I mean I completely understand that a player would stop or a coach would stop with the player if the trust is not here anymore, because it won't work. You have to trust your coach 100 per cent and believe what he's saying and believe he's the right person for you. Maybe she probably does, otherwise she might have changed. But again, she's incredibly loyal. It's a trait of her personality most all top coaches (or parents as shown in Chapter 1) in all games are those who transfer their failed ambitions as players (or in other activities) to their wards after they became coaches. For a coach to groom a world champion, what is needed is that crucial transfer of ambition or instilling of a burning desire in his student. It is not enough for a coach to make his students practice for hours on end. There is other work to be done.

*

The best examples of such coaches can be seen in boxing. Cus D'Amato, boxing's immortal coach who also coached Muhammad Ali, took Mike Tyson home and told his wife, 'here's a son for you.' From there to making him the world champion is the story of legend, as we have discussed earlier. The totality of their faith in each other is a lesson in human relationship and has answers to that difficult question: Why do we trust another person so completely? In the case of a sportsperson, his/her life is wrapped up with the life of his/her coach.

Fiction provides some answers here. Gardner in his searing, disturbing novel elevated the relationship of the coach and the boxer to surreal levels. The coach and his boxer are wanderers or journeymen in the dismal path of life where only rarely does the bright ray of sunlight filter through. Before the bout they are one. Their souls and their ambitions merge:[98] 'Stripped of his gloves, Ernie stood on the gym floor, panting and nodding while Ruben, squared off with his belly forward and hat brim up, moved his small hands and feet in quick and graceful demonstrations. "You got a good left. Understand what I mean? Step in with that jab. Understand what I mean? Get your body behind it. Bing! Understand what I mean? You hit him with that jab his head's going back, so you step in—understand what I mean?—hit him again, throw the right. Bing! Relax, keep moving, lay it in there, bing, bing, understand what I mean? Keep it out there working for you. Then feint the left, throw the right. Bing! Understand

[98] Leonard Gardner, *Fat City*, Pushkin Press, 2017.

what I mean? Jab and feint, you keep him off balance. Feinting. You make your openings and step in. Bing, bing, whop! Understand what I mean?"'

Do the boys understand the smaller lessons, the larger lessons? How it is all life and winning is part of it?

The personal coach is always on his toes. Though the medal will never be his and his reward is just reflected glory, he is a worried man—worrying for someone else, worrying for the medal which is not his, caring for the body which is not his, pummelling the biceps which are not his, crying over the hamstring as if it is his own leg oozing blood, weeping someone else's tears.

Here is where proximity between coach and ward comes in and that is also the reason why father–son/mother–daughter coaching alliances have worked wonders. In many cases the parents have been strict taskmasters, leading their kids to an early burnout. Other such extreme cases, however, do have great results. Many stars have been whipped into shape. Some of them don't mind losing their childhood, but others, like Agassi for instance, resent it.[99] Tottenham Hotspurs Korean forward Son Heung-Min is one who survived the most killing routine set for him by his father, who through a regimen that few kids will survive, made his son a great footballer. Here it is interesting to see how the father, Son Woong-jung, instilled ambition in his son and saw his shattered dreams come alive in his son.

The Tottenham forward's father Son Woong-jung was a former professional footballer who made it to a good level in South Korea. He had begun to coach his boys, making it his mission to guide them to the top, avoiding the pitfalls that he encountered.

---

[99] *The Guardian*, 8 March 2019.

'He gave us four hours of keep-uppies,' Son says. 'Both of us. After about three hours, I was seeing three balls. The floor was red (through bloodshot eyes). I was so tired. And he was so angry. I think this was the best story and we still talk about it when we are all together.'

'Four hours of keeping the ball up and you don't drop it. That's difficult, no?' Son recounts. 'When I was ten or twelve, he came in to coach my school team and we were training. The programme was for us to keep the ball up for forty minutes. When someone dropped the ball, my father would not say anything. But as soon as I dropped it, he made us all start it from the beginning.'

Son fondly remembers all this, but many kids rebel against such boot-camp techniques adopted by their parents and move away from the game. Methods adopted by the parent who is not a qualified coach often always goes wrong. Unless the parent has played the game to some level and developed a philosophy about sport and winning, it is not possible to groom a youngster.

Strangely enough, some untrained coach-fathers or mothers became big successes in remaking their kids into champions, driven solely by the lingering shame of their many defeats and jinxed ambition and the immediate possibility of the son reversing the fate that befell the father.

Booker Prize-winning author Aravind Adiga makes this the theme of his novel *Selection Day* (also on Netflix as a film) where a dictatorial father drives his two children to cricketing fame, against the wishes of one of them who wants to know where his mother has disappeared. The very notion is completely disturbing. There are larger issues involved, including whether such a child will have stunted mental growth. There is no evidence to prove so, though various behavioural problems in adulthood have been documented in this context.

Among such parent-coaches was the eccentric warrior Enzo Calzaghe,[100] 'itinerant musician turned trainer whose tough love transformed his son Joe into a celebrated world champion' as the obituary in *The Times* noted.

'Experts often scoffed at Calzaghe's coaching because he did not use training pads or bind his son's hands properly. They also accused him of being tactically naive. However, he had one attribute that trumped all his deficiencies. Super-middleweight world boxing champion Calzaghe Jr said: "He could kick up my arse and keep pushing me. If it wasn't for him, I would never have laced up the gloves in the first place. We stuck together through the ups and downs even when people were saying I should get rid of him because he had never boxed. But he knew exactly what to say at the right time."'

The *Time* obituary noted that Calzaghe admitted he was self-taught, but countered criticism of his abilities by training several other champions, including Enzo Maccarinelli (world title) and Gavin Rees. At the same time, the Newbridge Boxing Club in South Wales operated by Calzaghe Sr became one of the most successful gyms in Europe with a reputation for producing all-action boxers known for their work rate, attacking style and 'punches in bunches'. Calzaghe Sr's proteges, however, attested to his motivational techniques and eccentricity. Gary Lockett, the trainer and former boxer, called him an 'absolute nut job, always laughing.'

To his son Joe, however, he could be brutal. During training at the rundown Newbridge gym he shouted at Joe: 'Call yourself a f__ing champion? More like a f—ing chump.' Later they were hugging each other.

The Times published a picture of Joe hugging his father after his win over American opponent Roy Jones

[100] 'Enzo Calzaghe obituary', *The Times*, London, 19 October 2018.

in 2008. 'As a trainer I've been honoured to be part of the Joe Calzaghe story. As a father what more could you want?' he said at the end.

This is why many failed fathers do it—to hug the son who is holding aloft the belt. In that moment of triumph, their ambitions and achievements merge and become one. At that point, life is worth it.

One more story of a father–son pairing gives us an idea of the intensity of such a relationship and the oneness of the quest. John McPhee,[101] in his immortal article on the Arthur Ashe–Clark Graebner match relates meticulously how the father of tennis champion Clark Graebner, who played Arthur Ashe in the classic US Open semi-finals, groomed him. Here was sacrifice and caring.

When Clark was a beginner, Dr Graebner completely gave up his own tennis for five years, and every Wednesday and Saturday and at all other practicable times, he took Clark to a tennis court and patiently taught him the game. 'Every shot I hit now is built on the rudiments of my father's strokes,' Clark acknowledges. 'He taught me everything. I don't think he wanted to make me a champion. He just wanted to make me as good as I wanted to be. He hit balls at me for hundreds of thousands of hours, as if he were a Ball-Boy machine.'

The way a father teaches his son or daughter is a bit different from the professional coach training a young kid. The emotional aspect is cut off if the coach is not the parent, making a world of difference. The burden on the young player is less with an outside coach. What happens on the ground is not replayed at home.

Among the advocates of the collaborative process of coaching, unlike the radically obsessive coaching method

[101] John McPhee, 'Levels of the Game', *New Yorker*, 7 June 1969.

mostly seen in the father–son scenario, is Paddy Upton who lays out his concepts in great detail in *Barefoot Coach* (surely, he didn't have to pose barefoot on the cover to prove a metaphorical point!). Quoting a study which looked at this aspect of coaching, mental focus and so on, Upton says: '... the keys to promoting mental toughness do not lie in this autocratic, authoritarian or oppressive style. It appears to lie, paradoxically, with the coach's ability to produce an environment which emphasizes trust and inclusion, humility and service. This paradoxical approach to developing toughness may well serve as a foundational skill for coaches of the future as older fear-based models of coaching go by the wayside.'

Upton settles upon what he calls the collaborative style of coaching, which consists of understanding what the player needs, what his weaknesses are, instead of thrusting a work ethic down his body, so to say. 'Instruction-based coaching is characterized by an authoritarian, dogmatic and dictatorial approach where the coach's word is law. The collaborative style is essentially where coach and player work together what is ultimately best for the player and the team, with the coach employing influence more than power and the player assuming a degree of responsibility for their decisions and actions.'

Upton realized that few Indian players liked to listen to lectures on their game, so he cut that out and instead, talked individually or listened to what the players had to say. A coach who employs a coach-centred approach will feel the need to be in control. It's an approach where coaches assume the role of being the expert and set the agenda (so well brought out in *Selection Day*), which is most commonly about winning. And this is understandable, as most coaches are judged, hired and fired based on results, even though this remains a woefully incomplete and narrow measure of coaching success. It's like measuring a businessperson's success solely by how much money they make.

Upton goes on to reason why the instructional style is not long-lasting. Quoting John Whitmore, author of *Coaching for Performance,* he says that when power becomes a driving force in coaching, the intellectual flame that lights up the path to knowledge and progress is smothered.

This is a bit philosophical and one-sided. Though tyrannical coaching is not advisable and often ends up in a burnout for the kid, a little bit of stentorian teaching has always helped youngsters, many of whom learn out of fear and sometimes a pat on their tired backs gives them the impetus to do their best. Given the option to be lackadaisical or disciplined, children often choose the easy path. Only later in life do they realize the mistake and tell themselves, 'If only I had listened to my father.'

The domineering role of a coach or manager is most evident in team games like football and basketball. Here, the entire strategizing is left to the coach who sits outside, unlike in cricket. The thinking is outsourced. This has given rise to the accepted notion that footballers or basketballers have no real strategic brains since the thinking part is outsourced to the manager like in boxing. This is not the full truth. Team game players too develop high strategic thinking. The coach's role is mostly overestimated.

The reason is that while the larger strategy can be formulated from outside, what actually happens on the ground is quite different. Each player has his/her own personal strategy which he/she has evolved over the years, playing according to that, while trying to show that he/she follows some instructions from outside. When the football manager screams from beyond the lines, it is because he realizes that many players are not playing according to his instructions. Also, sometimes the opposing side has a strategy which he never foresaw, leaving his own larger strategy in a mess. The manager is just a father figure of sorts. He has the powers to hire/sell or pull out players or finish off their careers.

But most players play their own way and managers learn to leave them to their own wiles. You might even argue that managers are no more than glorified talent scouts. It is not possible for any manager to know in advance if a player he plans to hire will fit in well with his team's forward line or defence. This is because of varying styles of play. Top players do manage to adjust but these are all unknown elements in team formation.

Thrust upon managers, therefore, are qualities they may not even possess: team-builder, ace strategist, a philosopher, father figure. The truth is that even if I am given the Real Madrid team to manage for a lark, the team will most likely win the match. The reason is that the team is packed with top players, grandmasters of the game who can devise their own strategy while the play is on. Their forwards know when to strike, how to strike, how to stretch the defence and how to draw out the goalkeeper, for instance. Is more strategy required to score a goal? Truth be said, managers benefit more from a top team, than the other way round. Chief coaches or managers give the team a sense of unity and purpose more than anything else.

As I have emphasized earlier, top-ranked teams, like top-ranked tennis players or any top-ranked player win most or all of their matches. This notion of David felling Goliath is just faith or a belief in the sports fan's mind. It seldom or never happens. Sports fans all over the world suspend or ignore statistics and facts when going to watch their lower ranked team play and always hope for an upset.

What if the lower placed team gets more than expected penalties during a league season? Even then they will not win consistently or rise to the top. 'Penalties have no impact at all on whether the favourite wins: favourites win 51.3 per cent of games without a penalty, and 51.4 games with a penalty. It's true that underdogs win more often when there is a penalty than when there is not, but once again, the tests demonstrate that this fact has no statistical significance. We can put the increase down to chance. Match results appear to be the same with or without penalties. Penalties do not matter,' says Simon Kuper in *Soccernomics*.[102]

England's football manager of the national team, Gareth Southgate, said before the 2018 World Cup (England lost in the semi-finals), 'My job is to create an environment for the players where they are able to express themselves and feel the confidence we have in them.' This is the right estimate of a manager's job. Southgate also said before the tournament, 'It's going to be an exciting time watching these boys play. They have a hunger to press and win the ball back and want to play brave football. They want to be a bold and attacking team. We have lads that are so exciting and I want them to go into this tournament, really go for it good as they may be and not go back and think, "I wish I'd been a bit brave and tried something and been prepared to give the ball away."'

Here we see the manager playing the role of an emotional glue, a father figure for the team to cling on to.

[102] Simon Kuper and Stefan Szymanski, *Soccernomics*, Nation Books, 2014.

He surely sets the larger strategy but once the game starts, the players take over, often doing their own thing. Yet, a manager has to inspire, threaten and cajole in turn, plead and reason. Players have left teams, unable to bear the manager and his tantrums. Such players feel the manager is a destroyer who survives on the career of players. Or maybe survives on the defeated bodies of players lying broken inside the penalty area.

Managers have become the creators of footballing destiny. In an article typically and predictably titled 'What Next for Pep Guardiola?',[103] the writer pays huge tributes to the famous coach: '(Manchester) City have the most points, most shots, most goals and the most passes. They have been strolling away at the top of the league since the fifth week of the season.

'From August to April these PL [Premier League] champions have been a rare joy, a team that keeps the ball with the usual Pep-issue mania but come forward in a relentless swarm, spreading the game into every available part of the space whatever the score, whatever the time on the clock always unapologetically itself.

'For all its brilliance this City team are also a ruthlessly assembled winning machine.

'For all that Guardiola has somehow managed to retain not just the moral high ground but an air of likeable asceticism. He seems an oddly monk-like figure known for purity of his methods, the idealistic obsession with detail.

'At the same time, he is clearly a brilliant manager on a very basic level, venerated in England partly because so much of what he does is an upgrade on the old managerial tropes. Like a George Graham for the non-contact age, Guardiola spends hours drilling his defensive

---

[103] 'What Next for Pep Guardiola?', *The Guardian*, 17 March 2018.

line, enacting what is in effect a fluid version of moving up and down, together holding a piece of rope.'

A team needs a monk-like figure, a philosopher if you will, who can talk about the higher reaches, the need to keep the desire burning. To keep a bunch of millionaires toiling together is not an easy task for each one has his type of tantrums, just like the different types of toys they possess. A manager has to have the intellect to override all these factors.

Most of the top football managers are philosophers. French former manager and player, Arsène Wenger, was quoted by *The Times*, London as saying: 'I believe that anything in life, if it is really well done becomes art.' And again: 'If you read a great writer, he touches deep inside and helps you to discover something about life.'

Recalling all this, British journalist and former table tennis player, Matthew Syed, wrote: 'These words ring true of the greatest sides under Wenger, teams that ravished the imagination and in their way, turned the game of the people into art.'

A true intellectual can take a team to great heights because his mind can out-think all others. As we have seen here, there is a basic difference between coaching an individual and a team. The coach of a tennis player can take more credit for his ward's performance than a soccer manager can take for his team's showing.

Nowhere in the 100 years of the history of sport, could I find a coach as majestic and endearing as George Yeoman Pocock. He was not just a rowing coach—he was a builder of boats or shells and a philosopher and intellectual. He belonged to a family of boat-builders, his father having built boats for Eton school rowers for many years till he lost his job, which sent the Pocock family to poverty like thousands of others during the Depression.

George and his brother Dick went to Canada from England and worked in logging camps and other body-breaking jobs. Their presence in Vancouver was noticed since the family's reputation as boat-builders in Eton was well known. Finally, George landed up in Washington, where he made finely finished shells for university teams around the country.

Daniel Brown[104] in his classic book on the higher ideals of sport, which sold over a million copies, writes: 'George Pocock learned much about the hearts and souls of young men. He learned to see hope where a boy thought there was no hope, to see skill where skill was obscured by ego or by anxiety. He observed the fragility of confidence and the redemptive power of trust. He detected the strength of the gossamer threads of affection that sometimes grew between a pair of young men or among a boatload of them striving honestly to do their best. And he came to understand how those almost mystical bonds of trust and affection, if nurtured correctly might lift a crew above the ordinary sphere, transport it to a place where nine boys somehow became one thing—a thing that could not quite be defined, a thing that was in tune with the water and the earth and the sky above that, as they rowed, effort was replaced by ecstasy. It was a rare thing, a sacred thing, a thing devoutly to be hoped for. And in the years since coming to Washington, George Pocock had quietly become its high priest.'

George Yeoman Pocock is the coach every sportsman should have by his or her side as they navigate their life and careers, plumb the depths and scramble to the heights of glory. He was a builder of boats as well as champions.

---

[104] Daniel James Brown, *The Boys in the Boat: Nine Americans and Their Epic Quest for Gold at the 1936 Berlin Olympics*, Penguin Books, 2014.

CHAPTER NINE

Sport's Big Myths, Fallacies and Cuckoo Science

Losing consistently in sport poses terrible dilemmas not just for the loser, but also for coaches and commentators of sport. How do we explain the defeat? Where does the logic of this consistent losing lie? That is the reason why coaches and sports analysts fill up the gaps with ersatz science and bizarre logic.

The basic reasons for losing have been dealt with earlier—lack of proper practice, lack of planning or strategy (basic and higher), no burning desire, and in team games, basically no top-ranked players and a general lack of purpose. Individuals often have a sense of purpose but for a team to have a combined resolve and a purpose is much more difficult. Most consistently losing teams go to a tournament or match like lambs to slaughter. Neither hope nor resolve resides in such teams or individuals. Along with this has come up an impressive narrative that is mostly pop analysis and cuckoo science, which has settled down as received wisdom. A few of these narratives need to be specifically addressed, although some of these aspects have been covered in earlier chapters.

Cricket is the most analysed sport in India and England since highly paid commentators are involved and also because the game lends itself to analysis of every kind: scientific, social, physical and spiritual. A cricket Test lasts five days, giving commentators enough time for spontaneous invention. In India at least, theories invented by such commentators have passed on to other sport too.

Choking as a breathless theory

One of the more dubious but oft-heard expressions that has emerged from sport is the phrase 'choker'. If a team or a player loses after looking like winning or loses three or four times by narrow margins, they are termed chokers. This is the team that when in sight of a glorious victory, loses its senses and embraces defeat instead. The choking theory has gained ground especially because it gives a psychological twist to the habit of losing. This has also perpetrated the notion that mentally or physically weak populations (there is nothing like that in reality) are prone to this choking and hence Indian teams have lost to Pakistan many times both in cricket and hockey by just choking.

The mythical subtext of India–Pakistan rivalry is that since all those in the Pakistan team are meat-eating, Muslims have more daredevilry and courage. Weak populations (especially vegetarian Indians and Buddhists) are also meant to lose wars, since they don't have the grit to fight till death. India as a country and as a people have often been described thus, without any scientific backing.

The choking theory looks at sport and winning from the standpoint of the losers and gives no credit to the winners, suggesting instead that they won because the losers have a mental issue about winning, but there is nothing wrong with strategy, preparation and other factors. This notion is widespread in the world of sport from which I take a few examples.

Veteran sports commentator Sandeep Dwivedi, writing in the *Indian Express*,[105] subscribes to this theory that Indian teams have a choking tendency; they lose matches they could have won, or lose sight of victory pretty easily: 'Virtually every Olympics this millennium has featured an Indian hockey meltdown—always against a mid-level opponent, because of a late goal: Sydney 2000 … Poland sixty-ninth minute); Athens 2004 … Argentina (sixty-ninth minute)' and so on. Dwivedi, by this time seething with anger at this method of losing, goes on to say that the Indian cricket team too has this psychological issue of losing when it could have won. Most other cricket writers also subscribe to this theory.

'Our cricketers are no better. Regardless of what those puffy teasers, [the Board of Control for Cricket] BCCI-water marked commentators and other assorted social media spin doctors say, the India batsmen—those modern day brand ambassadors of everything uber cool—too turn into nervous wrecks in high-pressure situations. In the last nine months Virat Kohli's stubble-wearing top order have repeatedly panicked and perished, while chasing sub-300 winning targets—208 (South Africa, Cape Town), 245 (England, Southhampton) and 287 (South Africa, Centurion),' Dwivedi writes.

Well-known sportswriter and philosopher Matthew Syed[106] also subscribes to this theory of a psychological blockade that occurs inexplicably and makes a team lose. Syed was a table tennis star who represented Great

---

[105] Sandeep Dwivedi, 'We, the Chokers', *Indian Express*, 15 September 2018.

[106] Matthew Syed, *The Greatest: The Quest for Sporting Perfection*, John Murray, 2017.

Britain at the Sydney Olympics. Here's what he says about a match and what 'choking' means: 'Perhaps the most chastening lesson I learned as a sportsman was the time I choked. It happened at the Olympics Games in Sydney, an experience etched on my consciousness, the only time that I suffered a total meltdown in what was unquestionably the most important contest of my career. There seemed to be a breakdown in communication between mind and body, a catastrophic loss of feeling and touch, and a defeat so one-sided that my Olympic dream was over in thirty minutes flat.'

Syed has in many of his columns tried to get a hang on 'failure' and points to the psychological impact on a sportsman's performance, arguing that 'psychological' factors are often the difference between victory and defeat. 'Why do some athletes learn from failures and setbacks while others are overwhelmed by them?' he asks, but does not have a straightforward answer nor a solution to what he called 'choking'.

There is a difference in the type of 'choking' that Dwivedi and other Indian cricket writers and Syed analyse. Syed looks at individual performances and tries to get an answer to the inexplicable defeats by top individual players. The other 'choking' refers to teams losing after playing well in a match in which they could have won. Choking by individuals only refers to certain bad days, which any human being can have in any activity, physical or mental. However, if a once top player starts flopping in many matches in a year, it can only be that he has lost his game due to various reasons. Syed points this out as well.

'Choking is not limited to top sportsmen. Musicians, politicians and all manner of other performers have at times been afflicted by the curse of choking, suddenly and inexplicably unable to execute the skills they have spent a lifetime perfecting. You may have choked at some point too—unable to utter a word on a hot first date, unable to string a sentence together when giving a big presentation.'

Arthur Ashe,[107] perhaps the most intellectual sportsman, too favoured using the world 'choke' on many occasions, mostly I guess out of humility to describe why his opponent lost. He used the word to describe how he managed to defeat former World Number One Jimmy Connors, in the Wimbledon final of 1975. Both were coming out of tough semi-finals—Ashe had overcome Australian player Tony Roche and Connors had smothered the deadly serves of American player Roscoe Tanner. After he beat Connors, Ashe, as always candid and displaying his analytical skills, noted that roughly two-thirds of Connor's errors had fallen 'into the middle of the net.' 'He hardly ever put the ball behind the baseline. That's a sign of choking.' To which Connors, not one to take any condescending statement without a deadly return, retorted, 'I don't choke, my friend,' glaring at the reporter who had quoted Ashe, 'I've been playing too long to choke.'

This notion of being a choker is fairly well established and publicized. But in truth, there is no such thing as 'choking' as a factual mental or psychological disorder in any sport. In one-sided matches as well, the losing team knows in advance what awaits them. As a metaphorical notion, and as an analytical tool maybe, yes, we can tell that someone choked when going for the kill. We need to believe that 'choking' is just an excuse for not being able to win. Last minute defeats, which is Dwivedi's concern and Syed's notion of individual failure on certain days, are routine in sport and no larger lesson can be drawn from it due to the following reasons:

---

[107] Raymond Arsenault, *Arthur Ashe: A Life*, Simon and Schuster, 2018.

In any sport, any team can win or lose though upsets are rare in all sport. Including a mind game like chess. As I have said earlier, top-ranked teams almost always defeat lower ranked teams, unless they are closely ranked. In cricket, there are only eight good teams so this logic may not apply. Victory happens at the last minute in hockey or soccer or tennis or any game in equal measure and examples are many. In fact top-ranked players are often not surprised that they won. Victory is routine. Arthur Ashe said after his victory against Connors: 'If you're a good player and you find yourself winning easily, you're not surprised.'[108]

There is no rule in any sport that victory should be sealed in the first half of a game so that a victory is perfect and not due to any choking of the other team. That is not how games are designed. In tennis Slams, for example, many players have lost in the final fifth set due to just one shot going long, a micro error that changes their destiny after a four and a half hour battle waged alone. Is Dominic Thiem who lost to Nadal in five sets at the US Open 2018 a 'choker'? The score line read: 0-6, 6-4,7-5, 6 (4)-7 (7),7-6 (7-5). Thiem had beaten Nadal twice on clay before and he started out smashing Nadal for a love set or a 'bagel' as they call it. There was nothing called 'choking' here. Nadal has more than ten bagels in the last ten years but has got back to win all of those. So is he a player who chokes in the beginning? That is how tennis or any game is played. Many games are geared for a last-minute or last-gasp finish.

For instance, if the Slams had a rule that if any player loses 6-0 in any set, he is considered defeated, there would not be any last-minute 'choking'. In other sport too, last-minute losing is equal to first half losing.

---

[108] Arsenault, *Arthur Ashe: A Life*, p. 383.

The imagined notion of choking can thus be applied to any team or any player. If you really dig out all the stats of particular teams, you would find most teams have lost after leading or lost while being in a good position to win. These are the pleasures of sport.

Such notions gain currency because of the nationalistic way of analysing sport. Victory in sport is considered a nationalist glue. The question 'Why did India lose?' has to have an answer so a term is invented and pegged on to the team's performance. The performance of the other side is not appreciated. For example, if the Poland hockey team defeated India with a last-gasp goal it could be because Poland knew that Indian players were a bit short on stamina and it was effective strategy to attack at full throttle in the last ten minutes or so. For Poland, it was the victory of strategy, not because India 'chokes'.

The fact is that a team loses because it didn't have the muscle or the skill or the plan or the strategy to win. A team wins because it has all these things taken care of.

All matches lost in penalty shoot-outs are also last-minute defeats after 'dominating the proceedings during most of the game' as Indian reporters normally write.

Blaming the mind of 'choking' is just a convenient excuse. The real reason is that the other team had the gun power and bore calibre.

Hand–eye coordination, foot–eye coordination

There are other such 'accepted wisdom theories' that have prevented us from understanding defeat and victory in sport. Let's look at the 'scientific theory' of 'hand–eye coordination'. In Indian sport generally, a good player is described as one who had a brilliant 'hand–eye' coordination. Many coaches propagate this theory, which has gained momentum due to its frequent mention by 'water-marked commentators', to borrow a phrase from Dwivedi.

This scientific phrase became popular in cricket reporting in India due to the rise of Virender Sehwag, an unorthodox batsman who, throwing textbook to the winds, could smash any fast bowler to all sides of the park. I was witness to his amazing 309 in an India–Pakistan Test match in a dust bowl in Multan, Pakistan in 2004. Since his technique had no explanation and was counter to all accepted techniques of batting, Sehwag was branded as the man with an awesome 'hand–eye coordination'.

Scientifically, there is nothing called hand–eye coordination and so it can be termed cuckoo science. Even if our hand–eye coordination was one per cent defective, as it happens in the case of those with motor neurone disease or Parkinson's disease, we will not be able to even climb down a staircase. So in short, I have the same hand–eye coordination as Sehwag has. But I am not an opening batsman and definitely cannot smash any fast bowler. However, I can do a drop volley at the net on a tennis court, a reflexive action which calls for much 'hand–eye coordination' because I have trained myself to do so.

How does the hand and eye coordination work? For an explanation, we have to turn to cognitive scientist V.S. Ramachandran.[109] His classic *The Tell-Tale Brain* demolished many such theories and he also points to how many 'mumbo-jumbo' theories come to exist. This is due to what he calls 'linear thinking'. 'It is a common fallacy to assume that gradual, small changes can only engender gradual incremental changes. But this is linear thinking,

---

[109] V.S.Ramachandran, *The Tell-Tale Brain*, W.W. Norton & Company, 2012.

which seems to be our default mode for thinking about the world. This may be due to the simple fact that most of the phenomena that are perceptible to humans, at everyday human scales of time and magnitude and within the limited scope of our naked senses, tend to follow linear trends. Two stones feel twice as heavy as one stone. It takes three times as much food to feed three times as many people. And so on ...' That the 'hand–eye coordination' theory is the outcome of this highly deficient way of thinking or analysing is my conclusion.

Many theories on sport do not stand up to scientific scrutiny, including the Self One and Inner Self Two tennis theory of Timothy Gallwey propounded in *The Inner Game of Tennis*. That is because the brain is too complex and how a winner's brain is mapped is still a fully unanswered question.

Apart from our linear thinking, which produced the two sports theories mentioned as well as various others, another reason why many theories are faulty is that many of us, even the well educated sometimes, do not have metaphorical thinking, which is a higher function lodged in the cortex of the brain. Ramachandran explains this with reference to a doctor whose cortex was injured. Dr Jackson, with an injured cortex, could not explain the full metaphorical meaning of the common phrase: 'All that glitters is not gold', a very common and oft-used aphorism. The doctor said that it means that the gold you see cannot be pure gold and when you go to buy jewellery you can be cheated. The metaphorical meaning escaped the doctor. Dr Jackson had a disorder called 'metaphor blindness' according to Ramachandran. A large number of even educated populations suffer from such metaphor blindness and that is why they cannot use metaphors in speech or writing or cannot understand the range of such usage in books.

That apart, the hand–eye coordination theory can be rubbished by following what Ramachandran says about coordination of movements and how complex it is. One of the important (among many) parts of the brain that controls activity (hence sports too) is the left angular gyrus in the left parietal lobe. 'The left angular gyrus is involved in important functions unique to humans as arithmetic, abstraction and aspects of language such as word finding and metaphor. The left supramarginal gyrus, on the other hand, conjures up a vivid image of intended skill actions—for example, sewing with a needle, hammering a nail or waving goodbye—(*and hence crucial to Sehwag's hitting*) and executes them ... When I ask you to salute, you conjure up a visual image of the salute and, in a sense use the image to guide your arm movements.'

The other part of the brain that is crucial to an action like Sehwag hitting a ball or anyone doing anything for that matter is the right parietal lobe which is 'involved in creating a mental model of the spatial layout of the outside world, your immediate environs, plus all the locations (but not identity) of objects, hazards and people within it along with your physical relationships to each of these things. Thus you can grab things, dodge missiles (*Sehwag's speciality*) and avoid obstacles. The right parietal lobe, especially the right superior lobules, is also responsible for constructing your body image—the vivid mental awareness you have of your body's configuration and movement in space. Note that even though it is called an 'image', the body image is not purely a visual construct. It is also partly touch- and muscle-based.

Crucial to every human being and to skill-based games is this aspect of how the brain analyses visual information. 'Visual information from the retina gets to the brain via two pathways. One (the old pathway) relays through superior colliculus arriving eventually in the parietal lobe. The other (new pathway) goes via the lateral genicular nucleus (LGN) to the visual cortex and then splits once again into the "how" and "what" streams,' Ramachandran writes. The intention here is to show that everything cannot be just classified under 'hand–eye coordination' and be done with it. The logic that his hand is good, his eye is good, so he is a great batsman—that accepted notion is false.

So much more is involved in a Sehwag or Tendulkar or Federer hit. A visual image has to be first conjured up by the brain or the left supramarginal gyrus. This visual image that is conjured up could be the image that is set after years of practice. This could be why Federer can hit a backhand perfectly without even looking at the court on the other side of the net. Some of these functions clearly come to the aid of the sportsman.

Sehwag's record as an opening batsman and his unorthodox style are all the result of his dedicated and targeted practice from a young age. God or genes has no role to play in his batsmanship. Only Sehwag made Sehwag.

Another brain function we have to consider while trying to analyse sporting techniques is what even minor injuries can do to the brain. The person who has had an accident or was hit on the head may be seemingly normal after a week or so, but in many cases minor damages could have occurred, affecting crucial functions or visual ability.

For instance, there are many people who cannot see colour. Everything is black and white, whether it is an apple or a cake. This is due to the damage to a portion call V4 in the temporal lobe which scientists believe processes colour. Processing colour is very important in sport. Teams playing each other have different uniforms which mostly have contrasting colour combinations and cannot have similar colours, such as white versus pinkish-white clothes. If this is the case, players cannot distinguish in a split second, in the wink of an eye, if it is his partner in the forward line who is lying unmarked. In cricket, a player with a colour agnostic brain will have problems with the white ball and even the red one. So the entire act of a batsman executing a hook off a bouncer is the result of a sophisticated system or series of actions that happens in the brain with a visual image of that act stored in the brain.

One such case that Ramachandran mentions is that of a lady who due to a damage to the middle temporal area (MT) could not make out motion. Moving objects were a set of snapshots, even though everything else was all right. There's a lot happening inside our brain. What if a player cannot suddenly make out motion and everything is static for him?

David Epstein[110] quotes the scientific tests done by Janet Starkes to gauge reaction time. 'One woman's blink of light was another woman's fully formed narrative. It was a strong clue that one key difference between expert and novice athletes was in the way they have learned to perceive the game, rather than the raw ability to reach quickly,' Epstein concludes about some of Starkes's occlusion test results. In Starkes's occlusion tests of field hockey players, she found just what she had found in volleyball players and more. Not only were elite field hockey players able to tell faster than the blink of an eye whether a ball was in the frame (in lab tests), they could accurately reconstruct the playing field after just a fleeting glance. This holds true from basketball to soccer. It was

---

[110] David Epstein, *The Sports Gene*, Portfolio, 2014.

as if every elite athlete miraculously had a photographic memory when it comes to his/her sport. The question then is how important these perceptual abilities are to top athletes and whether they are the result of genetic gifts.

It is, however, not possible to conclude that the top players have any inherent faculties that a lower ranked player doesn't have. It is a question of developing these faculties, by playing, by reading, by just observing the world go by.

The well-known cognitive scientist and writer Oliver Sacks[111] recounts how he travelled with a neuroscientist to a remote hospital somewhere in British Columbia in a small plane piloted by the doctor himself. Just before his surgery, the doctor developed fits and grovelled on the floor for the duration of the attack while his colleagues watched. Sacks was in utter shock. After the attack, the doctor got up, dusted himself, had a cup of coffee and went to the operation theatre to do brain surgery. In the evening he piloted the plane back, with a slightly nervous Sacks on board.

So let's comfort ourselves with the thought that the brain has its quirks.

When Sehwag was not getting big scores towards the fag end of his career, he pointed to his declining eyesight as the reason for his decline. This needn't necessarily have been true—for you can play as well with spectacles which correct your vision. Mansoor Ali Khan Pataudi played with just one eye. Many mental and physical faculties of a person decline with age. Sometimes this decline is drastic as with the memory of a person who nears forty. If there was a general decline, Sehwag could not have continued playing even with perfect eyesight.

---

[111] Oliver Sacks, *The Island of the Color Blind*, Vintage, 1998.

Killer instinct

Closely aligned with the choking theory is the 'killer instinct' theory. For many years during which India had the Hindu rate of growth (2 to 3 per cent), India also had a Hindu rate of winning in international matches. Every Indian defeat, in hockey, cricket and in the Olympics where the performance was dismal (one medal was standard), we comforted ourselves with the conclusion that Indians generally lack a killer instinct. This notion segued well with the nationally accepted hypocrisy that Indians are a non-violent non-meat-eating people, so a 'killer instinct', was definitely lacking.

Like the choking theory, the killer instinct too is a defensive theory, not giving any credit to the skill and strategy of the other team, in this case mostly Pakistan. A team that wins is a team which has top-ranked players who reached those positions due to dedicated practice over the years, top dedicated coaches, strategies worked out over many hours of discussions. In specific terms, this killer instinct construct meant that when it came to barging into the penalty area, we Indian baulked because that would have meant hurting or injuring the defensive player.

Every physical activity calls for certain resolve. From a woodcutter to a badminton player, they all decide before the activity or game starts that they have to finish the job well. For that they come prepared with certain insights. Those who don't have such insights, lose. Additionally, it serves you well if you have made winning a habit. A player who has lost ten matches in a row is going to be quivering jelly before the start of the eleventh match, as would a team that has lost. It is not the lack of killer instinct because such an instinct does not exist in reality, except maybe as journalistic excess.

Muscle memory

Among physical aspects of sport, the condition of the muscles, of course, is primary. Generally, athletes with nicely toned muscles are said to have a perfect body and are hence ranked highly. But in high-skilled sports, big muscles are not an advantage. Tennis stars are a great example; for instance, most of them have beanstalk legs.

What then, is muscle memory? It is given much credence by coaches, most of whom believe that muscles act or move according to how they have been trained. So much so, they can move on their own after a certain period of practice. That is what I gather from the term 'muscle memory'. Recent research suggests that there could be some evidence that 'muscle memory' exists, though there is no conclusive evidence that muscle fibres can replicate the function of the brain and repeat actions that result in sports victories or physical achievements.

Gretchen Reynolds of the *New York Times*,[112] quoting a study, writes: 'If muscles have been trained in the past, they seem to develop a molecular memory of working out that lingers through a prolonged period of inactivity and once we start training again this "muscle memory" could spread the process by which we regain our former muscular strength and size. The findings suggest in effect that skipping workouts now need not guarantee enfeeblement later and if we forget what finesse once felt like, our muscles recollect.'

The issue here is whether any aspect of memory can be seen in the muscles. The study[113] gets close to a solution

---

[112] Gretchen Reynolds, 'How "Muscle Memory" May Keep Us Fit', *New York Times*, 25 March 2020.

[113] Marcus Moberg and others, 'Exercise Induces Different Molecular Responses in Trained and Untrained Human Muscle', US National Library of Medicine, August 2020.

but the findings are not convincing enough. 'Many of us probably think that muscle memory refers to our well documented ability to retain physical skills even without practice. Learn to ride a bicycle and you never forget. Ditto by and large for hitting a free throw, skiing or starting to walk as a child. These repeated movements apparently burn themselves into our motor neurons, scientists believe, and remain available for later retrieval from our brains and nervous system, whenever needed,' according to the newspaper report.

The hypothesis for the study by Swedish scientists was that muscle memory resides within the myonuclei found within muscles. The study looked at myonuclear behaviour during training, detraining and retraining and concluded: 'As there was no myonuclear increase or fibre growth following training in this study, we were unable to investigate a muscle memory within the number of myonuclei during training and retraining. However, changes in type II fibre size during training, detraining and retraining were positively correlated with changes in the myonuclear number which supports the "myonuclear domain theory".'

So physically, a muscle is able to recreate muscles that existed prior to the stopping of training but whether such muscles are able to act in a particular way is not known. Can a weightlifter who lifted a certain weight return to the sport after a break and sufficient retraining, lift the same weight or better it for certain? There is no conclusive evidence so far. That is because even weightlifting needs a lot of mental preparation. And if muscle fibres have some sort of memory fibre then the role of the human brain will have to be re-evaluated.

Champions as superhumans

Various theories abound, as discussed here, to show that a champion is born and has various physical and mental qualities that others do not have. Some of them have the veneer of science to support them. Closer scrutiny will show that these are mostly imagined and then statistically sealed. The truth lies elsewhere.

Michael Gleeson writing in *The Age*[114] contended that a champion tennis player can read a situation early, can foretell what shot is coming. In other words, he/she has more time in his/her hands to shape his reply. This has been attributed to intuition. 'Djokovic like other elite players intuitively knows sooner than other players where the serve is going,' Gleeson writes.

Quoting from experiments conducted at the Skill Acquisition Department of Victoria University, he writes: 'Average players react to the ball leaving the racquet. The best players don't. They know before the ball hits the racquet where the serve is going to go. On average it is a third of a second before the ball hits the racquet.'

This proposition is questionable. Anyone who has played tennis for a long time like I have, knows that it is not possible to figure out where a serve is going to go before it is hit. Even a normal player can have many ways of serving and many ways of hiding his intentions before serving. If such qualities of foresight are innate in a champion, why is it that they lose? Does Djokovic lose a match, because this particular faculty of his (knowing what is to come his way) did not function? Is this faculty something that functions only on select days or is it a switch-on, switch-off sort of faculty? Coming back from his injury, Djokovic lost to many players ranked below

---

[114] Michael Gleeson, *The Age*, Melbourne, 27 January 2019.

the fiftieth spot during 2017–18. What happened to this peculiar superhuman faculty of his during his low days?

Winning and losing is an outcome of complex factors, both human and external. Winning is not a crack of a thunderbolt. The incandescence of winning shows throughout your playing days. Dark days are rare. To ascribe winning to a rare natural faculty that top players possess, is a dubious proposition. Such theories also help propagate racial and other inexplicable notions of sport which suggest that winning is the monopoly of a few races, a few types of people due to privilege of birth.[115] For example in the late nineteenth century, naked profiles of African 'specimens' were used in the field of scientific racism as evidence of their subhuman and inferior status. This is the reverse of the theory propounded above—that some have superhuman faculties—by the Victoria University, which in its subtext lays out dangerous propositions.

Often, sportsmen are credited with superhuman faculties unseen in any others. This happens often in sports writing where profiles are written of certain players. Sport profiles have this weakness. The attribution of rare qualities often happens when the player is close to retirement and reporters who have covered them over the years, think it is their due to given them a send-off with a supernatural tag attached. Just before Indian wicketkeeper M.S. Dhoni played his last World Cup in July 2019, various reporters wrote him up. *The Indian Express*[116] published an article which squarely falls into this category of sport writing. The intention of the article was to show that Dhoni has exceptionally fast hands and

---

[115] *New York Review of Books*, September 2018.

[116] Sandip G., 'Stumper MS Dhoni: Fast Hands, Faster Brain', *Indian Express*, 4 May 2019.

a fast brain which help him carry out stumpings. One particular run out was described thus: 'It took just 1/16 of a second for the entire sequence to play out. Jadeja's slider whizzed past Chris Morris's bat and M.S. Dhoni whisked the bails. In the interim, the Morris back-heel had been fractionally airborne.'

Other instances of Dhoni's so-called superhuman speed are also given in the article and to back it up is the quote of the Indian fielding coach, R. Sridhar: 'It's the speed of his mind that stands out the most.' Sridhar credited this to be a term profoundly used in football—peripheral vision. 'While he's looking at the ball, the corner of the eye had always gauged where the stumps are and where the batsman's foot is ...'

So an entire sequence of scientific argument is put forth to suggest that Dhoni has superhuman powers embedded in him. To put it mildly, all this is an exaggeration for the following reasons:

Any World Cup or international wicketkeeper can stump with similar speed. That is why he is there in the team. Like other things. this is developed by practice and there is nothing superhuman about it.

Quick stumping happens when a series of things occur in sequence. Prime among them is that the ball has to spin past the stretched bat and an unbalanced batsman and come at a comfortable height to reach to the wicketkeeper. If the ball for some reason bounces high above the head of the keeper standing up to the stumps, it doesn't matter if you are a Dhoni or not, you will miss the stumping. So the ball has to come to you at a height above the stumps and near it at a comfortable height.

Everyone, including non-sportsmen, have the speed of mind and peripheral vision that Sridhar is talking of here. If you don't have peripheral vision, you cannot drive a car without banging into something. My uncle who drove a car at the age of seventy-five started bumping his car here and there. The doctor said he had lost his peripheral vision. Unless otherwise detected, everyone, other than those with major vision issues, have peripheral vision. It is not unique to Dhoni. In most sport, peripheral vision is displayed with high precision.

Soccer and basketball reporting is full of descriptions of superhuman efforts. In such reportage, the reporter is often influenced by the market value of the player. Such players are written up, especially before events like El Clásico, the football matches between rivals FC Barcelona and Real Madrid. Other players in the team whose contribution is no less are forgotten or dismissed as also-rans. Columnist Matthew Syed is a culprit in this regard as can be seen in his description of a header by Portuguese footballer Cristiano Ronaldo[117] in the Series A match of Juventus against Sampdoria in December 2019.

Even as the ball was leaving Sandor's (Hungarian footballer Sándor Kocsis's) foot, Ronaldo was computing the trajectory of the ball, its bend through the air, the degree of spin and where his head would need to make contact two seconds hence to propel the ball into the back of the net. 'These formidable calculations made possible by the synthesis of a keen practiced intelligence and years of painstaking practice—occurred in a fraction of a second. For at that point Ronaldo was already putting weight on his left (weaker) leg to make a leap that will remain in the annals of football for as long as this beautiful game is played. Perhaps leap is too banal a term. This was more a matter of a human taking flight, a slow-

[117] Matthew Syed, 'Cristiano Ronaldo's goal not so much as a leap as a human taking flight', *The Times*, 20 December 2019.

motion footage revealing that the Portugal forward had reached a height of 2.56 m above the height of the cross bar, roaring towards a ball like a precision-guided missile yet without its homing signal.'

The Ronaldo header was written up by many reporters, though many other players too have made such spectacular leaps. Most good headers can jump high. Ronaldo also used the shoulder of a defender to push himself higher. This looks supernatural because the player seems to pause a while at the apogee of the jump to execute a header—just like while executing a jump ball in basketball. It's just that hundreds of top footballers and basketballers can do the same. The trick here is to execute the header or the jump shot while on the way down rather than on the way up, giving the impression that the players floated in the air.

Such hype is the stuff of sport reporting or sport itself. This is how superstars are created and their reputation maintained.

Sportsmen are completely human, even though they are surreally tall or big-built. The halo around them is what we confer with our frenzied imagination.

Can sportsmen peak at will? Can they reserve their best for the Olympics?

One of the favourite excuses for defeat is that the player or the team did not peak in time or peaked early. Embedded in this belief is that you can play at your top form or peak performance only for a short period, so it's better to time it for the big events. This view also, sadly, has a nationalistic perspective. The narrative is that we lost because we peaked earlier.

Can a team which won an international tournament and then lost at the World Cup a month or two later, say it was because it peaked two months earlier? This does not stand any type of scrutiny because some teams and players can go on winning for ever and ever. Yes, teams cannot start winning soon after a long off-season but during the season, most teams can perform according to their peak level.

A team 'peaking' means that all players of the team should be playing at peak level in that tournament. Is it possible to engineer peak performances in such a way for all players in a team, such as all eleven in a cricket team? Looks difficult. When a player reaches the so-called peak, does it mean she/he cannot go any further?

However, in individual sport, especially in athletics, it is possible to increase the timings, the jump distance gradually from the start of the season. That is because a player is one person who, for instance, can run 100 metres during the pre-season at 10.9 or even 11 seconds, as he/she musters up enough strength or wait for injuries to heal. So in the first race of the season, the timing could well be 10.5 seconds, at which point the sprinter can rightly say, 'I haven't reached my peak speed yet.'

This factor is because sprint or most athletic events are speed-strength-endurance sports. Speed, endurance and strength (related in a way) can be easily controlled. In soccer, you cannot control or decide when to score a goal and then say 'I am only on the way to my peak form.' We have seen top sprinters shutter their speed once they are microseconds away from the finish. This is to prevent possible injury since they think their body is not fit enough to run at the blistering under ten seconds speed and injuries could result.

But in highly skilled sport (tennis, badminton, volleyball, basketball) and team games, can peaking be controlled by the player? Quite unlikely. No proof exists to show that Federer or Nadal can time their performance to perfection to win big tournaments. This is because they usually win. By 2017, Federer had seven twenty-plus match-winning streaks, while Nadal had six.

It is worthwhile to have a detailed look at this phenomenon of 'peaking at the right time'.

I am basing this assessment on a report in the *Indian Express*,[118] which concludes that even though Indian badminton star P.V. Sindhu consistently lost even in the early rounds over a certain period in 2018–19, there is nothing to worry about because she has a habit of winning in the big tournaments. This article betrays the complete danger of adopting a nationalistic view about an athlete's career which seeks to console Sindhu fans in India that all is not lost.

Secondly, the article has various false premises, the basic one being that Sindhu is a big tournament player and she is not fully revved up in lesser tournaments. A player who wins big should also win small. The reverse can never be true as can be seen from the Federer statistics. This conclusion in the *Indian Express* report came about two months after Sindhu lost in the first round of the All England Open Badminton Championships, which in any badminton player's plan, is the big Slam to win. But true, Sindhu 'peaked' in the World Championships in Basel, 26 August 2019. Overall, this win seems more a blimp than a recurring theme in her career.

Thirdly, the writer leans heavily on Sindhu's silver medals in the Rio Olympics and World Championship and Asian Games. Her multiple defeats to the same players, Tai Tzu-Ying and Carolina Marin, Nozomi Okuhara and Akane Yamaguchi over 2017, 2018 and 2019 are treated

---

[118] Tushar Bhaduri, 'Sindhu and the art of peaking in time', *Indian Express*, 5 April 2019.

as minor blimps in a career that is destined for Olympic glory. The writer ascribes it to the wrong premise that these players are talented while Sindhu is not. '(Her losses) has given rise to the narrative that she struggles in big matches, but she has to contend with a plethora of highly talented opponents.'

These arguments have multiple flaws. Firstly, you cannot say that the player you are supporting has the minor flaw of not being talented. There is no such thing as 'talent' alone, as I have shown many times in this book. Also, even going by the reporter's theory that Sindhu is not talented enough, then why the long-winded 'peaking' theory? The fact that Sindhu's troughs were getting wider in 2019 (despite her creditable World Championship win) should be worrying for those who see her as a Olympic gold prospect.

No one can deny that Indian players like Sindhu and many others from the Gopichand stable are world class material. But the burning desire to always win is not seen in their performances, just like many other sportsmen in India. The ambitions are limited. The inner anger should be like a halo around that player, often luminescent, sometimes a bit dimmer with contentment. Every move of the top player should be an animation of his desire. The calculated words, the swagger of intention, that pain behind the victory, the renewal of faith after defeat.

Mike Atherton switched from cricket writing to golf reporting to point to some of this burden of desire, just before the Augusta Masters of 2019.[119] 'To watch [Irish golfer Rory McIlroy] McIlroy grapple with his desire for the elusive Green Jacket has been to acknowledge a young man's struggles with the enormity of his talent ("why

[119] Mike Atherton, 'Rory McIlroy knows this is moment to join games' immortals', *The Times*, London, 10 April 2019.

me?") and with one of sports essential contradictions: that you can want something too badly, that you can try too hard. Equally, attempting to stay balanced and normal does not always fit well with a game that demands intense commitment. There are, after all, so many others prepared to drive themselves to the limit.

'To accommodate these challenges, McIlroy has often constructed an elaborate dance in the days leading to the off. Last year, he talked up the challenge and seemed to want to embrace it. This year, he has taken the opposite route and downplayed it.'

The interplay between desire, performance, thwarted ambitions is a complex phenomenon. A champion has to be able to swim in this swirl and yet be on top of it. Many drown after struggling to reach where the waters are very rough.

Ideally, before a big tournament, a player must go into a bubble along with his/her team of two or three. It is a space which is sealed off from various external tumults and the headwinds of contrarian thoughts. Here, constant attempts are made to focus, to practice relentlessly and to iron out the frailties that accompany any human endeavour. The player must play in lower ranked tournaments to get the mind into playing mode and also to check out the body and its thousand tendons that are stretching along with the mind to attain great heights.

To give an example of how important it is to play in lesser tournaments as a preparation for the Big One, here is one example from Federer's career. This is an excerpt from the match preview notes prepared by the Insight group that works with Tennis Australia, the governing body for tennis in Australia. 'Federer warmed up for the Australian Open at the 2018 Hopman Cup (for top tennis nations), winning all four of his singles matches—against [Japanese player] Yuichi Sugita 6-4, 6-3, Karen Khachanov 6-3, 7-6 (8), Jack Sock 7-6 (5), 7-5 and Alexander Zverev 6-7 (4), 6-0, 6-2. Switzerland won the Cup.' A tournament without much stress helps a player ease into the winning zone where only the champions reside.

For a Top Ten player in an individual sport to just practice hitting with a few others in an indoor court, to talk a few minutes with a coach, take the evening off to receive an award, to keep the big event at the back of the mind, instead of the front, is just not the right way. The player has to work himself up, with smaller victories, into an ethereal zone where victory is always just a handshake away and winning becomes an addiction.

CHAPTER TEN

Beautiful Losers, the Need to Win and the Impossibility of It All

There is no better way to try to understand the nature and logic of losing and winning than to look at sport. Nowhere is the passionate immediacy to succeed more in evidence than in sport. Apart from all the other reasons to chase sporting success, this immediacy is because time is always running out—ticking away as the player again slouches back to the bench after a first round defeat. If by thirty you haven't won a medal yet, you are still ranked 290 by the ATP, you are still warming the bench of your soccer team or club, you have to carry the burden of having been a loser. As they say in our parts: tenth class pass; BA attempt.

To at least attempt, is heroic. It is a terrible burden to carry for the rest of your life. Then if you are playing in the ticketless village maidan where the crowd is made of late night stragglers who stopped by on their way back from the neighbourhood toddy shop, you have to bear the shame of being hooted, like I have been. Those boos, let me tell you, echo for a long time.

Those who are on top of the world are, in fact,

constantly troubled by the visions of an imminent fall and of defeat. We all believe in the imagined notion that genius and success are closely interlinked, and a successful person can be spotted early on, his potential embellished by the grandeur of the genetic pool he belongs to. Early on, we succumb to the accepted belief that we are not destined for success and so we learn to share a comfort zone with mediocrity. That is how a huge majority of people console themselves.

In every sport, top-ranked players or teams dominate thoroughly. That is the reason why a large number of professional players and teams remain unknown. Four tennis champions—Nadal, Federer, Djokovic and Murray—won fifty-five out of the last sixty Slams (2018–19), showing the rest of the highly accomplished players, the impossibility of it all, how beyond reach the trophy really is. However, that doesn't deter the other ranked ATP circuit players from trying, from dreaming, from struggling. They go through the constant drudgery of travelling around the world only to lose and to continue such journeys again and again, dumping into their bags their soiled clothes that remind them of defeat and wasted chances, and then another court, another defeat.

Sport is considered a level playing field with its numerous rules that cancel out unfair advantages. Despite this, the leading countries, clubs or players always dominate and dominate thoroughly. In 100 years, India cannot hope to win the number of Olympic medals the USA or China wins. Upsets do happen, of course, but rarely, and only among closely ranked teams or players. If an Indian wins a gold medal, it is always an upset. Yet we all hope for upsets when we go to see a sport. There will always be fans cheering for the underdog. Sport is about the underdog and his claim to a place in the podium.

Gilles Müller, after about fifteen years on the ATP circuit, won his first title at thirty-four in 2017. That was indeed persistence. He constantly battled against self-doubt, against time, and failure was always round the corner. 'I was always kind of worried that time was running away and I was going to be one of those players that would never have a title. When that happened in Sydney, a lot of weight fell off my shoulders and it's a lot easier now. Now I am playing free and not thinking about the first title anymore. That's helped me a lot,' he was quoted as saying in the *New York Times*.

Canadian player Peter Polansky with a career high ranking of 110 in 2018 on the ATP tour could be one such man who is a big lesson for us in his determination to go through the gruelling tour, let's say, with not many titles in his bag. But luck has sometimes hugged him outside the court. In 2018 alone he got entry into the four Majors as a lucky loser, even though he lost in the third and last round of all qualifiers. A lucky loser is one who lost in the third and final round of qualifiers or 'qualies' but who gets an entry into the Majors due to late withdrawals from the main draw. The day before a Slam starts, some withdrawals are a given. Match referees then ask the players who lost in the third or last round to take a lucky dip, and those who get 1, 2, 3 get into the tournament proper. Sometimes the highest ranked among losers gets in. A first round loser in the Slams gets over $30,000 even if he loses. Polansky who lost all the first rounds made $100,000 in 2018–19, just by losing. (In 2019, he lost the third round of the Australian Open qualies to Indian upstart, Sumit Nagal.)

Polansky has his own philosophy with which he consoles himself. 'It's not the best accomplishment. But it's something that I think is super fun. I don't think it will ever happen again.'[120] He ran into Alexander Zverev in the first round of the US Open in 2018 and lost, 6-2, 6-1, 6-2. Polansky's journey continues. Some people are like, 'This is shameful, why are you proud of losing?' Polansky said. 'Some people take it too seriously.'

Sport needs resilience and fierce determination like Polansky's. At the age of eighteen, he sleepwalked out of a third-storey window and was seriously injured. Then no one would have thought he would soldier on, the very symbol of all what we admire in sportsmen and life's billions of journeymen.

My effort has been to help bridge that gap, drawing from scientific lessons written over the years by scientists who have been defiant and courageous and adding to it my own understanding gained by fifty years of watching, playing and writing on sport. I have only been like a manager of a basketball or football team, trying to put all of the big theories together in an effort to make a winning book or a book about winning and losing, how not to lose and even if you lose, to find out why.

The constant drilling into our children's mind about the need to win, is actually what makes this world go forward and what makes sport slowly break barriers. If all of us decide to take it easy, no boundaries can be stretched. It is a tough grind. At most points in that journey, every one of today's champions would have felt that it is better to give up because after all the sun will rise tomorrow as well.

That is why sport itself exists. The lowest ranked team believes it will win the next match. The 110th ranked player thinks he will be in the main draw. That is actually the right attitude.

---

[120] *New York Times*, 28 August 2018.

But for a world obsessed with success, it is so full of losers that we don't even care. We crowd around the winner's podium all the time. We forget to put a comforting hand around the loser's shoulder. So the beautiful loser has to bear it all by himself—console himself and renew his pledge.

Sean Fitzpatrick, New Zealand rugby captain who lost a World Cup final in extra time to South Africa in 1955, consoled himself thus: 'The sun will come up again. It might not be tomorrow it might not be next week. It might not be next month, but it will come up again eventually. You will feel good again.'[121]

Chris Robshaw, former England rugby captain who also suffered a World Cup loss in October 2015, went through the same emotions. 'I actually went away for a weekend to the middle of nowhere with (his partner) Camille and some of my friends to get away from it all. It did help but you need a lot of time, eventually you stand to feel better inside ...

'The World Cup will always live with me and the other guys. It will always be part of me and I will always have that scar no matter the success we have in the future. Even after all the wins recently. I don't think you'll be able to right those wrongs.'

Failures, specially the close ones, haunt you all your life. The moment before you die, when the last swish of clarity passes in front of your closing eyes, you see that failure ... you lament till the last breath.

The people whose success we try to replicate, thus setting up endless cycles and quests, are not those who were born to succeed and who had everything going for them. Most of them are cranks, largely self-taught,

---

[121] *The Guardian*, 28 March 2016.

clutching at some personal philosophy with exaggerated notions of their ability to succeed and often egged on by a romantic imagination. Some were driven by voices in the dark. The odds never deterred them. Even in their many failed ordeals, most of them stretched some boundary or the other and thus showed us the way. It was only much later that their greatness was recognized and they were pulled out of the abyss and installed in the city square.

One such man was the British long-distance runner Bruce Tulloh, generally unheard of, but who ran and ran. On a whim and the lure of a mention in the *Guinness Book of World Records*, he decided in 1969 to run 2,876 miles across the US at 45 miles a day, coast to coast. He was also inspired by the story of Don Shepherd, a South African who traversed his country in seventy-three days carrying a backpack filled with a plastic mug, a razor, some soap, a towel and a tube of glue to fix his running shoes.[122]

He spent a year writing an average of ten letters a month, looking for sponsors, until Commander Edward Whitehead, the boss of Schweppes and author of *How to Live the Good Life* put up the money. On the first day of his run, Tulloh collapsed after two hours. When his wife, a constant support by his side asked him, 'What next?', he asked for salt tablets. 'The first few weeks, going through the prairies and canyons was very exciting. Then it got like going to work. It became quite boring,' Tulloh is quoted as saying.

He finished the run in great style after Schweppes managed to close the roads in Manhattan and arranged for several journalists to run the last stretch with him. Tulloh arrived alone at City Hall, leaving the other runners

---

[122] *The Times*, 8 May 2018.

far behind. His timing was sixty-four days, twenty-one hours and fifty minutes. Now the ultra-run record for the distance is down to forty-two days, six hours and thirty minutes.

Tulloh did not give up running. Later. he spent three weeks with the Mexican tribe of Tarahumaras who could run a six-hour race after a hard day's work. They ran barefoot. Tulloh soon became a barefoot runner, saying the encumbrance of shoes slowed him down. It was failure that inspired his running. He could not get into his school team and from then onwards he wanted to prove a point. Tulloh believed that athletics was a rare sport in which a 'small man could beat a big one;. Of course, it is a rerun of the David–Goliath myth. His philosophy was: 'You should never accept what you are told. Always question it.' And how well he questioned it!

Later, he felt that he could have been a good marathon runner but said: 'The principle of laziness meant if you got in the team for running six miles there was no point doing twenty-six.'

Tulloh grew as a runner and inspired Peter Snell to break the world mile record and then ran a sub-four-minute mile himself. At the big stage where it mattered most, Tulloh failed. In Rome 1960, he could not win the 5000-metre race due to heat and lack of time to acclimatize. Gordon Pirie, another member of the British team lauded Tulloh: 'He ran with terrific courage against the adverse conditions of his body, but I had to carry him off after saving him from falling into the moat surrounding the track.'

Fate was not on his side. He aimed to win a medal in Tokyo 1964 but was laid low by measles. He would have gone to Mexico but realized that the high altitude was not for him and he retired in1967, almost unknown as a runner. It was a fascinating, sporting life so full of determination and fighting spirit. Yet it was marked by failure and misfortune.

Tulloh really existed in that intersect between achievement and failure, a self-consoler and a unrelenting chaser of goals who faced one setback after another. His callings were many, his achievements not as much. Yet he persevered. Fame and glory never embraced him while he was alive. But if there was a medal for never giving up, he would have got it.

Tulloh actually believed that his destiny was to become a novelist. Even that was not to be. He wrote a book on his running adventure (*Four Million Footsteps*) and the unforgiving trier as he was, at eighty he wrote a book *How to Avoid Dying* (*For as Long as Possible*) with his sense of irony intact. *The Times* obituary would have been the greatest accolade he got. Posterity remembered him and patted him on his back.

At the other end of the spectrum is situated Emil Zátopek who was one of the greatest athletes who ever lived. He gained immortality while he lived, gathering one Olympic medal after another, as we have discussed in earlier chapters. There is no success bigger than his, if we look at the odds stacked again him. He changed the meaning of human endurance, not just for running the way he did but for trying against odds. He was also the most generous man one could find in those difficult times in the 1960s and '70s. He won three golds in Helsinki, 1952. He paid the price of being a political opponent of the Russian communist regime, as a supporter of Alexander Kubeck's Prague Spring (a reform movement within the Communist Party) and it was a heavy one. After the Soviet invasion of Czechoslovakia he was despatched to work in a factory, sometimes breaking stones. Once near Litomysl, a woman asked her son to go and give some smoked meat to the distraught man. 'I am not the Zátopek you used to know,' the great athlete told the young boy. He was later rehabilitated and the Czech team wore his picture on their jackets at the Rio Olympics.

Was his success worth it? You might argue that success was his enemy for he was marked out by the Russian invaders. There is a larger lesson in Zátopek's story. The greatest success can also come embedded with darkness and defeat—success in sport does not guarantee everything. Fame also comes with its own footnotes.

Strangely, though, as we traverse this terrain, we can see that immortal men, many credited with being geniuses often saw themselves as failures during their life. The greatest among them and the poorest among them did not have the insight to realize that he was the greatest painter who ever painted. Leonardo da Vinci never saw himself like that. He avoided painting commissions, never finished any commission on time, never got paid much, nor did he ask for much. In fact, he never asked for money for the world's best-known most-viewed priceless painting, the *Mona Lisa*. He hadn't realized that he was a genius. He was a poor man, often sending long applications for jobs to aristocrats and kings in Italy and France. His resume travelled as much as some of ours, if that is any consolation.

The most heart-tugging part of Leonardo's life was that those paintings he carried with him from Florence, Milan, Rome and France were the ones he died with, the paintings by his bedside, yet unfinished yet waiting for some final touches. The paintings became him. In the small room in France where he lived during his last days, these paintings were found rolled up after he died. Among them was *Mona Lisa*. Like a sportsman trying relentlessly for a world record, Leonardo worked relentlessly in perfecting these paintings from 1503 to 1517 when he died.

There are parallels with such searches for eternity with a sportsman's search for a record or a medal. For a sportsman, reward is immediate. A painter or a scientist has to wait or die waiting for Time to make its judgement. Not everyone gets posthumous recognition like Leonardo da Vinci did—he believed that creativity needed time and that could be the reason why his partially finished paintings remained on the canvas or his murals on the many walls of chapels while he ruminated.

It is natural for a middle-level or low-ranked player to be described as a person who wasted his life on a road with a dead-end. Pathos and a badge of the tragic hero are appended to such athletes and they are seldom given farewells befitting the time they spent on the course or court. They are easily forgotten until by a twist of fate they, unwilling to give up, sometimes return as coaches and suddenly they seem to know the road where victory lies and can take their wards there.

In the late V.S. Naipaul's classic work *A House for Mr Biswas*, the protagonist is on a lifelong quest for the right house on a patch of earth to call his own. That quest for permanence and in a way, for glory, is a basic human trait. One house after another, one job after another, one tournament after another, we all journey to some goal. Biswas's longing and yearning is universal. And we all want to avoid 'to have lived without even attempting to lay claim to one's portion of the earth; to have lived and died as one had been born, unnecessary and unaccommodated.'

Warren Hastings is perhaps one of the most powerful, colourful and dominating characters in the East India Company history of colonial India. Andrew Otis[123]

[123] Andrew Otis, *Hicky's Bengal Gazette: The Untold Story of India's First Newspaper*, Westland, 2018.

recounts how much of a survivor he was and how he kept bouncing back, taking the relentless blows of destiny on his chin. His mother died in childbirth, his father abandoned him when he was young, and his grandfather sent him to a charity school where he often starved. His brief education at the famous Westminster School was cut short when his uncle died. Yet at seventeen, he sailed to India full of hope and determination. The blows came hard and thick. He just about escaped the Black Hole where 123 prisoners of the Nawab of Bengal died of suffocation. His first wife and daughter died. But Hasting survived all that, the death of his second wife, the loss of all his wealth. He kept coming back to keep playing, as it were. History remembers him for his success, but maybe not as a hero.

I sum up why failure in sport comes easily and success is a hard, never-ending climb.

Nine Ways to Win

1. No one is born a champion. You have to work hard to become one.
2. There is no sporting quality or gene you get from your parents. All you get is a physical frame and height, weight, eyesight, hair and so on. The rest of it you have to work hard for.
3. Nothing can be passed down because there is nothing called a cricketing gene, or a badminton gene. To play these games, various skills have to be acquired.
4. Once a player reaches a high level of achievement, say a tennis player who starts playing the Futures and Challengers, the point then is to develop a strategic mind, if he hasn't already. It requires certain mental powers to become a big player.

Along with the body, develop the mind and memory. Do memory exercises like all great men did. Sport is not just physical endeavour—it includes a sharp memory, an understanding of the levels of play of others, powers of observation, some reading, and most of all, intimate knowledge of the court or field of play and its dimensions, so intimate that you hit a perfect down-the-line in your dreams.

5. This mental capacity also helps you enter 'The Zone', a space where the person is in control of all his faculties, stays focused for the duration of the game, and his mind and body become one, with one purpose, one desire. Never go into a match like a lamb to slaughter, not knowing what the surface will play like, what the opponent's strong or weak points are.
6. Many sportsmen whom we think are great players still do not reach the top because they have either given up focused practising or do not realize the need to keep learning. Also go into the environments of excellence where either the coach or big players are drilling the notions of success. Make winning a habit.
7. Failure stares everyone in the face. The fear of failure is constant. Yes, failure is a stepping-stone. But at some point, you become an enemy of failure—but always question. Question even the coaches since they are not repositories of all wisdom. Often they are wrong.
8. Start early in whatever sport you choose. If you haven't started early, say at the age of twelve or thirteen, it is a difficult task. The toughest task is to choose the right sport. Don't go into a speed-

based game if you are a slow mover. Try out three or four coaches before you settle on one. Put all your faith in him or her.

9. If nothing goes right, stay back and accept it. That is what has happened to 99 per cent of the world's people. Life always throws up other possibilities.

Even the greatest poet (according to me), John Milton, started turning blind quite young, cutting short a great life. How more terrible can destiny be? But then Milton sat down and wrote the one great poem for this 99 per cent of humanity, who live in failure. The last line of poem, 'On His Blindness', is for all of us who never ascended the winner's podium in sport and life. 'They also serve who only stand and wait.'

If after all your endeavour, you still fail, and your dreams lie shattered, smash the ball one last time. Into your opponent's backhand court—let the ball sail over everything and sail beyond. If your sweat-soaked shirt hangs around your body adding to the burden of another defeat, sit down and think of all those years. In sport you can only persevere for so long. A sporting life is terribly short.

For you, there are other worlds to conquer. For all of us, thwarted ambition signals the very end of the purpose of our lives. To discover a new purpose is not easy. You have to become small again, learn again, experience defeat all over again. Many people have achieved a second life and fame, a failed player becoming a super coach, for instance. These are superhuman tasks. But go for it!

This poem by Naomi Shihab Nye captures most of the complexity of trying to be a champion and the pain that accompanies it:

The Rider

A boy told me
if he roller-skated fast enough
his loneliness couldn't catch up to him,
the best reason I ever heard
for trying to be a champion.
What I wonder tonight
pedaling hard down King William Street
is if it translates to bicycles.
A victory! To leave your loneliness
panting behind you on some street corner
while you float free into a cloud of sudden azaleas,
pink petals that have never felt loneliness,
no matter how slowly they fell.

There is always that cloud of azeleas with their pink petals that you will see on the roadside when you are walking back with the pain and loneliness of another defeat.